Political Tribalism in America

Political Tribalism in America

*How Hyper-Partisanship
Dumbs Down Democracy
and How to Fix It*

Timothy J. Redmond

McFarland & Company, Inc., Publishers
Jefferson, North Carolina

This book has undergone peer review.

ISBN (print) 978-1-4766-8310-2
ISBN (ebook) 978-1-4766-4696-1

LIBRARY OF CONGRESS AND BRITISH LIBRARY
CATALOGUING DATA ARE AVAILABLE

Library of Congress Control Number 2022034697

© 2022 Timothy J. Redmond. All rights reserved

No part of this book may be reproduced or transmitted in any form or by any means, electronic or mechanical, including photocopying or recording, or by any information storage and retrieval system, without permission in writing from the publisher.

Front cover images © 2022 Shutterstock

Printed in the United States of America

*McFarland & Company, Inc., Publishers
Box 611, Jefferson, North Carolina 28640
www.mcfarlandpub.com*

For Fang

"A sect or party is an elegant incognito designed to save a man from the vexation of thinking."
—Ralph Waldo Emerson. 2012. *The Heart of Emerson's Journals*. New York: Dover Publications. 49.

Table of Contents

Acknowledgments viii

Preface 1

Part I: Political Identities

1. The Nature of Political Tribalism 10

Part II: Political Opinions

2. Placing Party Before Policy 34

Part III: Political Information

3. Acquiring Political Information 56
4. Perceiving Political Information 76
5. Evaluating Political Information 99
6. Evaluating False Political Information 103
7. Evaluating Political Numbers 120
8. Evaluating Political Arguments 147
9. Evaluating Political Elections 168

Conclusion: Keeping the Republic 181

Chapter Notes 189

Bibliography 211

Index 227

Acknowledgments

This book wouldn't have been possible without the scholarship, assistance, and encouragement of so many others. While I would like to acknowledge them here, I do so fully aware that I won't be able to name them all or thank them enough. First, I would like to thank Michael Shermer (editor-in-chief of *Skeptic* magazine), Kendrick Frazier (editor-in-chief of *Skeptical Inquirer* magazine), and Adam Zaremski (editor of the *East Aurora Advertiser*) for not only publishing some of my previous work on critical thinking and politics but also allowing me to reproduce portions of that material here. I would also like to thank author Guy P. Harrison for reading some of that work and encouraging me to write this book. I was able to complete this project due in large part to his encouragement, guidance, and friendship. Second, I would like to thank Sarah Pankow, Carrie Fey-Daly, Lewis Vaughn, Lisa Parshall, Juan Carlos Moya, Marcus Miranda, and the anonymous reviewers for editing and evaluating this manuscript, either in part or in full. Their insights and suggestions were invaluable. Third, I am grateful for Charlie Perdue and all the staff at McFarland for embracing and supporting this project and for all of the writers and researchers who produced the material upon which this book is built. Fourth, I am deeply indebted to Emily S. Redmond for her incomparable illustrations and Dave Spataro for his exceptional photography. Also, many thanks to Jeff Milner for his permission to use the Led Zeppelin "Stairway to Heaven" image, Robert Lichter for permission to use the "office scene" image, and Alexander G. Theodoridis for permission to use the "Ascent of Man" and "Chaos at the Republican Gathering" images. Lastly, I would like to thank my family and, in particular, my wife. I wrote this book during a pregnancy, birth, and pandemic. My parents and in-laws contributed countless hours of childcare so I could write. So, too, did my wife. What's more, she never once wavered in her encouragement, nor in her willingness to do so much for so long while I was often struggling to write far too little for far too long. I love you, Rebecca.

Preface

> A supporter once called out, "Governor Stevenson, all thinking people are for you!" And Adlai Stevenson answered, "That's not enough. I need a majority."[1]
> —Scott Simon

In the summer of 1787, fifty-five delegates gathered at the Pennsylvania State House to craft a new plan of government. After four grueling months of deliberation and negotiation, the attendees produced *The Constitution of the United States of America*. When the convention adjourned, an eighty-one-year-old Benjamin Franklin slowly made his way outside where he was approached by a certain Mrs. Powell of Philadelphia. "Well, doctor," she asked, "what have we got? A republic or a monarchy?" Franklin turned to her and replied: "A republic, madam—if you can keep it."[2]

Some two centuries later, our republic is in a state of neglect and needs some attending to. In principle, a democratic system of government demands that a well-informed citizenry think critically about matters of public import. Yet the American people are not particularly well-informed about politics. Surveys have consistently shown that they are ignorant of even the most basic features of their government.[3] For example, a recent analysis by the Annenberg Public Policy Center found that only 26 percent of Americans were able to correctly identify the three branches of government as the legislative branch, the executive branch, and the judicial branch.[4] A 2006 study conducted by the McCormick Tribune Freedom Museum found that a paltry .01 percent of Americans knew that the five freedoms guaranteed by the First Amendment of the U.S. Constitution are the freedoms of religion, speech, press, petition, and assembly. Even more troubling is the fact that some 20 percent of those surveyed agreed that the First Amendment guaranteed "the right to own and raise pets" or "drive a car."[5]

Nor do many Americans think critically about politics. According to the democratic ideal—or what political scientists Christopher H. Achen and Larry M. Bartels call the *folk theory* of democracy—citizens should objectively acquire, perceive, and evaluate information, use that information to inform their political opinions, and allow those considered views to influence their decisions about which political party to support.[6] In short, the folk theory of democracy demands that members of the republic think like scientists who gather evidence and draw their conclusions accordingly. Unfortunately, many citizens subscribe to the *tribal theory* of democracy—a mirror image of the ideal—in which they first and foremost identify with a political party, and then proceed to uncritically adopt that party's opinions while subjectively processing information in a manner that is favorable to their partisan views and allegiances. As such, they think more like trial lawyers who "already know what they want to conclude ... and then go about seeking and construing evidence to favor that conclusion (Figure P-1)."[7]

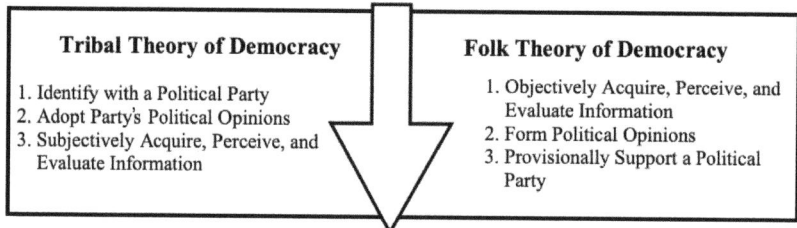

Figure P-1: The Folk and Tribal Theories of Democracy.

This is deeply troubling, for the tribal theory of democracy has several deleterious outcomes. As we shall see, Democrats and Republicans who adhere to its precepts tend to derogate members of the opposing party, adopt extremist views, misconstrue political information, undermine democratic responsiveness, and endanger peaceful transfers of power. Thus, if we hope to keep our republic, we must reject the tribal theory of democracy and strive for the democratic ideal by becoming better critical political thinkers. *Political Tribalism in America* is designed to assist citizens in that endeavor.

A Note on the Intended Audience

Political Tribalism in America was written as an ancillary text for students enrolled in an undergraduate political science, psychology, or critical thinking class. But it's also intended for casual readers who are interested in American politics and concerned about its increasingly tribal nature. Some people are undoubtedly untroubled by the tribal theory of democracy. They might be politicians, partisan media magnates, or purveyors of misinformation that stand to benefit from an unthinking electorate. Or, they might simply be devout partisans who prefer to put their tribe before the truth—as Congressman Earl Landgrebe (R-IN) did during the Watergate scandal when he said, "Don't confuse me with the facts. I've got a closed mind."[8] But there are also Democrats and Republicans of good faith—partisans who may not always abide by the folk theory of democracy, but are nevertheless committed to its pursuit. In the end, this book was written for, and in honor of, them—the partisans who want to be better thinkers, so they can become better citizens.

A Note on the Title

The book's title and subtitle delineate its subject matter in several important respects. For one, they allude to the name of the French philosopher Alexis de Tocqueville's classic treatise, *Democracy in America*. Originally published in two volumes—the first in 1835 and the second in 1840—*Democracy in America* primarily analyzed why democracy had succeeded in the United States well into the nineteenth century. By contrast, *Political Tribalism in America* explores a central reason why the commonwealth is wanting in the present-day—namely, the corrosive effect that political tribalism has had on the ability of Democrats and Republicans to think critically about U.S. government and politics. As such, while the treatment will touch upon concepts such as political sorting and polarization (Figure P-2), the bulk of the book will explore how *political tribalism*— or the attitudes and behaviors that arise from an affinity for one's own political party (partisanship), and a hostility towards an opposing political party (negative partisanship)—influences the means by which we acquire, perceive, and evaluate political information. Accordingly, the word 'dumb' isn't being used here to mean 'stupid' or 'ignorant,' but rather 'foolish' or 'unwise.' In other words, this book doesn't explore *what* Americans know— or don't know—about politics. It analyzes *how* Americans think about politics. And since several studies have shown that there is a weak correlation between intelligence and the tendency to think critically, it's an important read for all partisans, regardless of their political knowledge or IQ.[9]

> **Political Polarization and Political Tribalism**
> Polarization is the division into two sharply contrasting groups or sets of opinions or beliefs. Political scientists have generally identified three major types of political polarization:

1. **Policy Polarization**: Policy polarization is a process where extreme views on matters of public policy have increased over time. Example: If the average Democrat believes that the corporate tax rate should be 20 percent and the average Republican believes that it should be 10 percent at t_1, but 30 percent and zero percent, respectively, at t_2, the gap between their policy positions has grown or become more polarized.
2. **Party Polarization**: Party polarization occurs when partisans become more distinct from each other across a range of issues, and it occurs because of party sorting—a process in which conservative Democrats become Republicans, and liberal Republicans become Democrats. Party polarization is distinct from policy polarization because it can occur without the polarization of policy views.

Conservative Republican	Conservative Democrat	Liberal Republican	Liberal Democrat
0%	10%	20%	30%

Example: If a conservative Democrat believes that the corporate tax rate should be 10 percent and a liberal Democrat believes that it should be 30 percent at t_1, we can say that the average Democrat wants a corporate tax rate of 20 percent. If a liberal Republican believes that the corporate tax rate should be 20 percent and a conservative Republican believes that it should be 0 percent at t_1, we can say that the average Republican wants a corporate tax rate of 10 percent. But assume that the conservative Democrat becomes a Republican, and the liberal Republican becomes a Democrat at t_2. Now, the Democrats want an average corporate tax rate of 25 percent and the Republicans want one of 5 percent. Yet, that polarization was the result of people changing their parties, not their policy views.

Although most political scientists agree that political elites—that is, elected officials and activists etc.—have adopted more extreme policy views over time, they continue to debate whether there has been any meaningful policy polarization among ordinary voters. While some scholars believe that voters have experienced policy polarization, others counter that any increased difference in policy views between Democrats and Republicans is a result of party polarization instead.

3. **Affective polarization**: Affective polarization is the level of dislike for the other party compared to your own. If Democrats and Republicans gave an average "Feeling Thermometer" scale rating—where 0 is the most negative rating and 100 is the most positive rating—of 70 degrees to their co-partisans and 30 degrees to their counter-partisans at t_1, and say 72 degrees to their co-partisans and 10 degrees to their counter-partisans at t_2, the two parties can be said to have affectively polarized.

Figure P-2: Three Different Types of Political Polarization (Source: Nolan McCarty. 2019. *Polarization: What Everyone Needs to Know*. New York: Oxford University Press).

Next, this analysis will address the influence of political tribalism on Democrats and Republicans residing in the United States. Some 85 percent of U.S. citizens identify with one of these two political parties.[10] And while it would be interesting and important to explore the impact of political tribalism on minor parties—such as the Libertarian Party and the Green Party—doing so poses a challenge because so few people identify with those parties in surveys, thereby making them difficult to study systematically.[11] And while a recent study found that aspects of political tribalism have afflicted a handful of other democratic states—such as Canada, New Zealand, and Switzerland—its incidence has been most pronounced and analyzed in the United States.[12] As such, the experiments and examples cited in the text involve American politics. Nevertheless, I hope that the content covered herein will be edifying for partisans of all stripes in any country.

Finally, this book is prescriptive. The scourge of political tribalism yields a host of complex problems to which there are no simple solutions. Nonetheless, there are steps that we can take to ameliorate its most malignant effects. To that end, *Political Tribalism in America* proffers several concrete actionable remedies that can be used to reduce the influence of political tribalism in our daily lives. Some of these countermeasures are actions that can be taken rather quickly. Others are skills that will be decidedly more difficult to master. But they're all responsibilities of citizenship and should thereby demand our attention.

What This Book Is About

This book is organized according to the stages of the tribal theory of democracy. It commences with an examination of party identification (Part I), continues with an analysis of how our party attachments influence our political opinions (Part II), and concludes with an exploration of how our partisan identities shape the way in which we process political information (Part III).

Chapter 1 examines political tribalism. In particular, it will explore how partisanship and negative partisanship encourage Democrats and Republicans in the United States to stereotype, discriminate against, segregate themselves from, dehumanize, and even wish or inflict violence upon their political opponents. It will conclude with some suggestions on how to recognize the role that political tribalism plays in our own lives and how to extract ourselves from its grip.

Chapter 2 examines the formation of political opinion. It shows that our policy views—on everything from taxes and trade to health care and welfare—are often influenced more by our partisan attachments than by our interests and values or well-established facts. It will also explore how this state of affairs inhibits representative government and the obstacles that must be overcome if we ever hope to place policy before party.

Chapters 3 through 9 explore how political tribalism influences the ways in which we process information about public affairs. To start, Chapter 3 investigates the acquisition of political data. It describes how political tribalism encourages citizens to engage in *partisan selective exposure*—the inclination to seek information that they like and avoid information that they dislike. It also describes how partisan selective exposure can discourage deliberation and precipitate the polarization of policy views. The chapter closes with suggestions on how citizens can broaden their information diets and consider issues from various perspectives.

Next, Chapter 4 illustrates how political tribalism influences the way we perceive sources of political information. In particular, it will explore how Democrats and Republicans often deem balanced information as biased, and biased information as balanced. It will also provide readers with the skills needed to evaluate the objectivity of different sources in an effective manner.

Then, Chapter 5 will assess how partisanship and negative partisanship encourage *partisan motivated reasoning*—that is, the tendency to accept political information that we like (*confirmation bias*) and discredit political information that we don't like (*disconfirmation bias*). The remainder of the book will examine how partisan motivated reasoning influences the ways in which citizens evaluate information in various contexts.

For instance, Chapter 6 discusses the phenomenon of false political information. It shows how partisans are more likely to accept false information as true, and reject true information as false, when it aligns with their political predispositions. It also analyzes the spread of false headlines and articles, fabricated quotations, doctored photographs, and altered audio and video files in American politics, and provides the tools one needs to avoid being duped by such disinformation.

Chapter 7 explores how political tribalism can inhibit our ability to understand and work with numbers. It seeks to enhance one's numeracy by exploring five frequent sources of numerical bunk in politics: the dangling comparative, the meaning of "average," graphs, opinion polls, and the difference between absolute and relative change. Yet it also explores the fact that numeracy alone won't protect us from the ill effects of political tribalism, as numerate Democrats and Republicans have been found to accept inaccurate numeric information when it supports their partisan identities, and dismiss accurate numeric information when it does not.

Similarly, Chapter 8 describes how political tribalism clouds our ability to think logically by showing that Democrats and Republicans often dismiss good arguments from the opposing party while accepting poor arguments from their own. Next, it offers suggestions on how to avoid this trap by illustrating how to identify an argument's premises and conclusions, diagram an argument, evaluate an argument's premises, and locate logical fallacies.

Chapter 9 investigates the influence of partisanship and negative partisanship on the evaluation of electoral outcomes. Political tribalism often encourages the supporters of the victorious party to overly revel in their success and the adherents of the losing party to unreasonably dispute an election's result. To do so, however, is highly detrimental to the democratic process. As such, the penultimate chapter will explore the importance of a citizenry that is both magnanimous in victory and accepting of defeat.

Finally, the conclusion will provide a concise list of the tools detailed throughout the text. This summary will serve as a handy reference that critical political thinkers can use to resist the pull of political tribalism, and steer themselves toward the democratic ideal.

What This Book Is Not About

It is important to note that this book is not an attack on political parties. Political parties serve several important functions in a democratic society—from recruiting and running candidates to proposing and passing legislation.[13] What's more, our partisan identities can provide us with a sense of community and motivate us to become politically engaged.[14] This book, however, is an attack on political tribalism and its corrosive impact on the folk theory of democracy. Hence, *Political Tribalism in America* will not ask you to give up your party, but it will ask you to take up the responsibilities of citizenship. Similarly, this book is not an attack on any single political party. It will let others decide whether one party is more tribal than the other at this particular point in American history. Instead, the experimental studies described herein will show that succumbing to the siren song of the tribal theory is generally not a Democratic problem or a Republican problem, but a human problem.[15] As such, the book's lessons should be heeded by members of both political parties.

Lastly, this book is not meant to be a manual on how to attack members of the opposing party. It will undoubtedly equip readers with the ability to make plain how the tribal theory of democracy has distorted the thinking of their political opponents. Yet the primary purpose of this book is to help readers minimize the manifestation of political tribalism in their own lives, not in the lives of others. Surely, we should respectfully point out the epistemological errors in the thinking of any counter-partisan *and* co-partisan. But the research on behavioral contagion—or the tendency of people to copy the behavior of others—intimates that the most effective way to make others think critically about politics is to model that behavior ourselves. Doing so will neither be easy nor always enjoyable. But it is necessary. A representative government functions best when its citizens aspire to the folk theory of democracy. We will never reach the democratic ideal, but if we use the tools detailed in this book, we can approach it. And in so doing, we will have done our part to keep the republic.

Part I
Political Identities

Chapter 1

The Nature of Political Tribalism

> "A thousand years or more ago, When I was newly sewn, There lived four wizards of renown, Whose names are still well-known.... While still alive they did divide their favorites from the throng, Yet how to pick the worthy ones when they were dead and gone? 'Twas Gryffindor who found the way, He whipped me off his head. The founders put some brains in me, So I could choose instead! Now slip me snug around you ears, I've never yet been wrong, I'll have a look inside your mind, And tell you where you belong."[1]
> —J.K. Rowling

The Problem: Political tribalism encourages Democrats and Republicans to stereotype, discriminate against, segregate themselves from, dehumanize, and even wish or inflict violence upon their political opponents.

In the summer of 1954, the social psychologist Muzafer Sherif and his colleagues conducted an elaborate experiment that was designed to explore the nature of human tribalism. The researchers recruited twenty-two white, Protestant, middle-class, fifth-grade boys from Oklahoma City; divided them into two equal-sized groups; and invited them to spend several weeks at separate campsites situated on a 200-acre campground in Robbers Cave State Park. Although the boys were initially all strangers, they quickly took a liking to one another. By the first week's end, each set of campers had already developed a unique identity. One group began calling itself the "Rattlers" and designed a symbol to be imprinted on its t-shirts and hats. The other troop adopted the name "Eagles" and marched about camp singing songs and waving the group's flag. Both sets of campers developed norms regarding their preferred manner of talking, swimming, and dealing with bumps and bruises.[2] In short, each team had formed a sense of being a group.[3]

Then, near the beginning of the second week, Sherif informed each team of the other's existence. Immediately, the boys became agitated. Each group referred to the other as "outsiders" and "intruders," and threatened to "challenge them" and "run them off." And when the experimenters arranged a tournament between the two sides—with activities ranging from a treasure hunt to a tug of war—their mutual antipathies became even more entrenched. After a Rattler victory, the Eagles stole their "cheating" opponents' flag, set it on fire, and hoisted the charred remains. Following an Eagle triumph, the Rattlers raided their "cowardly" foe's camp, overturned their beds, and ripped their screens. When the Eagles responded in kind, a fistfight ensued and the counselors were finally forced to intervene. According to David Berreby, the author of *Us and Them: The Science of Identity*:

> Fourteen days after they had arrived as strangers, then, these look-alike boys, all born around the same time, from look-alike households, had turned into two exclusive, disdainful tribes, yelling "dirty bums" and "sissies" at their neighbors whenever their paths crossed. [And] it had all, ... as Sherif put it, ... been "produced from scratch."[4]

The Nature of Tribalism

Homo sapiens evolved in an environment in which being a member of a *tribe*—or social group that shared a common identity—was essential for survival. Our ancestors weren't particularly fast or strong. Nor were they equipped with claws or fangs. But when they worked together, our foregoers not only survived, they thrived. A cooperative tribe of human beings could effectively and efficiently hunt big game, gather fruit, and tend to the young, while watching for, and fighting back against, even the stealthiest and fiercest of predators.[5] Yet our forebearers also evolved in an environment in which their tribes competed for limited resources. Whenever a human tribe "exceeded their area's carrying capacity ... and [were] running out of food ... [they would] attempt to take either food, or food-producing land, from someone else."[6] Consequently, human beings evolved a predisposition to engage in *tribalism*—the tendency to assume that "[m]embers of the in-group (until they prove otherwise) are ... virtuous: friendly, cooperative, trustworthy, safe, and more [while] members of an out-group (until they prove otherwise) are ... the opposite: unfriendly, uncooperative, unworthy of trust, dangerous, and more."[7]

Tribalism, therefore, places a premium on the ability to distinguish between us and them. For it is not simply a matter of identifying who is in our group and who is not, it's a matter of discerning friend from foe. To that end, Homo sapiens employ *markers*—attributes that identify someone as a member of a particular group.[8] And although these markers may create a community that is, in many ways, imagined—by obscuring the differences among in-group members and the similarities between in-group and out-group members—their consequences are all too real.[9] If human history has taught us anything, it's that those who do not possess a particular marker will often be hounded and harmed by those who do.

In *The Human Swarm: How Our Societies Arise, Thrive, and Fall*, the biologist Mark W. Moffett notes that the "markers ... people [utilize] to unmask those who don't belong ... could fill volumes."[10] Everything from food and utensils to hairstyles and clothing can be used to distinguish us from them. Even the manner in which people count on their fingers can serve as a marker. For instance,

> When most Western Europeans (such as Germans, Austrians, Belgians, Italians, the Swiss, the Spanish, the Dutch, the Portuguese, the French, and the Scandinavians) count with their fingers, ... the thumb is always the first digit and represents number one, followed by the index finger (2), middle finger (3), ring finger (4), and finally the pinky finger (5). English speaking countries, such as the United States, Canada, and the United Kingdom typically count with the index finger as the first digit and end with the thumb to represent five.[11]

In fact, this marker figured prominently in Quentin Tarantino's 2009 film, *Inglourious Basterds*.[12] The movie, which traces various plots to assassinate Nazi Germany's leadership, features a tense scene in which a British spy impersonating a Nazi Captain orders three glasses of whisky from the Scottish Highlands at a tavern in German-occupied France. When he places his order, however, he does so by extending his three middle fingers rather than his middle finger, index finger, and thumb as Germans do. Upon seeing this, a Nazi Major pulls out his gun and declares, "You've just given yourself away, Captain. You're no more German than that scotch." A bloody Tarantinoesque shootout then ensues.[13]

Other markers are admittedly less mundane. For instance, religion is often used to discern who's in and who's out. One's religious identity can be determined by outward signs of devotion—such as the donning of a yarmulke, hijab, or cross—or even by one's familiarity with a given sect's beliefs and rituals. In his Netflix special *The Comeback Kid*, the comedian John Mulaney humorously notes how his lack of devotion was unwittingly revealed by his unfamiliarity with recent changes in the Catholic Church's liturgical practice.[14]

Chapter 1. The Nature of Political Tribalism

I grew up Catholic, I don't go to church anymore but I went on Christmas Eve with my parents because, you know, how you lie to your parents. So, we go into the church and I was like "I got this under control." And then I got schooled because they introduced a bunch of new shit. No, I was going through mass and I was batting like .400. And then in the middle of mass the priest said "Peace be with you," and everyone said "And with your spirit." And I was like the one pre–Y2K asshole going "And also with you!" … For those of you who aren't Catholic … there's a part in church where the priest says "Peace be with you," and for many, many years we all said "And also with you." … But they changed it to "and with their spirit," because that is what needed revamping in the Catholic Church. That was the squeaky wheel that needed the grease.

Of course, separating the faithful "us" from the infidel "them" has seldom been a laughing matter. One need only recall the bloodshed between Christians and Muslims during the Crusades, Catholics and Protestants during the Thirty Years' War, or Muslims and Hindus during the partition of India to be reminded of the horrors that religious tribalism can unleash.[15]

Notions of ancestry, ethnicity, and race have also served as markers throughout world history.[16] Recent DNA tests have shown that the mighty Aztec (1345–1521) routinely sacrificed outsiders to the sun god Huitzilopochtli.[17] From the late 1400s to the late 1800s, merchants from various Arab and European states sold tens of millions of Africans into slavery.[18] In 1915, Turkish nationalists murdered over one million Armenians in their quest to build a union that would include only "peoples of proven…. Turkic origins."[19] The Nazi regime annihilated some 6 million Jews in the Holocaust (1941–1945) because they were—as Adolf Hitler wrote in *Mein Kampf*—an inferior "people with definite racial characteristics" that would forever preclude them from being German.[20] In 1937, between 260,000 and 350,000 Chinese men, women, and children were slaughtered by the Japanese during the Nanjing Massacre due in part to the Japanese's belief that they "were racially superior to all the rest of the world, and that it was the destiny of Japan to control Asia."[21] From 1975 to 1979, the Khmer Rouge murdered anyone of Chinese or Vietnamese descent during the Cambodian genocide.[22] And in 1994, the Hutu used ethnic identity cards to facilitate their slaughter of the Tutsi in Rwanda.[23]

In the United States, of course, those with Native American ancestry were regularly killed or displaced while those with "one black ancestor" or "one-drop" of African blood were routinely enslaved, lynched, and discriminated against.[24] At the turn of the twentieth century, many of the leading opponents of immigration—who proudly traced their ancestry back to the passengers aboard the *Mayflower*—believed that America's "pure pedigree" was being "mongrelized" by the "barbaric blood" of "the lower races" from southern and eastern Europe.[25] During World War II, some 120,000 Americans of Japanese descent were forced into camps because they were perceived as a threat.[26] Even today, white nationalist groups in the United States use modern commercial personal genomics tests as a means of establishing their northern European ancestral bona fides. In fact, many white nationalists proudly post the results of their DNA tests on racist websites such as Stormfront. (These postings, however, don't always elicit the response that the posters were anticipating. When one user revealed that 61 percent of his DNA was European, another user replied: "I've prepared you a drink. It is 61 percent pure water. The rest is potassium cyanide…. Cyanide isn't water, and YOU are not White."[27])

Or consider language. In 2017, a Pew Research Center study found that a vast majority of participants in each of the 14 countries analyzed believed that the most important "measure of who is 'one of us' and who is not" was the ability "to speak [the national] language."[28] Indeed, Moffett argues that the intricacies of language—its subtle accents or culturally specific vocabulary—make it "almost impossible to replicate precisely unless you learned it growing up, giving languages a priority in unmasking the foreigner among us."[29] For example, the Bible's book of Judges (12:5–6) recounts how the Ephraimites attacked Gilead, were defeated, and then fled across the Jordan River. Their retreat, however, was cut off by Gileadean soldiers who were able to root out the fleeing enemy by detecting the latter's faint accent—particularly their inability to pronounce the "sh" sound. So, when the men of Gilead came upon a suspected Ephraimite, "they said unto him, Art thou an Ephraimite?" And "if he said, Nay," the men of Gilead "said unto him":

> Say now Shibboleth: and he said Sibboleth: for he could not frame to pronounce it right. Then they took him, and slew him at the fords of the Jordan. Forty-two thousand Ephraimites were killed at that time.[30]

Language's effectiveness as a marker is also evident in *Invasion, U.S.A*, a 1952 film that invites viewers to imagine that the United States had been overrun by an unnamed communist army. At the climax of the movie, we learn that the enemy has not only infiltrated the nation's capital, but that it has done so dressed in American uniforms—effacing the primary means through which a U.S. soldier could identify the enemy. Thus, when a U.S. military commander gives the order to "Double the companies guarding the White House [and] the Capitol … and have them challenge everybody, no matter what uniform," a plucky American G.I. uses language to expose the invaders.

    U.S. Soldier: Halt! Who goes there?
    Enemy Soldier: Company B, 183rd Infantry.

U.S. Soldier: The 183rd, that's an Illinois outfit, ain't it?
Enemy Soldier: Yes? Yes! Uh, Chicago, Illinois!
U.S. Soldier: Do you ever go see the Cubs play?
Enemy Soldier: Cub? A cub is a young animal. A bear![31]

In response, the U.S. soldier raises the alarm and draws his weapon, but, alas, he and his compatriots are outgunned, and the enemy is able to capture the seat of government.

In fact, the scene from *Invasion, U.S.A.* is a wonderful illustration of how even sports can serve as a human marker. A national sport is often a central feature of a nation's identity—whether it be hockey in Canada, rugby in New Zealand, cricket in India, or table tennis in China.[32] Here, it was the enemy soldier's inability to identify with America's pastime—by failing to recognize the reference to the Chicago Cubs baseball team—that ultimately unmasked him as an outsider.

Political Tribes in America

Humanity's penchant for dividing itself into identifiable tribes that are agreeable to those within and hostile to those without, has manifested itself in contemporary American politics. Since the mid-nineteenth century, the polity of the United States has largely been divided into two tribes—the Democrats and the Republicans. And over the course of the last several decades, these two tribes have become increasingly discernible by a series of markers ranging from language, race, ethnicity, and religion, to even sports and food.

Traditionally, many Democrats and Republicans declared their tribal loyalties by donning quasi-uniforms—such as campaign t-shirts or hats— that advertise their tribe's leaders, colors (blue and red, respectively) or totem animals (a donkey and elephant, respectively) (Figure 1-1).[33] This remains true to this day. In fact, a select few may even have their tribal loyalties tattooed on their bodies. A spate of Democrats took to Twitter and Instagram to share their new tattoos of Barack Obama after the president was reelected in 2012.[34] Numerous tattoo studios were similarly bombarded with requests for renderings of Donald Trump following the 2016 presidential election.[35]

As of late, however, political tribes in the United States have also become marked by language. While Democrats and Republicans routinely talk about the same issues, they do so in strikingly different terms. For instance, whereas Democrats talk about undocumented immigrants, gun safety, and consumer protection, Republicans speak of illegal aliens, gun control, and corporate regulation. This was not always the case. In

Figure 1-1: Partisans often wear campaign merchandise—such as 2020 Democratic presidential candidate Andrew Yang's "Make America THink again" or President Donald Trump's "Make America Great Again" hats—as quasi-party uniforms (Dave Spataro Photography).

fact, when the economist Matthew Gentzkow and his colleagues showed a group of participants several speeches by members of Congress from 1873 to 2016, and asked them to guess whether the remarks were given by a Democrat or a Republican, they found that if a speech was given prior the mid-1990s, participants were able to correctly guess the party only slightly better than chance. But by 2010, participants were able to identify the right party 73 percent of the time.[36]

Likewise, several decades ago, one would have been hard pressed to identify people as Democrats or Republicans based on their race, ethnicity, or religion, let alone their culinary habits and musical tastes.[37] But that too is no longer the case. Today, race and ethnicity can often be used to identify someone's political tribe.[38] Outside of white voters—who are somewhat more likely to identify with or lean toward the Republican Party than the Democratic Party (51 percent to 43 percent)—there are sizable racial and ethnic differences in partisan affiliation. A 2018 Pew Research Center survey found that 84 percent of African American voters "identify with or lean toward the Democratic Party [whereas] just 8 percent of black voters identify in some way with the Republican Party." Similarly, Hispanic American (63 percent to 28 percent) and Asian American (65 percent to 27 percent) voters are twice as likely to affiliate with the Democratic Party than the Republican Party.[39]

So too can religion. The Pew Research Center found that 68 percent of voters who are religiously unaffiliated identify with the Democratic Party while only 22 percent identify with the Republican Party. And while Jewish voters align with the Democratic Party (67 percent) more than the Republican Party (31 percent), Mormon voters are much more likely to identify as Republicans (72 percent) than as Democrats (22 percent). In

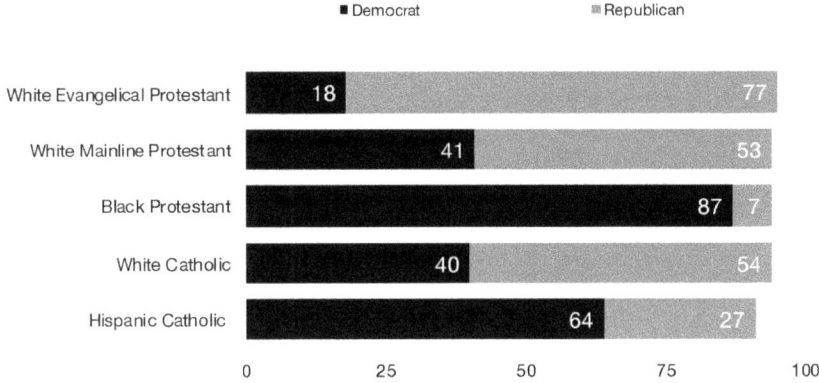

Figure 1-2: The percentage of White Evangelical Protestant, White Mainline Protestant, Black Protestant, White Catholic, and Hispanic Catholic Americans who identify as Democrats and Republicans (Source: Pew Research Center, 2018).

addition, while Hispanic Catholics and black Protestants are more likely to identify with the Democratic Party, white Catholics, mainline Protestants, and evangelical Protestants are more likely to identify with the GOP (Figure 1-2).[40]

In *Prius or Pickup? How the Answers to Four Simple Questions Explain America's Great Divide*, the political scientists Marc Hetherington and Jonathan Weiler found that Democrats and Republicans can even be identified by a suite of markers associated with their lifestyle choices. Someone who resides in an urban area and drives a foreign-made car is probably a Democrat, while someone who lives in a rural area and rides an American-made vehicle is probably a Republican. Someone who shops at Whole Foods and dines at authentic ethnic restaurants is more often than not a Democrat, while someone who frequents Walmart and eats at established chain restaurants is more often than not a Republican. Someone who swigs Starbucks coffee and microbrew beer is likely a Democrat, while someone who drinks Dunkin' Donuts coffee and Coors beer is probably a Republican. And someone who listens to country music and watches NASCAR or the television show *Duck Dynasty* is in all likelihood a Republican, while someone who enjoys everything but country music and tunes into soccer or the animated sitcom *Family Guy* is in all likelihood a Democrat.[41]

Simply put, fifty years ago one would have had to have seen a political sign on your lawn or a political sticker on your bumper to know whether you were a Democrat or a Republican. But today, one stands a good chance of identifying your political tribe simply by knowing whether your lawn is in an urban or rural area or whether your vehicle is foreign or domestic (no sign or sticker required). According to Lilliana Mason, a political scientist at the University of Maryland, College Park and author of *Uncivil Agreement: How Politics Became Our Identity*, being a Democrat or a Republican isn't just a single part of our identity anymore. Rather, partisanship has become "a mega-identity," a polestar around which many of our other identities have aligned. As such, "A single vote can now indicate a person's partisan preference as well as his or her religion, race, ethnicity, gender, neighborhood, and favorite grocery store."[42]

Political Tribalism in America

Unfortunately, the more that Democrats and Republicans have in common with themselves, the less they have in common with each other; and the less that one party has in common with another, the more contemptible that other party may appear. In a word, American politics has become more tribal. When asked to rate the parties on a 0–100 "thermometer" scale—where 0 is the coldest, most negative rating and 100 is the warmest, most positive rating—Democrats and Republicans gave an average rating of about 70 to their own party and 30 to the opposing party.[43] Similarly, 88 percent of Democrats and 91 percent of Republicans recently admitted that they have an unfavorable view of the opposing party.[44] In the parlance of political science, Americans have become affectively polarized (Figure P-2). And when Democrats and Republicans hold their political counterparts in such low regard, they are regrettably more willing to stereotype, discriminate against, separate themselves from, dehumanize, and even wish or inflict violence upon each other.

Partisan Stereotyping

Survey data shows that Democrats and Republicans routinely overestimate the extent to which the other party's supporters belong to party-stereotypical groups and hold party-stereotypical issue positions. For example:

- While most lesbian, gay, and bisexual (LGB) Americans are Democrats, most Democrats are not LGB.[45] Only 6.3 percent of Democrats are LGB. Yet Republicans estimate that a whopping 38.2 percent of Democrats are lesbian, gay, and bisexual. Members of the GOP similarly overestimate the percentage of Democrats who are African American or atheist. Likewise, while most Americans 65 years or older are Republican, most Republicans are not old.[46] In fact, just 21.3 percent of Republicans are 65+ years old. However, Democrats estimate that 44.2 percent of Republicans are aged. They also overestimate how many Republicans are evangelical Christians or earn over $250,000 per year.[47]

- Research has shown that Democrats and Republicans tend to overestimate the extremity of each other's views on a host of issues, ranging from affirmative action and abortion to immigration and race.[48] When asked to estimate what share of Republicans believe that immigration can strengthen the United States, Democrats guessed about half. In fact, almost nine in ten Republicans agreed. Likewise, while Republicans surmised that almost seven in ten Democrats support the idea of open borders, only three in ten said they do.[49] Whereas 57 percent of Democrats believed that a majority of Republicans agreed with discriminatory attitudes, only 22 percent of them reported even somewhat agreeing with them. And while Republicans believed that 63 percent of Democrats agreed with banning certain public figures from speaking on college campuses, only 34 percent of them even somewhat did.[50] In many instances, Mason notes, "our conflicts are largely over who we think we are rather than over reasoned differences of opinion."[51]

Democrats and Republicans also tend to associate the other party's members with a host of unenviable personal traits and character flaws. For instance:

- A 2016 survey revealed that around one-in-two Republicans believed that Democrats were more close-minded, dishonest, and lazy than other Americans. Among Democrats, one-in-three believed that Republicans were less intelligent than other Americans and nearly three-in-four held that members of the GOP were close-minded.[52]
- Similarly, not only do some 50 percent of Democrats and 40 percent of Republicans believe that their party is "morally right," but 35 percent of Democrats and 47 percent of Republicans also believe that members of the opposing party are immoral.[53] In fact, just over 40 percent of both Democrats and Republicans believe that their partisan counterparts are "downright evil."[54] As the journalist Thomas Edsall notes, "In real numbers, this suggests that 48.8 million voters … believe that members of the opposition party are in league with the devil."[55]

Partisan Discrimination

What's more, research has shown that Democrats and Republicans are readily willing to discriminate against each another. In 2015, the political scientists Shanto Iyengar and Sean J. Westwood asked several partisan subjects to read the resumes of a pair of graduating high school seniors and decide which of the students should receive a $30,000 scholarship. The catch was that one of the students was a Democrat and the other was a Republican—as evidenced by their respective leadership of the Young Democrats and Young Republicans. The participants received one of three different sets of resumes: one in which the students were equally qualified (Figure 1-3), one in which the Democratic student had a higher grade point average (4.0) than the Republican student (3.5), and one in which the Republican student had a higher GPA (4.0) than the Democratic student (3.5).

Applicant Highlights	
Arthur Wolfe	Jeremy O'Neil
Academic achievements	**Academic achievements**
4.0 GPA	4.0 GPA
Community involvement	**Community involvement**
Volunteer park ranger	Volunteer middle school math tutor
Habitat for Humanity volunteer	Red Cross volunteer
Extracurricular activities	**Extracurricular activities**
Bowling team	Art Club
President of the Young Republicans	President of the Young Democrats
Honor Society	Member of the marching band

Figure 1-3: When Democrats and Republicans were provided with a pair of "equally qualified" resumes like the one above, almost 80 percent awarded a scholarship to the student who shared their party affiliation (Source: Shanto Iyengar and Sean J. Westwood. 2015. "Fear and Loathing Across Party Lines: New Evidence of Group Polarization." *American Journal of Political Science*. Vol. 59, No. 3).

The results were disheartening. When the students were equally qualified, nearly 80 percent of Democrats and Republicans awarded the scholarship to the student who shared their party affiliation. Yet the vast majority of Democrats (70 percent) and Republicans (85 percent) awarded the $30,000 to their co-partisan even when the student from the opposing party was more qualified.[56] Another study found that Democrats and Republicans are some 20 percentage points more willing to cooperate with members of their own party than they are with members of the opposing party.[57] And still another revealed that Democrats and Republicans "choose to hear from those who are politically like-minded on topics that have nothing to do with politics ... in preference to those with greater expertise on the topic but have different political views."[58]

Partisan Segregation

In addition, many Democrats and Republicans appear unwilling to associate with members of the political opposition in any way, shape, or form. In 2015, Speaker of the House John Boehner (R–OH) admitted that he stopped playing golf with President Obama because "his office phone lines kept lighting up with angry callers" every time he did so.[59] In 2019, several Democrats were outraged when the liberal television host Ellen DeGeneres was captured on television sitting with former Republican president George W. Bush at an NFL football game.[60] First Lady Michelle Obama was booed when she attended a NASCAR event in the Deep South and Vice President-elect Mike Pence (R–IN) was jeered when he attended a performance of the Broadway musical *Hamilton* in New York City.[61] Moreover,

- Americans are 19 percentage points less willing to spend occasional social time with a member of the opposing party than with a member of their own party.[62]
- Thirty-one percent of Democrats and 27 percent of Republicans said that it would be harder for them to get along with a new person who moved into their neighborhood if that person belonged to the other party.[63]
- Slightly less than 10 percent of Democrats and Republicans report having spouses or partners that belong to the other party, and 19 percent of Democrats and 22 percent of Republicans said that they would "be unhappy if an immediate family member married someone from the other party."[64]

Dehumanization

But it gets worse. Much worse. A number of Democrats and Republicans have also evinced a willingness to view members of the opposing party as less than human. In "Men Against Fire," an episode of the British satirical series *Black Mirror*, a soldier named Stripe is in the process of hunting down humanoid mutants in a dystopian, post-apocalyptic future. He soon realizes, however, that these hideous beasts are nothing of the sort.

In reality, they are human beings who happen to be members of a despised group that has been marked for extinction. Stripe's hostility toward the so-called "roaches" had been induced by a brain implant that made him see his human targets as pale monsters with fangs and hear their cries for mercy as hostile, ear-piercing shrieks. It was only when this implant began to short-circuit that the true nature of his mission was revealed. He had not been engaged in a noble effort to save humanity from an inhuman threat. He was a participant in a genocide that had been launched to eliminate a group of people who were deemed to be genetically inferior.

The episode is an exaggerated depiction of what has come to be known as dehumanization. According to David Livingstone Smith, a professor of philosophy at the University of New England and author of *Less than Human: Why We Demean, Enslave, and Exterminate Others*, dehumanization is "the act of conceiving people as subhuman creatures rather than as human beings."[65] Dehumanized people can be portrayed as unclean parasites or vermin who must be exterminated lest they contaminate one with something harmful, bloodthirsty predators that must be killed in self-defense, or prey who can be hunted for sport.[66]

Sadly, examples of dehumanization—or at least examples of dehumanizing rhetoric—are ubiquitous throughout history. In colonial America, the Puritan minister Cotton Mather and then–general George Washington respectively wrote that Native Americans were "Ravenous howling wolves" and "beasts of prey."[67] During World War I, the U.S. government produced a poster that depicted Germany as a vicious ape. Amid World War II, the Nazi Heinrich Himmler referred to the Jewish people as a "bacillus" that needed to be destroyed, the Japanese called American soldiers "dogs," and the U.S. military portrayed the Japanese as "lice" whose "breeding ground" had to be annihilated (Figure 1-4). Prior to the Rwandan genocide in 1994, Hutus routinely characterized the Tutsi as "cockroaches." In 2004, the popular conservative radio host Michael Savage opined that the Iraqi prisoners who had been tortured in the Abu Ghraib prison by U.S. military personnel were "vermin" whose forcible conversion to Christianity would be "the only thing that [could] turn them into human beings."[68]

The use of such dehumanizing language and imagery can have devastating effects. Michelle Maiese, a professor of philosophy at Emmanuel College, suggests that most human beings "believe that people's basic human rights should not be violated—that crimes like murder, rape, and torture are wrong."[69] Life forms that are subhuman, however, are not typically extended the protections provided by our moral code. Once someone is dehumanized, therefore, they may be denied moral consideration. If exterminating a roach is not immoral, and a particular person is perceived as being akin to a roach, then exterminating that person is not regarded as

Chapter 1. The Nature of Political Tribalism

Louseous Japanicas

The first serious outbreak of this lice epidemic was officially noted on December 7, 1941, at Honolulu, T. H. To the Marine Corps, especially trained in combating this type of pestilence, was assigned the gigantic task of extermination. Extensive experiments on Guadalcanal, Tarawa, and Saipan have shown that this louse inhabits coral atolls in the South Pacific, particularly pill boxes, palm trees, caves, swamps and jungles.

Flame throwers, mortars, grenades and bayonets have proven to be an effective remedy. But before a complete cure may be effected the origin of the plague, the breeding grounds around the Tokyo area, must be completely annihilated.

Figure 1-4: An example of dehumanizing rhetoric, used by the United States during World War II, that portrayed the Japanese as less than human (*Leatherneck Magazine*).

immoral. As such, Smith notes that dehumanization operates by "dissolving our inhibitions and inflaming our destructive passions ... [thereby] empowering us to perform acts that would, under other circumstances, be unthinkable."[70]

Indeed, a host of studies show that dehumanized individuals and groups are more likely to be mistreated than those who are perceived to be fully human. Northwestern University's Nour Kteily found that people who dehumanized Arabs were significantly less likely to support Arab immigration and more likely to support drone strikes in the Middle East than those who did not see Arabs as subhuman.[71] A study by the psychologist Phillip Goff and his colleagues found that when respondents were subtly primed to associate black people with apes, they became more supportive of the violent policing of black criminal suspects. They also found that black defendants who were represented by apelike metaphors in the press were more likely to be put to death than those who were not described in a dehumanizing manner.[72] Another study by the psychologists Laurie A. Rudman and Kris Mescher found that men who dehumanized women were more likely to suggest that women who had been raped "deserved it" and that they would rape a woman "if [they] could be assured that no one would know and that [they] could in no way be punished" than men who did not.[73]

Disconcertingly, dehumanization is present in American politics. Former Senate Minority Leader Harry Reid (D–NV) referred to Donald Trump as "the Republican Party's.... Frankenstein monster" and *New York* magazine depicted President Trump as a pig on its cover. Fox News host Jeanine Pirro referred to Democrats as "demon-rats" and President Trump's son Eric suggested that anyone wanting to investigate ties between his father's presidential campaign and the Russian government in 2016 were "not even people."[74] Such sentiments are not uncommon. One 2019 survey revealed that around 20 percent of Democrats and Republicans believe that members of the opposing party "lack the traits to be considered fully human" and should be "treated like animals."[75] A study by the political scientists Alexander G. Theodoridis, James Martherus, and Andy Martinez found "a pronounced willingness by both Democrats and Republicans to asymmetrically dehumanize members of the out-party." In fact, 77 percent of those queried "rated their political opponents as less evolved than members of their own party" on the "ascent of man" scale (Figure 1-5).[76]

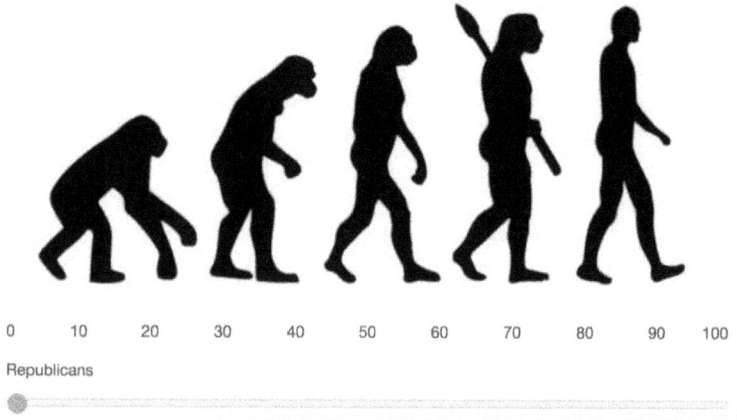

Figure 1-5: In 2019, Theodoridis, Martherus, and Martinez found that 77 percent of partisans rated their political opponents as less evolved than members of their own party on the "ascent of man" scale (Alexander G. Theodoridis, James Martherus, and Andy Martinez. 2019. "Party Animals? Extreme Polarization and Dehumanization." *Political Behavior*. July. Reproduced with permission of Alexander G. Theodoridis).

Chapter 1. The Nature of Political Tribalism 25

> **Chaos at Republican Gathering**
>
> 07/05/2014 03:18 PM MDT
>
> A Fourth of July Republican Party cookout at the Fairgrounds started out peaceful, but quickly spiraled out of control. After a fight broke out between two of the roughly 5,000 attendees, the crowd began charging for the exits. More than two dozen adults sustained minor injuries, and a small child's arm was broken.

Figure 1-6: Partisans who read a vignette about either Democrats or Republicans (as seen here) fighting at a party gathering are more likely to dehumanize the participants if they are counter-partisans instead of co-partisans (Alexander G. Theodoridis, James Martherus, and Andy Martinez. 2019. "Party Animals? Extreme Polarization and Dehumanization." *Political Behavior*. July. Reproduced with permission of Alexander G. Theodoridis).

In addition, Theodoridis and his colleagues asked a group of partisans to read a vignette describing a fight that broke out at either a Democratic Party or Republican Party gathering, and note whether they agreed or disagreed with the statement: "These people are like animals." The only difference between the two scenarios was the party responsible for sponsoring the event (Figure 1-6). Yet while 34 percent of Democrats agreed that the revelers were "like animals" when the vignette described a group of Republicans, only 26 percent of them agreed when the scenario involved their fellow Democrats. Likewise, while 43 percent of Republicans were eager to dehumanize Democrats, only 31 percent were willing to do so when the vignette implicated members of the GOP.[77]

Lethal Partisanship

While our political tribes—which have increasingly become "mega-identities" marked by race, religion, and lifestyle—can activate our tribal instincts to stereotype, discriminate against, separate from, and dehumanize our political opponents, they can also encourage us to approach members of the out-party with fear. In *Why We Are Polarized*, the political commentator Ezra Klein wrote:

> Imagine two Democrats. One of them, Rick, is white, straight, and conservative. He attends an evangelical church, lives in a rural area, and belongs to a union. The other, Sarah, is black, gay, and liberal. She's skeptical of religion, lives in Los Angeles, and identifies as a feminist. Rick, looking at the candidacy of George W. Bush, would find some of his identities under threat—Bush is a Republican and hostile to unions—but other identities would modulate his panic: like him, Bush is an evangelical Christian, a white man, a conservative, respectful of rural culture. John Kerry, meanwhile, is a pro-union Democrat, but he's also a liberal urbanite who evinced little understanding of rural America or the evangelical church. This is the kind of Democrat who would at least have considered voting for Bush.
>
> Sarah, by contrast, would look at Bush and see all her identities under threat simultaneously: he's a Republican, an evangelical, a white man, a conservative. He shows little respect for urban life, for atheists, and he backed a constitutional amendment to ban gay marriages. This is the kind of Democrat who would fear Bush, who would see him as a genuine danger to her life, who would do almost anything to see him defeated.[78]

In short, when a political party becomes our "mega-identity," the opposing party won't simply be viewed as a threat to our party, it will be seen as a threat to our race, our religion (or lack thereof), and our very way of life. No wonder Democrats and Republicans have increasingly come to fear the other party. In fact:

- Fifty-five percent of Democrats and 49 percent of Republicans say they are "afraid" of the other party.[79]
- Forty-one percent of Democrats and 45 percent of Republicans believe that the opposing party's policies are a "threat to the nation's well-being." Similarly, 56 percent of Democrats and 70 percent of the GOP believe that the opposing party is "a serious threat to the United States and its people."[80]
- And 41 percent of Democrats and a whopping 61 percent of Republicans think of members of the other political party as enemies instead of political opponents.[81]

Regrettably, when one political tribe feels threatened by another, it may wish ill-fortune upon their opponents and even desire that they become the target of violence. As the political scientists Nathan P. Kalmoe and Lilliana Mason found, *lethal partisanship*—or the tendency of Democrats and Republicans to rationalize, endorse, or take pleasure in the harming of their political adversaries—is disconcertingly alive and well in the United States.[82] For instance:

- Seventeen percent of Democrats and 7 percent of Republicans report that they have "wished that someone would physically injure one or more politicians" from the opposing party.
- Just over 10 percent of Democrats and Republicans believe that it is "OK for [members of their own party] to send threatening and intimidating messages to [opposing party] leaders."
- Just under 10 percent of Democrats and Republicans maintain that "it is OK for an ordinary [member of their party] in the public to harass an ordinary [member of the opposing party] on the Internet, in a way that makes the target feel unsafe."
- Almost 10 percent of members of both parties believe that it is justified for their own party "to use violence in advancing their political goals."
- And 20 percent of Democrats and 15 percent of Republicans think that "we'd be better off as a country if large numbers of [the opposing party] in the public today just died."[83]

These percentages are relatively small. Nevertheless, they do represent tens of millions of Americans, and it only takes one of these lethal partisans to inflict great harm. In June 2017, James Hodgkinson opened fire on a group of Republican members of Congress who had gathered at a park in Alexandria, Virginia, to practice for the annual bipartisan Congressional Baseball Game for Charity. In all, the gunman shot five people, including House Majority Whip Steve Scalise (R–LA). Prior to the shooting, Hodgkinson had posted several statements on social media that were hostile toward the Republican Party, including one in which he referred to President Trump as "inhuman" and another in which he wrote "Trump has Destroyed our Democracy. It's Time to Destroy Trump."[84] In October 2018, Cesar Sayoc was arrested for mailing pipe bombs to a dozen Democratic party leaders, including former President Barack Obama and former Secretary of State Hillary Clinton. Convinced that President Trump's critics were "dangerous, unpatriotic, and evil," the Florida man took to Facebook and declared that "Satan Sent Obama to Destroy America" and that the "Swamp had to be drained!" He even drove a van that featured images of Obama and Clinton with crosshairs superimposed upon their faces.[85] The fact that there are perhaps tens of thousands of Americans—like Hodgkinson and Sayoc—who endorse something as undemocratic as the use of violence against their political opponents is, to say the least, unnerving. Yet so too is the fact that so many more are willing to stereotype, discriminate against, separate themselves from, and dehumanize their political opponents. We must do better.

> **What We Can Do:** As critical political thinkers, we should (1) recognize the role that political tribalism plays in our own lives and limit its influence by (2) focusing on what unites Democrats and Republicans rather than what divides them and (3) cultivating relationships with members of the other party.

"We, as modern Americans," Lilliana Mason writes, "probably like to think of ourselves as more sophisticated and tolerant than a group of fifth-grade boys from 1954.... But the Rattlers and Eagles have a lot more in common with today's Democrats and Republicans than we would like to believe."[86] Similar to the Rattlers and Eagles of Robbers Cave State Park, Democrats and Republicans have coalesced into two unique tribes that not only favor their in-group but also devalue the out-group in a myriad of ways. Nevertheless, we can take certain steps to alleviate the poisonous impact that political tribalism has on our body politic.

Recognize the Role that Political Tribalism Plays in Our Lives

In the opening scene of HBO's political drama, *The Newsroom*, news anchor Will McAvoy suggests that "the first step to solving any problem is recognizing there is one."[87] Many of us believe that political tribalism is something to which others succumb. But as the American physicist Richard Feynman said, "the first principle is that you must not fool yourself—and you are the easiest person to fool."[88] We all need to plumb the depths of our own in-party affinities and out-party enmities and honestly assess the degree to which political tribalism has infected our lives. To that end, we should pay particular attention to how politics makes us feel. For instance:

- Does our breathing speed up or our hearts beat faster when someone criticizes our political party?
- When a political scandal erupts, do we feel deflated when the participants are members of our own party, and a sense of relief and righteous indignation when they are not?
- Do we take pleasure in the political failures of the other party, irrespective of the real-world implications?[89]

If we feel as though we are being personally attacked while watching either Fox News or MSNBC, or anxiously search for the party affiliation of an unfamiliar politician accused of impropriety, or hope—in our heart of hearts—that the economy will suffer a downturn while the opposing party's president is in office, we are exhibiting the hallmarks of political tribalism. Furthermore, we should also be mindful of how political tribalism can influence our behavior. For example:

- Have we adopted a number of qualities typical of members of our political party, or belittled those qualities emblematic of members of the opposing party?
- Do we underestimate the diversity within each political party, and use overly broad referents such as "we" and "they?"
- Have we chosen to befriend those who share our partisan affiliation, and eschew those who do not?
- Do we use epithets—rednecks, Repugnicans, libtards, or snowflakes, et cetera—when describing members of the opposing party?[90] Have we dehumanized or aggressed someone because they are a counter-partisan?[91]

If we drive a Dodge Ram while deriding those who drive a Toyota Prius, or claim that "Republicans are racist" or "Democrats are unpatriotic," or overestimate the number of Democrats who are LGB or Republicans who are rich, or avoid a colleague at work because they identify with the opposing party, or cut off drivers with Donald Trump and MAGA bumper stickers on their vehicles, we are displaying the telltale signs of political tribalism. Fortunately, once we recognize that there is a problem, we can take steps to address it.

Focus on What Unites Us Rather than What Divides Us

One way in which we can mitigate the influence of political tribalism in our lives is by making a concerted effort to look for the similarities between ourselves and our partisan counterparts as opposed to the differences. For instance, imagine that you were tasked with grouping the three images of a baseball, baseball bat, and football depicted below (Figure 1-7). How would you proceed?

You could place the image of the baseball and the baseball bat into a "baseball" group and the football into a "football" group. Or you could place the baseball and the football into a "ball" group and the baseball bat into a "not a ball" group. Alternatively, you could place all three objects into one group ("sports") or even three separate groups (perhaps "round,"

Figure 1-7: Just as there are similarities and differences between the baseball, baseball bat, and football depicted above, there are also similarities and differences between human beings (illustrations by E.S. Redmond).

"long," and "oblong"). The point is that any of these options are possible. The same logic indubitably applies to human beings. As David Berreby notes,

> Human beings are unusually alike. We're also, each of us, unique. From these two facts, it follows that measurable, objective differences will always exist between *any* two groupings of people, and that any two groups, no matter how different, will be the same on many other measures.[92]

Yes, Democrats and Republicans have increasingly become divided by race and religion and lifestyle. Yet as Perry Bacon, Jr., and Dhrumil Mehta of *FiveThirtyEight* note, "Just because the parties are trending in a certain direction doesn't mean they're fully there."[93] In fact, there are tens of millions of Americans who defy their party's stereotypes. If we seek a similarity with a member of the opposing party, therefore, we will most assuredly find one. At the very least, we should recognize the fact that Democrats and Republicans are all Americans. For research has shown that just reminding partisans of that naked truth alone can substantially reduce the animus they express toward members of the other party.[94]

Cultivate a Relationship with a Member of the Other Party

In "The Least Politically Prejudiced Place in America," Amanda Ripley of *The Atlantic* reports that the people residing in Watertown, New York, are more likely to live near, and be married to, people who disagree with them politically than most Americans, and "When people know members of the other political tribe intimately, as neighbors, friends, or spouses," she writes, "they correct for the ... negative stereotypes, ... distrust, ... and awkwardness [that] typifies limited intergroup interaction." Accordingly, the people of Watertown "tend to be less likely than

Americans elsewhere to say they'd be upset if a family member married someone from the other party," and they are "more likely to describe their political opponents as more 'patriotic' and less likely to describe them as 'selfish.'" Even the founders of the local pro-life organization and Planned Parenthood are dear friends. "It's never been contentious," one of them said, "You know, we *know* each other."[95]

The residents of Watertown serve as a reminder that the power of political tribalism can be reduced by forging relationships with members of the opposing political party. Numerous studies have found that frequent and sustained contact between people belonging to different groups leads them to be more accepting of the group to which they don't belong.[96] A 2011 study by Thomas F. Pettigrew, Linda R. Tropp, Ulrich Wagner, and Oliver Christ found that this is particularly true of inter-group friendships.[97] A recent Pew Research Center survey revealed that partisans who have a lot or some friends in the other party are less likely to have "very cold" feelings about the people in that party. While 49 percent of Democrats without at least some Republicans friends rate members of the GOP as "very cold," only 31 percent of Democrats with at least some Republican friends consider them as such and Republicans with at least some Democratic friends are half as likely to rate Democrats as "very cold" than are members of the GOP with few or no Democratic friends (62 percent vs. 30 percent).[98] Unfortunately, only 31 percent of Democrats and 39 percent of Republicans have "a lot or some" friends in the opposing party.[99] Yet, if Justice Antonin Scalia—a staunch conservative—and Justice Ruth Bader Ginsburg—a steadfast liberal—were able to bond over their love of opera, Democrats and Republicans should be able to connect with a cross-partisan colleague, neighbor, or family member over some shared hobby or interest.[100]

Ezra Klein argues that "when our identities separate us from each other, they can be a moat, widening the distance between us.... [But] when we share identities with each other, they can act as a bridge."[101] It is imperative that we, as critical political thinkers, not only find some bridges between ourselves and members of the opposing party, but that we also be willing to cross them. If we do, we will be less willing to give in to the dictates of political tribalism, and, as we shall see, few things are more important for our republic than that, because the effects of political tribalism on the democratic ideal can be downright devastating.

Part II
Political Opinions

CHAPTER 2

Placing Party Before Policy

"When a party leader vocalizes a strong opinion on an issue, many people just accept that view. In the mind of the voter, it's replacing a hard question ('How do I feel about international trade taxes?') with an easy question ('What team am I on, and how would they answer this question?')."[1]
—Brian Resnick

The Problem: Political tribalism encourages Democrats and Republicans to prioritize their political party over their political opinions.

American politics is dominated by two increasingly adversarial tribes: the Democrats and the Republicans. As we have seen, these two tribes have become well-marked by uniforms, language, race, ethnicity, religion, and even lifestyle. Yet according to the democratic ideal, Democrats and Republicans should be marked, first and foremost, by their considered political opinions. The folk theory of democracy presumes that voters study the issues, adopt their positions, and identify with the party that best represents their views. Unfortunately, the folk theory is largely a mirage.

The manner by which a voter comes to identify with the Democratic or Republican Party is undoubtedly complex and continues to be a matter of debate. Some political scientists underscore the role of genetics, and some accentuate the socializing influence of parents and spouses.[2] Still others emphasize the desire to belong to a group of "people like me" and "people I like."[3] Yet, few (if any) argue that our partisan identities are derived from an objective and rigorous review of the issues. To the contrary, decades of research has shown that a substantial swath of the American electorate operates under the tribal theory of democracy in which voters initially identify with a party and then proceed to either ignore or adopt that party's political views.[4]

Ignoring One's Party's Views

Take, for instance, so-called *unsorted* voters. Unsorted voters are balloters who have issue positions that generally contrast with those of their political party—such as a pro-life Democrat or a tax-and-spend Republican. In *The Partisan Sort: How Liberals Became Democrats and Conservatives Became Republicans*, the political scientist Matthew Levendusky notes that as recently as 2004 only about half of the Democrats and Republicans surveyed agreed with their party on the issues of abortion (52 percent), guaranteed jobs (51 percent), guaranteed health insurance (50 percent), and defense spending (45 percent).[5] In *The Ambivalent Partisan: How Critical Loyalty Promotes Democracy*, the political scientists Howard G. Lavine, Christopher D. Johnston, and Marco R. Steenbergen similarly found that 20 percent of Democrats and 17 percent of Republicans were unsorted on economic issues, such as a government-guaranteed income, and 15 percent of Democrats and 33 percent of Republicans were unsorted on social issues, such as laws protecting homosexuals from job discrimination.[6] This isn't the stuff of which democracies are made.

Adopting One's Party Views

Fortunately, the number of unsorted voters in the United States has substantially declined over the course of the last half-century (see Party Polarization in Figure P-2).[7] Unfortunately, a sorted voter can undermine the democratic ideal just as much as an unsorted one. At first glance, this charge seems nonsensical. After all, a *sorted* electorate—one composed of voters whose issue positions align with those of their political party—is a defining feature of the folk theory of democracy. But all sorts are not created equal. There are two ways in which voters can sort; they can either change their party to align with their issue positions, or they can change their issue positions to align with their party. While the first method cleaves to the democratic ideal, the second one does not. Lamentably, sorted voters have generally chosen party over policy.[8] As reported by Lavine, Johnston, and Steenbergen:

> Rather than switching parties to accommodate their substantive preferences, the empirical evidence indicates that the voters tend to do the opposite. They

sort by altering their policy preferences to fit with their standing party attachments. Thus, an unsorted liberal Republican is more likely to become a sorted conservative Republican than a sorted liberal Democrat.[9]

And therein lies the problem. Of course, citizens should identify with the political party that best represents their views. But their party should not determine their ill-considered views. Rather, their well-considered views should determine their party. To do otherwise, Lavine, Johnston, and Steenbergen continue,

> … implies that voters' substantive opinions are less a reflection of systematic thought about desired end states than they are reflexive accommodations to socialized partisan attachments. So rather than reasoning that "I favor a progressive tax system because I value social equality (or have a low income)," it is "I favor a progressive tax system because I am a Democrat and that's what Democrats favor."[10]

In fact, one finding after another indicates that if the Democratic and Republican parties were to suddenly change their stances on the issues, many of their members would follow suit. This is exactly what one would expect if the voters had sorted themselves according to the dictates of the tribal, rather than folk, theory of democracy. Consider just a few examples:

- In June 2015, Republican Donald Trump declared his candidacy for the presidency. During his announcement, the real estate tycoon said, "I will build a great wall.… I will build a great, great wall on our southern border."[11] At the time, the proposal had considerable support among voters in both parties. Between 2005 and 2015, multiple polls showed that between 40–50 percent of Democrats and 60–70 percent of Republicans supported building a barrier along the U.S.–Mexico border. As the wall became a common theme at Trump's campaign rallies and a focus of his presidency, however, partisan approval of the measure diverged.[12] By 2019, Democratic support for the wall had plunged to just 6 percent while Republican support had surged to 82 percent.[13]
- A recent HuffPost/YouGov poll found that the American people's policy views regularly shifted when they were given partisan cues. When asked if they favored "requiring background checks for buying and selling guns," 87 percent of Democrats and 62 percent of Republicans said yes. Yet when respondents were asked, "Do you support or oppose President Obama's plan to require background checks for buying and selling guns," 91 percent of Democrats and

Chapter 2. Placing Party Before Policy

42 percent of Republicans expressed support.[14] Similarly, when asked, "Barack Obama has praised the idea of universal health care. Do you agree or disagree with Obama about universal health care?," 82 percent of Democrats and 16 percent of Republicans agreed. But when universal health care was associated with Donald Trump, Democratic support plummeted to 46 percent while Republican support surged to 44 percent. When voters were asked, "Donald Trump believes that the policy of affirmative action should be kept in place. Do you agree or disagree with Trump about affirmative action?," some 43 percent of Democrats and 33 percent of Republicans agreed. But when affirmative action was associated with Barack Obama, Democratic support increased to over 60 percent while Republican support declined to just above 10 percent.[15]

- In 2004, 39 percent of Democrats and 40 percent of Republicans supported the North American Free Trade Agreement (NAFTA)—an international agreement signed by the governments of Canada, Mexico, and the United States to create a trilateral trade bloc in North America. During the 2016 election, however, then–Republican presidential nominee Donald Trump forcefully spoke out against the agreement, calling it "the worst trade deal maybe ever signed anywhere, but certainly ever signed in this country."[16] By February 2017, 67 percent of Democrats and 22 percent of Republicans supported NAFTA.[17]

The evidence that voters routinely place party before policy isn't simply borne out by survey data; it's found in lab experiments as well. In a famous 2003 study, the psychologist Geoffrey Cohen devised two versions of a welfare policy—one which provided stringent benefits and another which was quite generous (Figure 2-1). As expected, pilot testing revealed that Democrats preferred the generous policy to the stringent one, and Republicans preferred the stringent policy to the generous one.[18]

Stringent Policy	Generous Policy
$250 per month to a family with one child	$800 per month to a family with one child
Extra $50 per each individual child	Extra $200 for every additional child
Partial medical insurance	Full medical insurance
Benefits limited to 1.5 years	Benefits limited to 8 years

Stringent Policy	Generous Policy
No food stamps	Additional $2,000 in food stamps
No housing	Extra subsidies for housing
No day care	Extra subsidies for day care
No job training	Job training program
No paid work	Guaranteed job after benefits ended
No college tuition	Two years paid tuition at community college

Figure 2-1: In general, Democrats tend to support more social spending than Republicans. Nevertheless, Democrats and Republicans will respectively champion "stringent" and "generous" welfare policies when informed that their parties endorse such measures (Geoffrey L. Cohen. 2003. "Party Over Policy: The Dominating Impact of Group Influence on Political Beliefs." *Journal of Personal and Social Psychology*. Vol. 85, No. 5).

But when Cohen presented Democrats and Republicans with these welfare policies *and* a report detailing the political parties' positions on the proposals, he found that "the stated position of one's political party ... overwhelmed ... the policy's objective content."[19] Cohen continued,

> Regardless of whether the policy was generous or stringent [Democratic] participants supported it if told that Democrats supported it and they opposed it if told Democrats opposed it. Likewise, [Republican] participants supported the policy if told that Republicans supported it and they opposed it if told Republicans opposed it.[20]

In 2018, the political scientists Michael Barber and Jeremy C. Pope similarly asked Republicans about their positions on ten contemporary political issues—ranging from increasing taxes on the wealthy and raising the minimum wage, to enforcing penalties on women who obtain abortions and allowing teachers to carry guns on school property. One-third of the participants were simply presented with the policy statements and asked whether they agreed or disagreed; another one-third were presented with the policy statements, notified that "Donald Trump has said that he *supports* [emphasis added] this policy," and asked whether they agreed or disagreed; and the final one-third of respondents were presented with the policy statements, informed that "Donald Trump has said that he *opposes* [emphasis added] this policy," and asked whether they agreed or disagreed (Figure 2-2).

Chapter 2. Placing Party Before Policy

Control Condition
Please indicate whether or not you support or oppose the statement: To increase the amount of taxes paid by the wealthy. Do you support or oppose increasing the amount of taxes paid by the wealthy? Support Oppose Don't know
Liberal Trump Condition
Please indicate whether or not you support or oppose the statement: To increase the amount of taxes paid by the wealthy. Donald Trump has said that he supports this policy. How about you? Do you support or oppose increasing the amount of taxes paid by the wealthy? Support Oppose Don't know
Conservative Trump Condition
Please indicate whether or not you support or oppose the statement: To increase the amount of taxes paid by the wealthy. Donald Trump has said that he opposes this policy. How about you? Do you support or oppose increasing the amount of taxes paid by the wealthy? Support Oppose Don't know

Figure 2-2: The control, liberal Trump, and conservative Trump "Tax hike on the wealthy" policy queries given to subjects in Barber and Pope's study. The researchers found that Republican support for, or opposition to, various policies was strongly influenced by whether or not Donald Trump was said to be for or against them (Michael Barber and Jeremy C. Pope. 2018. "Does Party Trump Ideology? Disentangling Party and Ideology in America." *American Political Science Review*. Vol. 113, No. 1).

Once more, the results revealed that "group loyalty is the stronger motivator of opinion than are any ideological principles." On average, when Donald Trump was reported to have a liberal position on an issue, Republicans were 16 percentage points more likely to take the liberal position, and when he was reported to have a conservative position on an issue, Republicans were almost 10 percentage points more likely to take the conservative view, than Republicans in the control group.[21] When it comes to policy, many Democrats and Republicans are reminiscent of Walt Whitman in his *Song of Myself*—they can "contain multitudes."[22]

Rather Fit In Than Figure Out

Some voters will elevate party over policy because it requires far less time and cognitive effort. Why bother going through the trouble of thinking when political parties and pundits are so willing to tell us what to believe? Other voters, however, will cleave to the tribal theory of democracy for the psychosocial benefits it provides.[23] The advantages of belonging to a tribe are manifold. According to the psychologist Marianna Pogosyan,

> Bonds with other people can become causes of happiness. Supportive social networks can act as buffers against stress. The feeling of being connected to others can be a protective factor against depression.... On the other hand, when social ties come undone and connections are severed, the resulting social injuries may not only become sources of copious ill-effects but may also affect our brains in similar ways as physical injuries would. Thus, as some neuroscientists have suggested, human beings could be wired to feel pain when we are bereft of social connection, just as evolution has wired us to feel pain when we are deprived of our basic needs (e.g., food, water, and shelter).[24]

We are a tribal species—one that depends upon the emotional (as well as material) support bestowed by the groups to which we belong. Accordingly, a partisan has much to gain from being a party member in good standing. When we toe the party line, we will likely feel welcomed in our homes and classrooms and accepted in our churches and communities. But when we express support for the views of the opposing party—a party that is often seen as dangerous, immoral, and even unhuman—we run the risk being shouted down or even thrown out. If one's very well-being depend upon one deferring to their party's doctrinal positions, so be it. The cost of doing otherwise is often too awful to contemplate.[25]

By contrast, the benefits of elevating policy over party pale in comparison. In *Competing Motives in the Partisan Mind: How Loyalty and Responsibility Shape Party Identification and Democracy*, the political scientist Eric W. Groenendyk notes that "because each person can cast only a single vote ... the probability of casting the decisive vote in any large-scale election approaches zero." As a result, he continues, "the expected policy benefits to be derived from policy-oriented voting approaches zero." Therefore, the political benefits to be derived from elevating policy over party are likely to be dwarfed by the psychosocial benefits of placing party before policy.[26] A pro-life Democrat or a pro-gun control Republican welcomes an awful lot of risk and very little reward. The odds that their contrarian views would engender a change in the

Chapter 2. Placing Party Before Policy 41

nation's abortion or gun laws are nil, but the chances that their positions would take a toll on their personal relationships are comparatively high.[27]

Nonetheless, while it may be reasonable to elevate party over policy from an individual's point of view, it can be downright devastating to a republic. In 1968, Garrett Hardin published an article titled "The Tragedy of the Commons" in the journal *Science*. In his essay, the American ecologist argued that if a group of cattle herders were provided with a common tract of land upon which each of their cows could forage, the ranchers would invariably destroy that pasture by overgrazing. According to Hardin,

> The rational herdsman concludes that the only sensible course for him to pursue is to add another animal to his herd. And another; and another…. But this is the conclusion reached by each and every rational herdsman sharing a commons. Therein lies the tragedy. [When] all men … pursue [their] own best interest … [it] brings ruin to all.[28]

Soon thereafter, the term *tragedy of the commons* came to be used by social scientists to describe any situation in which individuals—acting in accordance with their own self-interest—behave in a way that is contrary to the common good. For instance, the Yale psychologist Dan Kahan argues that the tragedy of the commons can be used to explain why Democrats and Republicans respectively maintain unscientific beliefs about politicized issues like nuclear power and climate change. When a Democrat protests the construction of a nuclear power plant or a Republican drives a gas-guzzling vehicle, they are sending a social signal about the tribe with which they identify.[29] As the Harvard psychologist Steven Pinker writes, "certain beliefs become symbols of allegiance … [and] people affirm or deny these beliefs to express … who they *are*." Pronouncing "the wrong opinion on a politicized issue," therefore, "can make one an oddball at best—someone who 'doesn't get it'—and a traitor at worst."[30] If you attempt to discuss the benefits of nuclear power at the vegan potluck, or the costs of anthropogenic climate change as your friends set out for an evening of "rolling coal"—that is, belching black smoke from a modified vehicle at those driving in an electric car—you may find yourself uninvited to the next dinner party or joyride.

Yet, while holding these unscientific beliefs may serve the self-interest of the individual, they can run counter to the interests of the community. Call it the "Tragedy of the Belief Commons."[31] Sure, it may be reasonable for some Democrats to believe that the scientific consensus on the safety of nuclear power is misguided, but it is devastating for society as a whole. According to Eric Armstrong, the associate editor of the progressive magazine *The New Republic*, "one of the environmental movement's biggest victories in the past 50 years—crippling the expansion of nuclear power—has actually done irreparable harm to the environment." He continues:

> For more than 60 years we've had access to one of the cleanest, safest, most environmentally friendly forms of energy available. And the reputed party of science and environmentalism has fought tooth and nail against it every step of the way. The damage inflicted has been lasting and severe. Energy vacuums are always filled. For each nuclear reactor proposal protested in the streets or that languished and died at the feet of lawmakers, something else took its place. In America, that means that coal, the dirtiest and deadliest source of all, overwhelmingly filled the void. And still today, only 30 percent of Democrats support increased use of nuclear power, compared to 54 percent of Republicans. Imagine the accusations of science-denial that would be hurled at Republicans if these roles were reversed.[32]

Likewise, it may be reasonable for Republicans to disbelieve the scientific community's overwhelming conclusion that human behavior is the leading cause of climate change, but it's dangerous to the common good. Whit Ayres, a Republican strategist, notes that denying climate change has "become yet another of the long list of litmus test issues that determine whether or not you're a good Republican." So, when President Trump declared that anthropogenic climate change was a "total ... hoax" and pulled the United States from the Paris Accord—an historic international agreement seeking to mitigate global warming—most Republicans cheered. All the while, "scientists have ... drawn concrete links between the planet's warming atmosphere and changes that affect Americans' daily lives and pocketbooks, from tidal flooding in Miami to prolonged water shortages in the Southwest to decreasing snow cover at ski resorts."[33] The tragedy of the commons is quite commonly tragic.

Critical Thinking and Politics

When we examine the nexus of critical thinking and politics, it yields four possible outcomes: (1) citizens can refuse to think critically and put policy before party, (2) citizens can think critically and put policy before party, (3) citizens can refuse to think critically and put party before policy, or (4) citizens can think critically and put party before policy (Figure 2-3).

Chapter 2. Placing Party Before Policy 43

1. Don't Think Critically / Vote Policy	2. Think Critically / Vote Policy
3. Don't Think Critically / Vote Party	4. Think Critically / Vote Party

Figure 2-3: The intersection of critical thinking and politics could theoretically result in four outcomes: (1) citizens who don't think critically and vote based on policy, (2) citizens who think critically and vote based on policy, (3) citizens who don't think critically and vote based on party, (4) and citizens who think critically and vote based on party. While the first outcome is—for all intents and purposes—impossible, and the second reflects the democratic ideal, the third and fourth options respectively include unsuitably sorted and unsorted voters who reside in the realm of political tribalism.

The first alternative is oxymoronic. Policy voting, by definition, requires critical thinking. Surely, citizens can't vote for well-considered policies if those policies weren't well-considered to begin with. For its part, the second outcome reflects the democratic ideal. Hence, citizens in the upper right-hand corner of Figure 2-3 are *suitably sorted*—that is, they objectively study the issues and vote for whichever party best represents their examined views. By contrast, the third and fourth alternatives reside in the realm of political tribalism. The lower left-hand corner of Figure 2-3 is composed of voters who are unwilling to spend their cognitive resources on critical political thinking. Their ranks include *accidentally sorted* voters—who adopt the policy views of their party even though they would've endorsed those positions had they given them some critical thought—and *unsuitably sorted* voters—who adopt the policy views of their party even though they would've rejected those positions had they given them some critical thought. Lastly, the inhabitants of the lower right-hand corner of Figure 2-3 are *unsorted*. These voters—upon reflection—reject the policies of their party, but not the party itself. In short, while they have borne the cognitive responsibilities of citizenship, they have not embraced its psychosocial ones. Accordingly, unsorted voters will frequently experience *cognitive dissonance*—a state of tension that occurs whenever a person holds two attitudes that are inconsistent or participates in an action that goes against their beliefs, ideas, or values.[34] To relieve this distress, some of these voters might engage in "issue reprioritization."[35] For instance, they might place less importance on certain issues than they otherwise would because their personal views are at odds with the positions of their party. If one disagrees with their party on issues *a*, *b*, *c*, and *d*, but agrees with their party on issue *e*, they could simply tell themselves that *e* is far more important than *a—d*. Others might engage in "issue reorientation" and change their policy positions outright. Here, if one disagreed with their party on issues *a—d*, they could simply tell themselves that they had initially been in error and that upon further reflection, they have decided to revise their views. For instance, the political scientist Ian Anson found evidence of this phenomenon when Democrats and Republicans were faced with unfavorable economic data. He writes:

> Partisans perform mental gymnastics by changing the way they think the economy works. When stock market performance runs in conflict with the partisan economic narrative, partisans become less likely to say the stock market matters at all for the broader economy.... [In essence,] when they learn "inconvenient facts," Americans seem to be more than willing to revise their underlying understanding of the world to accommodate the new information in line with the partisan narrative. Rigid in party loyalty, yet limber in mind, Republicans and Democrats can deftly vault past disconfirming information to land in vastly different economic realities.[36]

Unfortunately, the unsuitably sorted and unsorted's reticence to take up the cognitive and psychosocial responsibilities of citizenship is not without cost. For when we refuse to objectively analyze the issues, or we fair-mindedly examine the issues but ignore or rationalize away any unwelcomed results, we undermine the very foundation of representative democracy.

Dumbocracy in Action

A well-functioning republic requires an electorate that is composed of suitably sorted voters. For the sake of explanation, assume that the Democratic Party supports policies x, y, and z and that the Republican Party does not. Next, imagine a body politic comprised of six suitably sorted Democrats (D) and four suitably sorted Republicans (R). These voters have objectively evaluated the issues, have allowed those evaluations to inform their policy views, and have obliged those policy views to guide their party identification and vote choice. Accordingly, the Democratic party would win this election and pursue policies x, y, and z. In a word, the policies of the nation would echo the policy preferences of a majority of the people (Figure 2-4). This is the democratic ideal—a responsible electorate begets a responsive government.

But note how easily a troop of tribal citizens can disrupt that paradigm. Take a constituency that includes two unsuitably sorted Democrats (USD)—that is, voters who refuse to take up the cognitive responsibilities of citizenship (Figure 2-5). Although the four suitably sorted Democrats and four suitably sorted Republicans would adhere to the folk theory

Chapter 2. Placing Party Before Policy

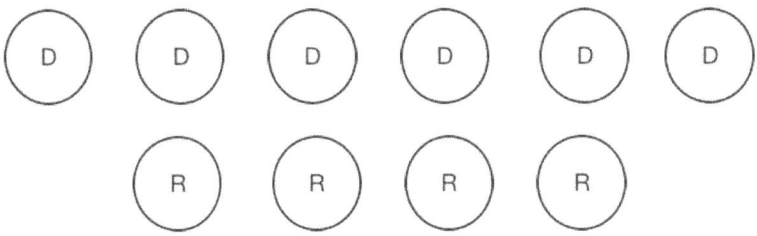

Figure 2-4: An imaginary electorate composed of six suitably sorted Democrats (D) and four suitably sorted Republicans (R) would beget a responsive government.

of democracy, the two unsuitably sorted Democrats would not. Instead, they would unthinkingly support their party even though they would've opposed their party's platform had they given it some thought. As a result, the Democrats would win the election with 60 percent of the vote (4D + 2 USD) and pursue a suite of policies that would, in reality, be opposed by 60 percent of the people (4 R + 2 USD).

Or consider a constituency that includes two unsorted Democrats (UD)—voters who have borne the cognitive duties of citizenship but not its psychosocial ones (Figure 2-6). In theory, unsorted voters aren't a problem for the democratic ideal. If the electorate in Figure 2-6 were to abide by the folk theory of democracy—and vote policy over party—no trouble would ensue. In that instance, the unsorted Democrats would side with the GOP and elect Republicans who, once in office, would do their level best to prevent policies x, y, and z from becoming

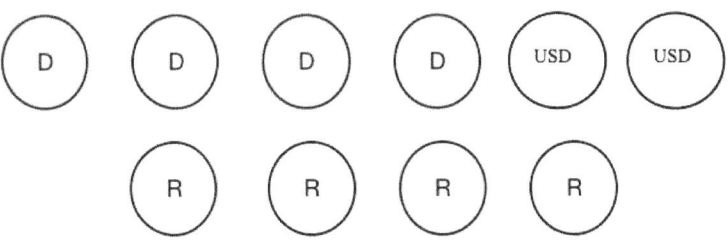

Figure 2-5: An imaginary electorate composed of four suitably sorted Democrats (D), two unsuitably sorted Democrats (USD), and four suitably sorted Republicans (R) would beget an unresponsive government because the unsuitably sorted Democrats failed to assume the cognitive responsibilities of citizenship.

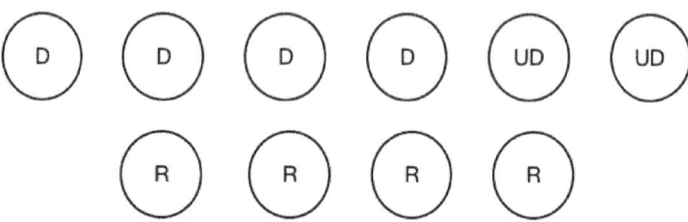

Figure 2-6: An imaginary electorate composed of four suitably sorted Democrats (D), two unsorted Democrats (UD), and four suitably sorted Republicans (R) would beget an unresponsive government because the unsorted Democrats failed to assume the psychosocial responsibilities of citizenship.

law. Once again, a responsible electorate would beget a responsive government.

In practice, however, unsorted voters in the United States seldom put policy above party. As we have seen, research shows that unsorted voters tend to subscribe to the tribal theory of democracy which encourages "Republicans with liberal issue positions [and] Democrats with conservative ones ... [to] betray their policy preferences and vote their party loyalty."[37] Unfortunately, if the unsorted Democrats in Figure 2-6 do ignore their conservative views and vote with their party, 60 percent of the electorate (4D + 2UD) would choose representatives that support policies opposed by 60 percent of the people (4R + 2UD). In sum, an electorate with enough unsuitably sorted or unsorted voters is an electorate that will beget an unresponsive government. And an unresponsive government is, at its heart, an undemocratic one.[38] Therefore, we should do our level best to ensure that we take up residence in the upper right-hand corner of Figure 2-3 and situate ourselves among the suitably sorted.

> **What We Can Do:** It is important that critically thinking citizens place policy over party. To that end, we should (1) assess whether our political opinions truly are our own and, if not, (2) assume the cognitive and (3) psychosocial burdens of citizenship.

We like to believe that policy forms the fundamental basis of our politics. As Lilliana Mason notes, if policy is the foundation of our politics, then our "political fights in American politics are ... *about* something"

Chapter 2. Placing Party Before Policy

and our elections are referendums *on* something.[39] But if our policy views are derived from our party—as opposed to an extensive and objective analysis of the issues—then the fundamental basis of our politics is party, and our policy fights and elections are nothing more than vacuous political pep rallies. Regrettably, we have seen that tens of millions of Americans do just that. And while it might be reasonable from an individual's point of view to avoid objectively analyzing the issues or to ignore or even change one's interests and values to remain in good standing with one's partisan tribe, it's tragic from the perspective of our political community. We must do better, and we can begin by taking an inventory of our policy views.

Assess Whether Our Political Opinions Are Truly Our Own

We like to envision ourselves as paragons of the democratic ideal. We believe that while others may let their political parties do their thinking for them, we most assuredly don't. This self-image, however, is likely a mirage. To understand how, give some thought to the bicycle. You may have owned or operated one at some point in your life and perhaps that experience provided you with a basic understanding of how the vehicle functions. If so, the following task should be rather easy. The box on the left contains a sketch of a bicycle (Figure 2-7). Please take a moment to draw in the missing pieces of the frame, the pedals, and the chain (the correct answer can be found at the end of the chapter).

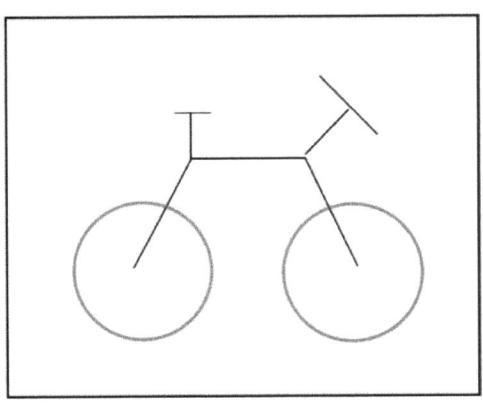

Figure 2-7: The image above is an incomplete illustration of a bicycle. Please complete the image by drawing the missing pieces of the frame, the pedals, and the chain (Rebecca Lawson. 2006. "The Science of Cycology: Failure to Understand How Everyday Objects Work." *Memory and Cognition*. Vol. 34. 1667–1675).

So, how did you do? If this seemingly simple exercise turned out to be more trying than you had anticipated, you're in good company. In fact, when the psychologist Rebecca Lawson of the University of Liverpool presented this challenge to a group of participants, almost 50 percent were unable to correctly complete the task. And they didn't just flunk—they flunked badly. In fact, many of the mistakes were of such a magnitude that they would've rendered the bicycles inoperable. And yet prior to completing their sketches, these very same subjects claimed to possess a reasonable command of a bicycle's mechanics. In a word, they were ignorant of their own ignorance.[40] The participants exhibited what psychologists call the *illusion of understanding*—a cognitive bias in which people overestimate their own knowledge due to the fact that they don't know what they don't know and, as a result, often mistake what little knowledge they have for a lot.[41]

The illusion of understanding is plainly evident in politics. In a 2013 study, the cognitive scientist Philip Fernbach and his colleagues found that participants readily admitted to having strong opinions on, and an intimate knowledge of, several political issues ranging from a cap-and-trade system for carbon emissions to a national flat tax. And when asked *why* they believed what they believed, the subjects had several reasons at the ready. Certainly, one can imagine Democrats passionately expounding upon the dangers of climate change, or Republicans waxing eloquently about tax cuts and economic growth et cetera. But when Fernbach and his colleagues asked them to explain *how* these policies worked, the participants were unable to describe even the most basic details involved. The study's subjects were overly opinionated about policies of which they were unduly ignorant. As such, Fernbach concluded that the confidence citizens tend to have in their political opinions is unjustified because "they know less about [public] policies than they think they do."[42] A little dose of humility would surely go a long way in making our politics more palatable.

In his poem *An Essay on Criticism*, Alexander Pope writes, "A little learning is a dangerous thing; drink deep or taste not the Pierian Spring, there shallow draughts intoxicate the brain; and drinking largely sobers us again."[43] While the tribal theory of democracy beckons us to take shallow draughts from the pool of political information, the folk theory of democracy demands more—it demands that we drink deep. To that end, we should make a habit of probing the limits of our political knowledge. We should pick a policy that we're passionate about and attempt to explain it in a comprehensive and mechanistic manner. To do so, we can create a graphic organizer—like the one depicted in Figure 2-8—and have a go at describing the policy's details. Then, we can try to indicate some reasons in favor of, and in opposition to, the policy, as well as any evidence in support of those justifications.[44]

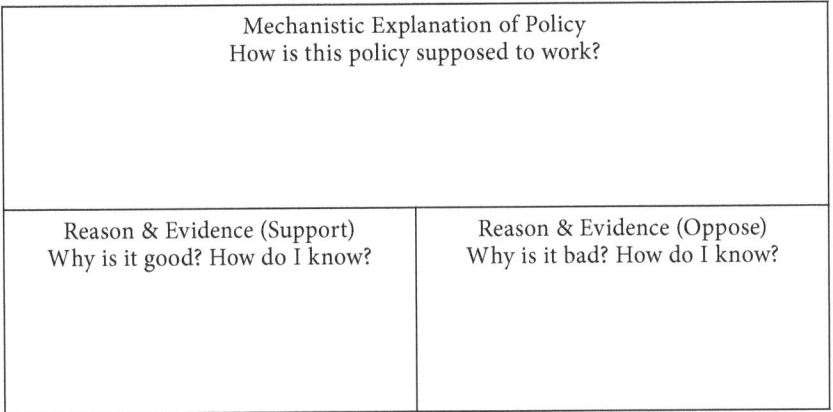

Figure 2-8. The graphic organizer above is a template that can be used to gauge our understanding of a given policy issue. First, we should try to provide a purely mechanistic explanation of how a policy is supposed to work. Then, we should attempt to provide reasons both for and against that policy and provide evidence that illustrates whether or not those reasons are likely to be true. If we can't explain how a policy would work, *and* provide an equitable list of reasons in support and in opposition to that policy, *and* honestly evaluate the evidence (or lack thereof) in support of each of those reasons, then we shouldn't take a firm stance on that issue.

If we support a flat tax, but can't explain *how* one would work; or we can list several of its alleged benefits but few of its purported costs (or the costs that we do cite are just snarky characterizations of the opposing side's point of view); or we can't reference any specific evidence that supports the arguments put forth; perhaps we might admit to ourselves that our party attachments are a cause, rather than an effect, of our policy views. And if that's the case, then we must move beyond the superficial talking points provided by our party—and the illusions of understanding they induce—and conduct a thorough and objective analysis of the issue. Of course, if we don't have the time or inclination to do so, so be it. But we should, at the very least, start to show some humility and stop passionately supporting or opposing a policy about which we know so little.

Assume the Cognitive Responsibilities of Citizenship

Fortunately, some Democrats and Republicans are willing to assess the issues in view of their interests and values. In fact, Lavine, Johnston, and Steenbergen found that "a nontrivial portion of the electorate" is composed of partisans who—unlike their more tribal counterparts—place policy before party and thus "reliably approximate the 'good citizen.'"[45] In point of fact, the trio of political scientists presented a group of subjects with an excerpt from a newspaper article detailing two competing health care proposals. Some of the participants were randomly assigned an extract that was devoid of any partisan cue (see the "No Party Cue" column in Figure 2-9). Alternatively, the other subjects received a clipping that included a mismatched partisan cue: the liberal policy was attributed to the Republicans, and the conservative policy was attributed to the Democrats (see the "Mismatched Party Cue" column in Figure 2-9).[46]

No Party Cue	Mismatched Party Cue
… The first policy … [gives] government a greater role in the provision of coverage. The plan would require large businesses to provide health care to employees or pay a tax that would go into a government fund. Individuals without employer coverage would be allowed to buy into the government employees' plan. This plan would come at a greatly reduced cost and would be partially funded using the money collected from non-providing businesses. The second policy … seeks to [increase] competition between insurance providers. The plan proposes to give Americans a tax credit equal to about half the cost of covering a typical family. Families could then go out and choose a preferred provider in the market. In addition, the plan would allow individuals to purchase coverage across state lines in an attempt to increase competition between providers, thus lowering costs.	… The first policy, **supported by about 90 percent of Republicans, but only 10 percent of Democrats** [emphasis added], … [gives] government a greater role in the provision of coverage. The plan would require large businesses to provide health care to employees or pay a tax that would go into a government fund. Individuals without employer coverage would be allowed to buy into the government employees' plan. This plan would come at a greatly reduced cost and would be partially funded using the money collected from non-providing businesses. The second policy, **supported by about 90 percent of Democrats, but only 10 percent of Republicans** [emphasis added], … seeks to [increase] competition between insurance providers. The plan proposes to give Americans a tax credit equal to about half the cost of covering a typical family. Families could then go out and choose a preferred provider in the market. In addition, the plan would allow individuals to purchase coverage across state lines in an attempt to increase competition between providers, thus lowering costs.

Figure 2-9: Democrats tend to support "government-run health care" more than Republicans, who routinely endorse a more "free-market" approach. This largely remains the case for partisans who ascribe to the folk theory of democracy—even when they are told that their party endorses the opposite position. By contrast, partisans who adhere to the tribal theory of democracy generally align their policy views with those of their party. When tribal Democrats are informed that their party supports a "free-market" health care system and tribal Republicans are told that the GOP favors a "government-run" approach, they will likely follow suit.

Their results revealed that about 80 percent of the folk and tribal citizens in the "No Party Cue" condition chose the "correct" policy—which for Democrats was the government-sponsored health care plan, and for Republicans was the tax-cut based health care plan. Yet the presence of party cues exposed significant differences between the two groups. Here, while 69 percent of the folk citizens who received a party cue selected the correct policy, only 49 percent of the tribal citizens did so. In short, a large percentage of folk citizens read the policy details and settled on a view that was at odds with the stated position of their party. In contrast, a substantial percentage of tribal citizens preferred to heed the call of their party and fall in line, simply refusing to read any further or think any deeper about the issue before them.[47]

These findings are encouraging, for they show that it is possible to hue to the democratic ideal. What's more, Lavine, Johnston, and Steenbergen found that folk citizens are neither more intelligent nor less partisan than their tribal counterparts. They are just more willing to temper their partisan loyalty when their party pursues policies that violate their values and interests. They were ready to assume the cognitive responsibilities of citizenship, and for that they should be both congratulated and emulated.[48]

Assume the Psychosocial Responsibilities of Citizenship

Investigating political issues without the crutch of political tribalism is no easy task. As the remainder of this book will attest, it is time-consuming, cognitively taxing work. Yet the challenge of developing well-informed positions may pale in comparison to that of making our contrary views known to our tribe. The mere thought alone is enough to buckle many a knee. Be that as it may, we must summon the courage to do so (if we can do so safely). If we want to hold on to our republic, we may just have to let go of our tribe. This is a big ask, but it can be done. Consider the case of Derek Black.

In 2016, the Pulitzer Prize-winning journalist Eli Saslow published an extraordinary article about Derek Black in *The Washington Post*.[49] Black was the heir apparent of the white nationalist movement. In fact, he had been reared for that role by his father, Don Black, and his godfather, David Duke—both former grand wizards of the Ku Klux Klan. Seemingly, Black was a white supremacist success story. By his twenty-first birthday, he had already participated in numerous neo–Nazi conferences, launched a white nationalist website for children, and hosted a daily radio show where he expounded upon his belief that the United States was in the midst of a "white genocide" in which white identity and culture was being destroyed by non-white immigration and miscegenation.[50]

In 2010, Black enrolled at New College in Sarasota, Florida. He quickly adapted to college life—he attended parties, discussed philosophy, and played guitar on the balcony of his dorm room. He also formed new friendships, including ones with an observant Jew and an immigrant from Peru. And although he continued to participate in the white nationalist movement and embrace its beliefs, Black did so quietly. Nevertheless, those ties were eventually unearthed and publicized on a New College message board by a fellow student in 2011. His friends were stunned. Black proceeded to move into an off-campus apartment and live by himself. Although he continued to attend class, he largely evaded public spaces. Black sought to avoid his classmates, and they duly ignored him.

Then one day, after several months had passed, Black received a text message. It was from Matthew Stevenson, the Jewish student he had befriended the previous year. The two hadn't spoken since Black had been outed as a white nationalist, and with good reason. When Black's history was made public, Stevenson began to scour the internet for evidence of his old friend's alternate life. What he found was nauseating, particularly the anti-Semitic comments that Black had posted on his father's website declaring that "Jews are NOT white" and that "They must go." Nevertheless, Stevenson decided to invite Black to a Shabbat dinner which he prepared for a small group of students at his apartment each Friday night. Surprisingly, Black accepted. The evening was understandably awkward but cordial. He returned the following week, and the week after that. Black repeatedly dined with an eclectic group that included Jews, Christians, atheists, African Americans, and Hispanics. And as the years passed, he increasingly tempered his views and then began to abandon them altogether.[51]

Soon after graduation, Black took out his laptop and drafted a letter. He wrote, "A large section of the community I grew up in believes strongly in white nationalism, and members of my family whom I respect greatly, particularly my father, have long been resolute advocates for that cause. I was not prepared to risk driving a wedge in those relationships. [But] ... I have resolved that it is in the best interest of everyone involved to be honest about my slow but steady disaffiliation from white nationalism. I can't support a movement that tells me I can't be a friend to whomever I wish or that other people's races require me to think of them in a certain way or be suspicious of their advancements." Black emailed his letter to the Southern Poverty Law Center—an organization that monitors the activities of extremist hate groups in the United States—and asked it to publish the letter in full.[52]

Chapter 2. Placing Party Before Policy

The following afternoon, Don Black came upon the post online. He called his son to inform him that he had been hacked. When Derek told his father that the letter was real, his dad hung up on him. In the weeks ahead, Derek's mother would refuse to speak with him and his father would declare that he wished he had never had a son. Black would reconnect with his immediate family in time, but their relationship remains strained. His connection to the extended white nationalist tribe, however, has been entirely severed. "They were my community," Black said. "I [lost] everyone I had grown up knowing and caring about."[53] "When I left, I left alone and I spent a lot of years alone."[54] Fortunately, his connection to humanity as a whole has never been stronger.

When Democrats or Republicans conduct objective issue analyses, they assume the cognitive responsibilities of citizenship. But when the results of those exertions put them at odds with their fellow party members, they're faced with an additional question: Should they shoulder the psychosocial obligations of citizenship as well? It's a daunting question, for doing so carries the prospect of losing one's tribe and all of the support they provide. Thus, if doing so would place anyone in any kind of danger, it would be best to keep one's well-informed views between themselves and the ballot box. But if we are able to bear that burden, it is imperative that we do.

In his farewell address, George Washington warned that while the "spirit of party ... is inseparable from our nature, ... [its] baneful effects ... [and] mischiefs ... are sufficient to make it the interest and duty of a wise people to discourage and restrain it. [For] a fire ... demands a uniform vigilance to prevent its bursting into a flame, lest, instead of warming, it should consume."[55] Currently, the flame of political tribalism consumes our politics. If we want to do our part to contain that blaze, we have to first become critical political thinkers. The purpose of this book is to help readers in that endeavor, and it is that undertaking to which we shall now turn.

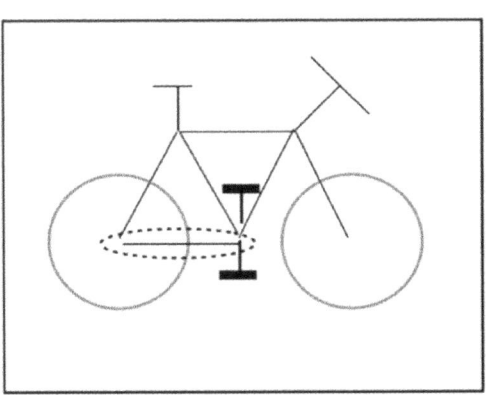

Figure 2-10: The image above presents a complete version of the bicycle depicted in Figure 2-7, including a functional frame, chain, and pedals (Rebecca Lawson. 2006. "The Science of Cycology: Failure to Understand How Everyday Objects Work." *Memory and Cognition*. Vol. 34. 1667–1675).

Part III
Political Information

Chapter 3

Acquiring Political Information

"The more power we have over the data that comes in, the better able we are to shelter ourselves from uncomfortable truths—from facts that challenge our preconceptions and misperceptions.... With news and data that is tailored to our prejudices, we deprive ourselves of true information. We wind up wallowing in our own false ideas, reflected back at us by the media. The news is ceasing to be a window unto the world; it is becoming a mirror that allows us to gaze only upon our own beliefs."[1]

—Charles Seife

The Problem: Political tribalism encourages Democrats and Republicans to seek information that supports their views rather than information that does not.

In 1954, Dorothy Martin claimed that she was receiving messages from an alien civilization located on a planet named Clarion. The suburban housewife from Oak Park, Illinois, believed that she had been chosen by these space beings to inform her fellow mortals that the world was going to end in a great flood on December 21. The extraterrestrial telepath soon gained a following of some thirty people—many of whom had quit their jobs, gave away their possessions, bid farewell to their family and friends, and moved into Martin's home to prepare for the cataclysm. According to Leon Festinger, Henry Riecken, and Stanley Schachter's classic account, *When Prophecy Fails: A Social and Psychological Study of a Modern Group that Predicted the Destruction of the World*, the troop believed that they would "survive the flood and ... be taken to Clarion [where] they would be spiritually indoctrinated [before being] sent back to a cleansed and innocent earth to repopulate it with good people who 'walked in the Light.'"[2]

On the morning of December 17, Martin divined that a flying saucer would arrive in her backyard that afternoon and transport the group to safety. Members—who were instructed to prepare for the voyage by removing all metal from their persons—proceeded to expunge coins from their pockets, watches from their wrists, zippers from their trousers, and eyelets from their shoes. But the spacecraft never arrived. Nevertheless, disappointment dissipated when some members of the group indicated that the incident had been a "practice session … so that when the real time arrived, things would go smoothly." What's more, Martin received a new message that a flying saucer would arrive later that evening to pick up the chosen. Once again, the group exited the channeler's home and waited for three hours, lingering in the frigid cold with their collective gaze transfixed on the nighttime sky. Alas, the spacecraft failed to materialize. Now, members spoke of a "test of faith," and encouraged each other to take heart. Finally, on December 20, Martin prophesized that a space man would knock on the front door at 12:00 a.m. and escort the chosen to a saucer. As the hour approached, the believers donned their overcoats and footwear, and sat motionless in the living room. Midnight came and went, but the special visitor never showed up. The membership increasingly became distraught—while some began pacing the room, others were on the verge of tears. But at 4:45 a.m., another dispatch was received and it spoke of a miracle: "The cataclysm had been called off. The little group, sitting all night long, had spread so much light that God had saved the world from destruction."[3]

Soon thereafter, fissures began to form. While some members continued to trust Martin's powers of prophecy, others became disillusioned and distanced themselves from the group. Interestingly, Festinger and his colleagues found that those who abandoned the bunch and its false beliefs did so because they were "surrounded by people with opinions openly opposed to their own and heard arguments that could serve only to increase … their doubts." In contrast, members who "were in the constant presence of fellow believers during the period following disconfirmation … were able to accept the rationalization [that their faith had averted the flood] … and regain confidence in their original beliefs." In the end, the authors concluded that the "presence of supporting co-believers" was an "indispensable requirement" for the maintenance of false belief.[4]

The story that unfolds across the pages of *When Prophecy Fails* should give pause to those with an interest in American politics. Like Dorothy Martin and her bevy of devotees, many Democrats and Republicans have chosen to reside in the "presence of supporting co-believers." As described in Chapter 1, almost 20 percent of Democrats and Republicans have expressed an unwillingness to socialize with a member of the opposing party.⁵ In fact, only 31 percent of Democrats and 39 percent of Republicans have "a lot or some" friends from the opposing party, and fewer than 10 percent of Democrats and Republicans have cross-partisan spouses or partners.⁶ But our preference for the like-minded isn't just found in the company we keep. It's also revealed in the information we seek.⁷

Partisan Selective Exposure

In George Orwell's dystopian novel, *Nineteen Eighty-Four*, Big Brother—the ostensible leader of the totalitarian state of Oceania—uses a misnomered agency called the "Ministry of Truth" to amplify official government messages and silence contrary points of view. First published in June 1949, Orwell's harrowing narrative continues to resonate. According to professors Abbott Gleason and Martha Nussbaum, "countless American [readers] … have identified with [the novel's] depiction of the struggle of the lone individual against an omnipresent … state that conducts a systematic and relentless assault against truth."⁸ But the fascination with Big Brother and the Ministry of Truth has obscured a more mundane method of thought control, one far more common yet no less pernicious: *partisan selective exposure*. Partisan selective exposure is the tendency to seek sources of information that reinforce one's pre-existing political views.⁹ And whether Democrats and Republicans partake in partisan selective exposure because they hope to avoid the pain of having their views challenged, or revel in the pleasure of having them confirmed, this inclination to engage in self-censorship is far more likely to direct "a systematic and relentless assault against truth" than any contemporary American political leader or government agency.¹⁰ In short, we have met Big Brother, and he is us.

The Big Brother Within

Researchers have uncovered ample evidence of partisan selective exposure in the lab. For instance, in 2006 the political scientists Milton Lodge and Charles S. Taber provided subjects with a list of sixteen sources that contained arguments about affirmative action and gun control. Eight of the sources were liberal—such as the Democratic Party, National Association for the Advancement of Colored People, and Citizens Against Handguns, and eight of the sources were conservative—like the Republican Party, Committee to End Preferences, and the National Rifle Association. Then, the researchers asked the participants to select and read eight of the sixteen arguments. What they found was that "participants were more likely to read the arguments of a sympathetic source than to expose themselves to an opposing point of view." In fact, partisans selected arguments from like-minded groups 70–75 percent of the time.[11]

In 2011, a professor of communications studies, Natalie J. Stroud, placed a series of neutral (*The Economist*), liberal (*The Nation*), and conservative (*National Review*) magazines on a waiting room table and surreptitiously recorded people's reading choices. While Democrats were willing to spend about half of their time skimming through a conservative magazine, Republicans only spent about 20 percent of their time reading a liberal magazine. What's more, when Stroud proceeded to offer a free magazine subscription to the study's participants, Democrats tended to subscribe to *The Nation* and Republicans to the *National Review*.[12] In a separate experiment, Stroud created a Google News website that displayed a series of articles from CNN and Fox News. Once again, she found evidence of partisan selective exposure: "Democrats tended to choose articles from CNN and … Republicans tended to choose articles from Fox News."[13]

Some Democrats and Republicans are so averse to hearing information from the opposing party's perspective, that they are even willing to forgo potential pecuniary benefits. In 2017, Jeremy A. Frimer, Linda J. Skitka, and Matt Motyl presented participants with a choice: read an opinion piece on same-sex marriage with which you agree and be entered into a raffle to win seven dollars, or read an opinion piece on same-sex marriage with which you disagree and be entered into a raffle to win ten dollars. The result? The authors found that partisans have a strong "aversion toward learning about the views of their ideological opponents." Indeed, 61 percent of conservatives and 64 percent of liberals "gave up the chance to win extra money in order to avoid hearing from the other side." The study yielded similar results for the issues of legalizing marijuana, abortion, climate change, and gun control.[14]

Evidence of partisan selective exposure, however, hasn't just been found in the confines of academic laboratories. It's been found in the real world as well. Fifty years ago, the vast majority of Americans acquired their news from one of the three network nightly newscasts—homogenous programs that provided a "point-counterpoint" perspective on the events of the day. But the development of partisan cable news shows, talk radio, and Internet websites has created a more fragmented information environment that allows voters to choose news sources that singularly share their political predispositions.[15] And tens of millions of Americans have opted to do just that.[16]

In her book, *Niche News: The Politics of News Choice*, Stroud reports that Democrats tend to watch CNN or MSNBC, and Republicans tend to watch Fox News. In fact, strong Democrats "have a 0.05 probability of naming Fox News their most watched cable news outlet and a 0.58 probability of naming either CNN or MSNBC." Similarly, strong Republicans "have a 0.47 probability of naming Fox News their most watched cable news network and a 0.14 probability of naming either CNN or MSNBC."[17] Furthermore, the incidence of partisan selective exposure among cable news viewers appears to be increasing. In *How Partisan Media Polarizes America*, the political scientist Matthew Levendusky reports that an equivalent percentage of Democrats and Republicans watched Fox News ($\approx$ 45 percent) in 2000. But by 2010, the proportion of Democrats who tuned in to the network declined to just 35 percent while the proportion of GOP viewers soared to 69 percent.[18]

The hallmarks of partisan selective exposure can also be found on talk radio and the Internet. Stroud reports that in 2004, 13 percent of Democrats and 3 percent of Republicans listened to liberal talk radio. By contrast, 25 percent of Republicans and 1 percent of Democrats tuned in to conservative talk radio. In like manner, she found that "Those accessing liberal Web sites nearly universally identified as liberal Democrats and those accessing conservative Web sites nearly universally identified as conservative Republicans."[19] The same appears to be true of social media. Take Twitter, a social networking service where users share and access content with others whom they have chosen to "follow." A study by Itai Himelboim, Stephen McCreery, and Marc Smith found that Twitter users tend to follow others whose political views are in accord with their own, and share links that correspond to their political leanings. Nearly 82 percent of the sources shared by Democrats were liberal while only 5 percent were conservative, and over 75 percent of the sources shared by Republicans were conservative while just 3.2 percent were liberal. As such, the authors conclude that Twitter users are "unlikely to be exposed to cross-ideological content."[20] Or consider Facebook. Users on Facebook send each other "friend requests" which, when accepted, enable them to share everything from pictures and videos to articles and opinions. But a study by Eytan Bakshy, Solomon Messing, and Lada Adamic shows that Facebook users have five politically likeminded friends for every one friend from the other end of the ideological spectrum. Additionally, only 24 percent of the hard news stories shared by liberal friends and 35 percent of the hard news stories shared by conservative friends had any cross-cutting content.[21] In addition, data from the Pew Research Journalism Project shows that 44 percent of "consistently liberal" Facebook users and 31 percent of "consistently conservative" users say that they have "hidden, blocked, defriended, or stopped following someone" because they disagreed with their political views.[22]

Partisan Selective Exposure In, Partisan Selective Exposure Out

To make matters worse, our tendency to engage in partisan selective exposure may be amplified by computer algorithms.[23] An algorithm is a sequence of well-defined steps or procedures intended to produce a particular output from a given set of inputs. Facebook, Amazon, and YouTube all employ algorithms that respectively utilize a user's clicks, previous purchases, or views to recommend similar articles, products, or videos that the user might also enjoy.[24] That sounds rather benign, but it can be highly problematic, for if an algorithm's inputs are marred by partisan selective exposure, then its outputs will similarly be spoiled. When Internet users seek sources of information that reinforce their pre-existing political views in the present, computer algorithms all but ensure that their views will be further fortified in the future. Partisan selective exposure in, partisan selective exposure out.

For example, the Brookings Institution reports that Facebook's News Feed algorithm will reduce cross-cutting political content for Democrats who customarily click on links for liberal websites by 8 percent, and for Republicans who traditionally click on links for conservative websites by 5 percent.[25] In the same way, when patrons search for a book on Amazon.com, an algorithm will present them with an array of similar titles under the "customers who viewed this item also viewed" and "frequently bought together" features. A Republican who purchases *Trump: The Art of the Deal*, therefore, will be prompted to pick up *Trump: The America We Deserve*, and a Democrat who acquires Hillary Clinton's memoir of the 2016 presidential election, *What Happened*, will be encouraged to buy her autobiography, *Living History*. Given the influence that partisan selective exposure and Amazon's algorithm can exert, it's unsurprising that a 2004 study of the company revealed that "buyers of liberal books buy only other liberal books, while buyers of conservative books buy only other conservative books."[26] As for YouTube, a recent investigation by *The Wall Street Journal* divulged that the online video-sharing platform's algorithm recommends content that is not only ideologically aligned with, but also more extreme than, a viewer's initial search.[27] Reflecting on these findings, Zeynep Tufekci, then an associate professor at the School of Information and Library Science at the University of North Carolina, wrote,

> At one point during the 2016 presidential election campaign, I watched a bunch of videos of Donald Trump rallies on YouTube.... Soon I noticed something peculiar. YouTube started to recommend and autoplay videos for me that featured white supremacist rants, Holocaust denials, and other disturbing content.

Since I was not in the habit of watching extreme right-wing fare on YouTube, I was curious whether this was an exclusively right-wing phenomenon. So, I created another YouTube account and started watching videos of Hillary Clinton and Bernie Sanders, letting YouTube's recommender algorithm take me wherever it would. Before long, I was being directed to videos of a leftist conspiratorial cast, including arguments about the existence of secret government agencies and allegations that the United States government was behind the attacks of September 11. As with the Trump videos, YouTube was recommending content that was more and more extreme than the mainstream political fare I had started with.[28]

Nevertheless, more research on YouTube's algorithm needs to be done. For while an analysis by Rebecca Lewis confirmed that the platform "makes it easy for audience members to be incrementally exposed to, and come to trust, ever more extremist political positions,"[29] a study by Mark Ledwich and Anna Zaitsev concluded that the "data suggest that YouTube's recommendation algorithm actively discourages viewers from visiting radicalizing or extremist content."[30]

In total, however, the evidence is clear: Democrats are more likely to subscribe to liberal-leaning magazines, listen to liberal talk radio, watch MSNBC, and access liberal websites than Republicans, and Republicans are more likely to browse conservative-leaning magazines, tune in to conservative talk radio, watch Fox News, and visit conservative sites online than Democrats. Simply put, many citizens engage in partisan selective exposure. Unfortunately, the implications for our democracy are significant.

The Effects of Partisan Selective Exposure

When voters consume political content from a singular point of view, they often develop beliefs and behaviors that are at odds with the democratic ideal. Consider the following:

- Democrats and Republicans who engage in partisan selective exposure exhibit higher rates of out-party animus than those who don't. In fact, while subjects who watched neutral media sources averaged an opposing party feeling thermometer rating of 30.4 degrees, those who viewed partisan news sources had a mean rating of just 20.9 degrees.[31]
- Partisan selective exposure similarly reduces levels of inter-party trust. Compared to their more omnivorous compatriots, Democrats and Republicans who consume a partisan media diet are 17 percentage points more likely to believe that the other party would do what is right only "once in a while" or "almost never."[32]

- Consuming like-minded media also makes viewers less willing to vote for an out-party candidate and more willing to consider an electoral victory by the opposing party as illegitimate.[33]
- And Democrats and Republicans who practice partisan selective exposure are 17 percentage points less likely to support bipartisan compromise than those who watch neutral or cross-cutting programs.[34]

Yet, the most disconcerting effect of partisan selective exposure may be its propagation of *policy polarization*—or the divergence of political attitudes to ideological extremes (Figure P-2).[35] Democrats and Republicans who encounter one-sided, pro-attitudinal political information tend to construe it as highly credible and persuasive. Consequently, they will move in the direction of that content and their views will become more immoderate.[36] For instance, policy polarization has been found to occur when partisans participate in political discussions with like-minded others. In 2007, David Schkade, Cass R. Sunstein, and Reid Hastie conducted a telling experiment. First, they surveyed a collection of participants' opinions "on three of the most controversial issues of the day: Should states allow same-sex couples to enter into civil unions? Should employers engage in affirmative action by giving a preference to members of traditionally disadvantaged groups? Should the United States sign an international treaty to combat global warming?" Next, they divided the subjects into several like-minded groups and instructed them to discuss the topics thoroughly. Finally, the participants were asked to restate their opinions on each of the three issues. When the authors compared the subjects' policy views before and after their chat, they found that "after discussion, people are likely to move toward a more extreme point in the direction to which the group's members were originally inclined."[37] According to Sunstein,

> Discussion made civil unions more popular among liberals [and] ... less popular among conservatives. Liberals favored an international treaty to control global warming before discussion; they favored it more strongly after discussion. Conservatives were neutral on that treaty before discussion; they strongly opposed it after discussion. Mildly favorable toward affirmative action before discussion, liberals became strongly favorable toward it after discussion. Firmly negative about affirmative action before discussion, conservatives became even more negative about it afterward.[38]

Thus, when like-minded groups converse, their members not only become more similar to one another, they also become more different from members of other-minded groups. Sunstein continues,

> Before members started to talk, many groups displayed a fair bit of internal disagreement. The disagreements were reduced as a result of a mere

fifteen-minute discussion.... Group members showed far more consensus after discussion than before. It follows that discussion helped to widen the rift between liberals and conservatives on all three issues. Before discussion, some liberal groups were, on some issues, fairly close to some conservative groups. The result of the discussion was to divide them far more sharply.[39]

Policy polarization has also been found to result from watching partisan cable news programs. In 2013, Levendusky conducted an experiment in which he assessed the political opinions of participants both before and after they watched a liberal (MSNBC), conservative (Fox News), or neutral (PBS *NewsHour*) news clip. His findings showed that some 33 percent of partisans who viewed a like-minded news program became "noticeably more extreme." Further, Levendusky found that the more partisan the participant, the more polarized they became. He concluded that "partisan media increase polarization not by polarizing moderates, but by increasing polarization among those already away from the political center. [In short,] ... like-minded media take people who are already somewhat extreme and make them *even more extreme*."[40] In 2018, James N. Druckman, Levendusky, and Audrey McLain conducted a similar study that yielded several important results. To begin, the trio of political scientists confirmed the fact that the policy views of both Democrats and Republicans polarize after they consume congenial partisan news. Yet they also found that when Democrats and Republicans were exposed to like-minded news *and* engaged in conversation with like-minded others, their views "polarized substantially further" than those exposed to the news programs alone. In other words, "partisan media exposure polarizes, but adding homogeneous discussion polarizes even more." Finally, the study revealed that people's policy views polarized even when they didn't watch any partisan news but conversed with those who did. In fact, the effects of participating in a discussion with like-minded others were more than twice as large as the effects of watching a congenial cable news program. The authors suggest that "the effects of discussion alone are substantially larger than the effects of direct media exposure ... because exposure only provides information, whereas discussion not only provides relevant information but also generates strong conformity pressures when in homogeneous groups."[41] People want to be perceived well by their fellow group members, and if that requires adjusting their policy views towards a group mean that is more extreme than their own, so be it.[42]

To be fair, the effects of partisan selective exposure aren't all bad. For example, the preference for like-minded information has been found to increase political knowledge and political participation, both important components of a properly functioning democracy.[43] Yet if that knowledge is solely one-sided and that participation is motivated by animus, intolerance, and zealotry, they aren't without cost. As Lilliana Mason opines, "an electorate that is emotionally engaged and politically activated on behalf of prejudice and misunderstanding is not an electorate that produces positive outcomes."[44]

What We Can Do: As critical political thinkers, we should (1) assess the role that partisan selective exposure plays in our own lives, (2) engage our curiosity, (3) seek out contrary points of view, and (4) deliberate with those with whom we disagree.

In the fall of 1787, the Constitution of the United States of America was sent to each of the states for their approval. Without delay, a furious debate ensued. Certainly, people argued about slavery, representation, and the powers of government. But they also debated the nature of debate itself. Opponents of the Constitution favored a confederation of small, homogeneous republics because they believed that discourse in a large diverse nation was unworkable. Robert Yates—a New York judge who penned a series of essays under the pseudonym Brutus—wrote, "In a republic, the manners, sentiments, and interests of the people should be similar. If this not be the case, there will be a constant clashing of opinions; and the representatives of one part will be continually striving against those of the other. This will retard the operations of government, and prevent such conclusions as will promote the public good."[45] Advocates of the Constitution vehemently disagreed. In *Federalist No. 70*, Alexander Hamilton argued that the heterogeneity of a national republic would actually enhance the nation's well-being because "the differences of opinion, and the jarring of parties in [the legislative] department of government ... often promote deliberation and circumspection."[46] In *Federalist No. 51*, James Madison insisted that within an "extended republic, ... and among the great variety of interests, parties, and sects which it embraces, a coalition of a majority ... could seldom take place on any other principles than those of justice and the general good."[47] A diversity of views begets deliberation, and deliberation begets better results.

Ultimately, the arguments advanced in support of the Constitution prevailed. The charter was officially established in 1788 and has remained in effect ever since. But its vision of a deliberative republic is under threat. Many citizens reside in separate ideological enclaves that are more reminiscent of the homogeneous republic envisioned by Yates than of the heterogeneous one imagined by Hamilton and Madison. More and more, Democrats and Republicans inhabit different neighborhoods and join distinct social groups. They watch divergent news channels, listen to disparate radio programs, read dissimilar books and magazines, and visit distinctive websites. Many Democrats and Republicans reside in different social circles—both online and off—and never the twain shall meet. But democracy demands disputation. It dictates that Democrats and Republicans be willing to exchange arguments for and against political matters in the public square.[48] As Cass Sunstein argues:

> [a republic requires] not only a law of free expression but also a culture of free expression, in which people are eager to listen to what fellow citizens have to say. Perhaps above all, a republic, or at least a heterogeneous one, requires arenas in which citizens with varying experiences and prospects, and different views about what is good and right, are able to meet with one another and consult.[49]

Yet, as Frimer, Skitka, and Motyl note, when voters engage in partisan selective exposure, they replace the "marketplace of ideas with two isolated, noncompeting monopolies ... [and] it's a scary situation if, in this deeply partisan moment in U.S. history, the one thing both sides have in common is a lack of curiosity about what the other thinks. For talking past each other is deeply unhealthy for our entire political system."[50] Hence, if we intend to live in a Hamiltonian and Madisonian republic, we need to stop digesting information as if we reside in a Yatesian one.

Assess the Role that Partisan Selective Exposure Plays in Our Lives

First, we should assess the presence of partisan selective exposure in our own lives. We can start by asking ourselves questions such as the following:

- Do I watch partisan programs on MSNBC or Fox News rather than more neutral news shows like PBS *NewsHour* or the NBC, CBS, and ABC nightly news?
- When I read political news online, do I exclusively visit websites that have a reputation for being liberal—such as *The Huffington Post* and *Dailykos*—or conservative—such as *Drudge Report* and *TownHall*?
- When I peruse political news online, do I tend to click on, read, and share content that is aligned with my political opinions?
- If I am a Democrat or a Republican, do I read political books and magazines written exclusively from a liberal or conservative point of view, respectively?

- Do I wholly follow liberals or conservatives on Twitter, or have I unfriended people on Facebook because I disagreed with their political views?

Lastly, it's important to remember that we can answer "no" to all of the questions above and still be plagued by the scourge of partisan selective exposure if we discuss politics with someone who would answer "yes." Analyses have suggested that anywhere between 10 and 34 percent of Americans engage in partisan selected exposure.[51] But even though the majority of Americans do not bathe themselves in like-minded news, they may very well have their policy views be polarized by the minority that do.[52] As the political scientists Andrew Guess, Benjamin Lyons, Brendan Nyhan, and Jason Reifler write, "the danger is not that all of us are living in echo chambers, but that a subset of the most politically engaged and vocal among us are."[53] So, by all means, ask yourself the questions above. But you should probably pose them to the people with whom you talk politics as well.

Engage Our Curiosity

Second, Democrats and Republicans should do their best to cultivate a sense of curiosity. From the tale of Pandora to the trial of Galileo Galilei, the history of humankind has been unkind to the inquisitive. Yet, in *Curious: The Desire to Know and Why Your Future Depends on It*, author Ian Leslie argues that epistemic curiosity—or the drive to acquire knowledge and understanding—is not a malignant trait to be shunned, but a beneficent state to be nurtured.[54]

Among the many advantages of curiosity is its ability to reduce partisan selective exposure. In 2017, Dan Kahan, Ashley Landrum, Katie Carpenter, Laura Helft, and Kathleen Hall Jamieson conducted an experiment in which they gave subjects a choice of news articles either in support of, or in opposition to, their existing political beliefs. They found that those subjects with low levels of curiosity "displayed a marked preference for information consistent with their political predispositions." Yet participants with high levels of curiosity exhibited a desire for information that was contrary to their partisan beliefs. In fact, curious Democrats and Republicans were respectively 44 percentage points and 20 percentage points more likely to choose an antagonistic article to read than their less curious co-partisans. As such, the research team concluded that curiosity is a sure way to promote "engagement with information that is contrary to individuals' political predispositions."[55] So, how can we cultivate our curiosity?

For starters, we can internalize the mantra: "I don't know, but let's find out."

- I don't know: We have to do away with the pretense that we're policy wonks. The odds are, we aren't. But that's okay. Once we recognize that we have gaps in our political knowledge, we can take steps to fill them in.[56]
- Let's find out: And we can do so by holding a running conversation—with ourselves or with others—in which we ask open-ended questions such as: What do you believe? What reason do you have for this belief? How did you verify that reason?[57]

Seek Out Political News that Contradicts Our Personal Opinions

Third, when we expose ourselves to contrary points of view, we should do so in an intentional manner. The research on the effects of eschewing partisan selective exposure is not particularly encouraging. Some analyses have revealed that consuming contrary points of view can actually exacerbate political polarization. A study led by sociologist Christopher Bail of Duke University found that Republicans and Democrats who followed elected officials and presidential candidates of the opposing party on Twitter became "substantially more" and "slightly more" likely to polarize, respectively.[58] Although the effects for Democrats were not statistically significant, the fact remains that neither group moderated their views in the face of out-group exposure.[59] Likewise, Levendusky found that when Democrats and Republicans who "strongly agree" with their party's issue positions watched a cross-cutting cable news program, their views became more extreme.[60]

That being said, Levendusky also discovered that partisans will moderate their attitudes when they consume cross-cutting media they deem to be credible.[61] Thus, when we set about seeking information from the opposing party, we need to be careful. We should avoid the other party's most polarized voices and sample those that we find to be relatively reasonable and trustworthy, if not always agreeable. If you're a Democrat, don't spend time watching Fox News's primetime lineup; tune in to *Fox News Sunday* instead. If you're a Republican, you don't have to watch MSNBC, but you can read the editorial pages of *The New York Times* or *The Washington Post*. And we don't need to apologize for unfriending a not so friendly foil on Facebook, or unfollowing a trouble-making troll on Twitter. But we might give products such as "Escape Your Bubble"—a

Facebook plug-in that inserts news stories aligned with the opposing party into a user's News Feed, or "FlipFeed"—a Twitter plug-in which allows you to see the feed of a random, anonymous user of a different political persuasion, a try.[62] Or try "The Flip Side"—a service that sends emails with brief summaries from both liberals and conservatives on important issues of the day.[63] Lastly, to paraphrase a sentiment expressed in Julia Galef's book *The Scout Mindset: Why Some People See Things Clearly and Others Don't*: If reading or listening to someone doesn't make you feel more compassion towards their perspective, then keep looking.[64]

Deliberate with Those with Whom You Disagree

Finally, we must make a concerted effort to deliberate with those on the other side of the aisle. We might find cross-partisan discussions uncomfortable and difficult. We might even go so far as to agree with Linus, who, in the 1966 Halloween special, *It's the Great Pumpkin, Charlie Brown*, opined that we should never discuss "religion, politics, and the Great Pumpkin."[65] But some important research—at least as far as discussing politics in concerned—says otherwise.

For one thing, conversations between Democrats and Republicans have the potential to reduce affective polarization. Diana Mutz, a professor of political science at the University of Pennsylvania and author of the book *Hearing the Other Side: Deliberative versus Participatory Democracy*, found that citizens who talk politics with members of the opposing party are, on average, 15 percentage points more tolerant than citizens who do not. Indeed, deliberators are more likely than non-deliberators to believe that those with whom they disagree are "good people."[66] The psychologist Peter Coleman reports that opponents who engage in cross-party conversation often learn to treat each other with dignity and respect.[67] The political scientist Erin Rossiter found that cross-party conversations have the power to improve "how partisans feel and think about opposing party members." For example, participants who had political conversations with members of the out-party were more likely to give their partisan opponents a favorable rating—that is, a value greater than or equal to 50 degrees on a feeling thermometer—than participants who had not been similarly engaged (38 percent to 25 percent, in turn). What's more, cross-party dialogue was found to reduce the likelihood that members of one party would refer to members of the other party as "closeminded, hypocritical, mean, or selfish."[68]

In the same way, heterogeneous political discussions have been found to produce *policy depolarization*—a situation in which the policy views of opposing partisans move closer together or even overlap.[69] Policy depolarization can occur when Democrats and Republicans' opinions become more moderate—or shift toward the middle, away from the extremes. If Alex and Barbara respectively believe that the corporate tax rate should be 30 percent and 10 percent before conversing, but 20 percent afterwards, their views have depolarized. Yet it's important to note that policy depolarization can also take place when the issue positions of members of one party move toward the middle or even approach the opposite pole, while the views of the other party relatively stay put. In 2021, James Fishkin, Alice Siu, Larry Diamond, and Norman Bradburn found that while 89 percent of Democrats and 36 percent of Republicans initially supported the Deferred Action for Childhood Arrivals plan (DACA)—which allowed some individuals who were brought to the United States illegally as children to avoid deportation—95 percent of Democrats and 61 percent of Republicans approved of the program after deliberating with members of the opposing party. As such, a 54 percentage-point gap between the percentage of Democrats and Republicans who supported DACA had been reduced to 34 percentage points. Likewise, while 38 percent of Democrats and 85 percent of Republicans initially opposed so-called "Baby Bonds"—or the proposal that "the government fund a bond for each child that will accumulate in value until the child turns 18 to then become usable for higher education or other essentials for a start in life"—79 percent of Democrats and 95 percent of Republicans disagreed with the plan after cross-party talks. Here, a 47 percentage-point gap between the percentage of Democrats and Republicans who opposed Baby Bonds shrunk to just to 16 percentage points. Note that while the number of Democrats who supported DACA increased, the gap between the number of Democrats and Republicans who approved of the plan decreased because the number of Republicans who supported the program increased even more. Likewise, while the number of Republicans opposed to Baby Bonds increased, the gap between the number of Democrats and Republicans who disapproved of the program decreased because the number of Democrats who opposed the program also increased more than twofold.[70]

What's more, evidence suggests that cross-party deliberation can even result in better thinking. A 2019 study by Feng Shi, Misha Teplitskiy, Eamon Duede, and James A. Evans found that politically heterogeneous teams of Wikipedia editors "engage in longer, more constructive, competitive, and substantively focused debates … [and] create articles of higher quality than politically homogeneous teams."[71] Research by the political scientists Elif and Cengiz Erisen has revealed that partisans with diverse social networks are more likely to have complex thoughts about issues such as abortion and capital punishment than partisans who are surrounded

Chapter 3. Acquiring Political Information

by like-minded others. When Democrats and Republicans converse, they are exposed to different dimensions of the matter at hand and resultantly develop a less one-sided and more nuanced view of the issue, steeped in reason as opposed to opinion.[72]

Finally, deliberating with "the other" may even culminate in more optimal decisions.[73] To understand why, ponder the following question:

> Paul is looking at Linda and Linda is looking at John. Paul is married but John is not. Is a person who is married looking at a person who is not married?" There are three possible answers: "Yes," "No," and "Cannot be determined."

So, which do you choose? In their book *The Enigma of Reason*, the cognitive scientists Hugo Mercier and Dan Sperber report that most people selected "Cannot be determined" due to the fact that Linda's marital status is unknown. If you agree, consider this argument:

> Linda is either married or not married. If she is married, then she is looking at John, who is not married, so the answer is "Yes." If she is not married, then Paul, who is married, is looking at her, so the answer is "Yes" again. So, the answer is always "Yes."

Now which do you choose? When presented with this explanation, the authors note that a majority of the respondents who selected "Cannot be determined" immediately changed their answer to "Yes," and they did so despite the fact that they had been "extremely confident" about their initial choice.[74]

For Mercier and Sperber, this seemingly insignificant example is teeming with significance. In particular, it reveals that "when people who disagree but have a common interest in finding the truth or the solution to a problem, exchange arguments with each other, the best idea tends to win."[75] This may be true for mathematical and logical problems, as illustrated by the example above, but does it hold for more intractable dilemmas which involve deeply social, political, or economic commitments as well? There is some evidence to suggest that it does. In fact, Mercier and Sperber contend that "argumentation has already proven its ability to effect large-scale moral and political change."[76]

For instance, the Atlantic slave trade was an unquestioned fact of life in Britain for over two hundred years. Yet in 1787, a dozen abolitionists met in a London print shop and founded the Society for Effecting the Abolition of the Slave Trade. The group worked tirelessly to educate the public about the abuses of the nefarious practice and encourage its eradication. One of its members, Thomas Clarkson, crisscrossed the countryside accumulating evidence related to Britain's participation in the buying, transporting, and selling of human beings. He toured slave ships, interviewed

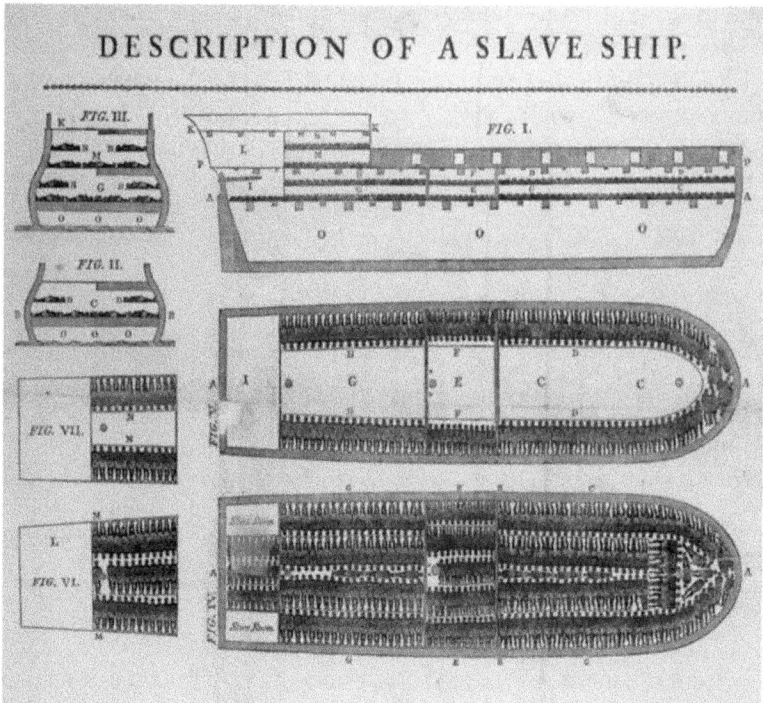

Figure 3-1: This illustration is a depiction of a slave ship that was included in Thomas Clarkson's *An Abstract of the Evidence Delivered Before a Select Committee of the House of Commons* (1790). The British abolitionist's diagram—which depicts how enslaved Africans were packed into the hold of a slave ship—appeared in newspapers, books, and pamphlets throughout the United Kingdom and was used to raise awareness about the horrors of the Middle Passage.

witnesses, and pored over muster rolls so he could calculate the trade's horrifying mortality rate. This evidence—which was reproduced in thousands of pamphlets, editorials, and books—provided irreproachable support for the arguments put forth to abolish the slave trade (Figure 3-1).[77]

To be sure, slave traders and owners responded in kind. But it was the opposition that triumphed in the debates that transpired in the nation's papers, pubs, and public meetings. According to Clarkson, "Day after day we beat our opponents out of the field, ... giving numerous individuals proper ideas concerning [the slave trade], and of interesting them in our favor."[78] Hundreds of thousands of Britons were inspired to boycott sugar produced by forced labor and sign petitions against the "inhuman traffic." As a result, Parliament abolished the slave trade in 1807, and it did so despite the fact that the decision resulted in economic dislocation, higher taxes, and the death of some 5,000 members of the British Royal Navy who lost their lives enforcing the measure.[79] The exchange of arguments changed minds, and it changed the course of history.

Of course, not everyone will be willing to change their minds when confronted with better reasons. The remainder of this book will illustrate the fact that when people seek to uphold their party rather than search for the truth, their ability to evaluate information in a biased manner is broad. Nevertheless, Mercier and Sperber maintain that it's not limitless. "Thomas Jefferson was not unduly optimistic," the authors conclude, when he wrote,

> Truth is great and will prevail if left to herself, that she is the proper and sufficient antagonist to error, and has nothing to fear from the conflict, unless by human interposition disarmed of her natural weapons, free argument and debate, errors ceasing to her dangerous when it is permitted freely to contradict them.[80]

How to Deliberate with Those with Whom You Disagree

Given the centrality of deliberation in a democratic society, we should all engage in political conversation with members of the opposing political party. To facilitate that process, there are several guidelines that we can follow. For instance,

- Find a Good Partner: Deliberate with a member of the opposing party who is interested in having a productive conversation. As Coleman writes: "Think with the best of *Them*."[81] There is no need to engage with someone who is verbally abusive and purposefully antagonistic.
- Assume the Best: Assume that your partner is well-intentioned, intelligent, and patriotic, etc. If they are presumed otherwise, the conversation is doomed from the start.[82]
- Pursue Understanding, Not Victory: Have a conversation, not a debate. The objective is to understand your partner's points of view, not defend your own.[83] Try to understand what your partner believes and why they believe it. In doing so, they might come to understand your reasoning, or see that their reasoning was flawed. Or perhaps you will discover that you were in error.[84] At the very least, you will learn where your partner stands, and why.
- Focus on Sources: Rather than attack your partner's information per se, ask them how they know that information. In a word,

what is the source of their information? Then, discuss the quality of that source and offer up high-quality resources that present an opposing point of view. For example, the psychologist Joshua Coleman suggests that if someone raises what you believe to be a dubious point, you could say something like this:

> That … might be right, but I've been reading a lot these days that goes counter to that. Do you mind if I send you an article or video about that? It would be good for us to look at both and see what we think.[85]

- Focus on Epistemology: Gently ask questions that might expose a problem, contradiction, or a lack of consistency in your partner's thinking.[86] If your companion claims to support President Trump because the stock market hit record highs during his time in office, you could ask, "Did you support President Obama as well, since the stock market set several all-time record highs during his administration?" Or, if your companion claims to support President Biden because the NASDAQ closed at record highs during his time in office, you could ask, "Will you support a future Republican president if the stock market hits a new high on their watch?"
- Listen: If we don't listen, we cannot hope to understand. Don't overwhelm your partner with a barrage of counterarguments. Instead, ask open-ended questions, and then listen. Next, ask more open-ended questions.[87] Also, resist the urge to jump in and speak before having heard and processed your partner's answers.[88]
- Play the Long Game: Deliberation isn't a panacea for all that ails American democracy, nor is it a quick fix. Nevertheless, continue to converse with members of the opposing party, for as John Stuart Mill said, "It is hardly possible to overstate the value … of placing human beings in contact with other persons dissimilar to themselves, and with modes of thought and action unlike those with which they are familiar. Such communication has always been … one of the primary sources of progress."[89]

According to Levendusky, "partisan selective exposure is a real, significant, and important trend."[90] Many of us reside in what the political scientist Brendan Nyhan has dubbed "a choose your own adventure" informational environment.[91] And far too often, we have chosen to pursue not the best information, but the best information that proves us right. When we do, we resemble Dorothy Martin's band of end-time ufologists; ensconced in an ideological enclave, so suffused with certainty and devoid of deliberation that we are incapable of discerning the fact that the edifice of our beliefs is firmly grounded in error. Nonetheless, even if we were to follow the advice above, and avoid the vicissitudes of partisan selective exposure, we still wouldn't satisfy the demands for the folk theory of democracy. It isn't enough to expose ourselves to contrary points of view; we also have to perceive and evaluate what we are seeing and hearing in an objective manner. As we shall see, that is far more difficult than one might assume.

CHAPTER 4

Perceiving Political Information

"Two people meet on opposite sides of a river. One shouts to the other, 'How do I get to the other side of the river?' The other responds, 'You are on the other side of the river.'"
—Unknown

The Problem: Political tribalism hinders the ability of Democrats and Republicans to accurately perceive partisan bias in sources of political information.

On a chilly day in November 1951, the Princeton Tigers and Dartmouth Indians participated in a pugnacious, penalty-riddled football game. The bout became particularly combative during the second quarter, when Princeton's All-American halfback, kicker, and quarterback, Dick Kazmaier, was forced to leave the game with a broken nose and concussion. Although Princeton went on to win by a final score of 13–0, the contest continued to be waged in the student press. Princeton's newspaper declared that blame "for the disgusting exhibition ... must be laid primarily on Dartmouth's doorstep," as their team made "a deliberate attempt to cripple Dick Kazmaier." Their opponent's periodical, however, had a different take. According to an article published in the *Dartmouth*, "Medical authorities have confirmed that as a relatively unprotected passing and running star in a contact sport, [Kazmaier] is quite liable to injury [and] his particular injuries ... were no more serious than is experienced almost any day in football practice." Yes, "the game was rough and did get a bit out of hand," but the paper made plain who was responsible. After all, the *Dartmouth* reminded its readers, "most of the roughing penalties were called against Princeton."[1]

A few weeks later, professors Albert H. Hastorf of Dartmouth College and Hadley Cantril of Princeton University showed identical footage of the game to a host of students at both institutions, and instructed them to record the number of infractions committed by each team. While the participants from Dartmouth concluded that the number of penalties perpetrated by the two squads were about equal, the students from Princeton determined that the Indians had committed twice as many infractions as their Tigers. Although the two groups of students had watched the exact same film, it was as if they had witnessed an entirely different game. In fact, in many ways, they had. Hastorf and Cantril explained that the two groups of students experienced a different game because that game was shaped by their respective school allegiances.[2] In other words, who we are often influences what we see, and nowhere is this more evident than in politics.

In 2012, Dan Kahan and his colleagues asked a bipartisan group of participants to watch a video of a political demonstration. The film—which was some three and a half minutes long—showed a group of protestors gathered near the entrance of a building, helmeted police officers, and a handful of pedestrians who at various points in time would approach the building, veer away, and leave the scene for good. While half of the subjects were told that the demonstrators were protesting abortion outside of an abortion clinic, the other half believed that the demonstrators were protesting the military's "don't ask, don't tell" policy—which prohibited openly gay, lesbian, or bisexual persons from serving in the military—outside of a military recruitment center. The participants were then asked whether the police were justified in stopping the protest because its participants had threatened members of the public who were seeking to use the facility in question.[3]

	Abortion Clinic Protesters as Threatening	Military Recruitment Center Protestors as Threatening
Democrats	56%	35%
Republicans	62%	83%

Figure 4-1: The percentage of Democratic and Republican subjects who perceived the abortion clinic and military recruitment center protesters as threatening (Source: Dan M. Kahan, David A. Hoffman, Danieli Evans, and Jeffrey J. Rachlinski. 2012. "They Saw a Protest: Cognitive Illiberalism and Speech-Conduct Distinction." *Cornell Law Faculty Publications*. Paper 400).

The results of the study, which are summarized in Figure 4-1, reveal a significant inter-party difference in perception. Republicans, who generally opposed abortion and supported "don't ask, don't tell," and Democrats, who broadly supported abortion rights and opposed "don't ask, don't tell," were both 21 percentage points more likely to see the demonstrations as hostile when they disagreed with the protesters' point of view.[4] Thus, many Republicans who would perceive the actions of a person protesting abortion as lawful, would view the same behavior as criminal if the protestor had been advocating for gay rights. Likewise, many Democrats who would perceive the actions of a person protesting "don't ask, don't tell" as impassioned dissent, would cry incitement if the demonstrator had been protesting abortion.[5] Simply put, political tribalism fits us with either red or blue tinted glasses that color everything we see. And nowhere is this more evident in politics than in our perceptions of partisan bias in the media.

Perceiving the Unbiased as Biased

The U.S. news media hasn't been polling well. A September 2016 Gallup poll revealed that "Americans' trust and confidence in the mass media ... dropped to its lowest level in Gallup polling history."[6] That same month, an NBC News/*Wall Street Journal* survey found that only 19 percent of respondents had a "very positive" or "somewhat positive" view of the American press.[7] Disapproval of the U.S. news media, moreover, spans the political spectrum. The University of Chicago's General Social Survey recently revealed that only 9.5 percent of Democrats and 4.4 percent of Republicans had a "great deal of confidence in the press."[8]

In part, the American people disapprove of the news media because they believe its reporting exhibits a partisan bias.[9] In fact, almost 90 percent of U.S. adults contend that members of the media are "regularly influenced by their personal views when covering politics," and estimate that 62 percent of the news they "read in newspapers, see on television, or hear on the radio" is politically slanted.[10] As with the public's lack of confidence in the press, the impression that the news media is suffused with political bias is a bipartisan one.[11] To be sure, Democrats rely on and trust a wider variety of sources than Republicans.[12] Still, a 2016 Pew Research Center survey found that 87 percent of conservative Republicans—who generally assume that liberal journalists pull the news to the left—and 73 percent of liberal Democrats—who often suspect that conservative owners push the news to the right—agreed that media organizations "tend to favor one side over the other" when they cover political issues.[13]

Yet the notion that the nation's mainstream news media is generally steeped in partisan bias is not supported by scientific study.[14] In 2000, Dave D'Alessio and Mike Allen of Michigan State University conducted a meta-analysis to determine the degree to which the mainstream media actually exhibits a partisan bias. The authors evaluated fifty-nine studies that analyzed partisan media bias in presidential election campaigns from 1948 to 1996, and concluded that there is "no evidence whatsoever of ... bias in the newspaper industry. To the extent that there are newspapers whose coverage is biased in favor of Democrats, they are offset by newspapers whose coverage is based in favor of Republicans." As for network television, news coverage of presidential campaigns exhibits "a very small, and not completely consistent, liberal bias." In contrast, major newsmagazines were found to have a slight pro–Republican slant, but the bias was so marginal that it "can easily be dismissed as insubstantial." In summary, D'Alessio and Allen maintain that their findings reveal "an aggregate, across all media and all elections, of zero overall bias."[15] In 2012, D'Alessio expanded this data set and updated his analysis to include a total of ninety-nine studies, several of which examined the 2000, 2004, and 2008 presidential elections. The result was no different. The net effect of partisan bias in the media, he concluded, was zero. A 2016 study by Ceren Budak, Sharad Goel, and Justin M. Rao— which employed almost 800 participants to classify nearly 11,000 political articles on the Internet—similarly concluded that "the major online news outlets—ranging from *The New York Times* ... to *Fox News*—have largely neutral, descriptive reporting of U.S. politics."[16] Additional studies have come to the same conclusion.[17] The American public's perception that the mainstream news media is politically slanted is simply not substantiated by the evidence.[18] Yet if that's the case, why do so many partisans believe otherwise? And what can we do to perceive the press more clearly?

What We Can Do: Before we conclude that a news report is biased against our party, we should make certain that we haven't (1) succumbed to the expectation bias, (2) surrendered to the hostile media effect, (3) misconstrued the adversarial or structural biases of the press as a partisan bias, (4) mistaken opinion-based content for news content, or (5) misinterpreted unfavorable facts as opinion.

The Expectation Bias

The *expectation bias* occurs when our expectations about an outcome influence our perceptions of that outcome. To illustrate this point, go to http://jeffmilner.com/backmasking/stairway-to-heaven-backwards.html, click on the "play forward" button, listen to the clip of Led Zeppelin's "Stairway to Heaven," and follow along with the accompanying lyrics (Figure 4-2). Trust me. It's well worth the effort.

Now, click on the "play in reverse" button, and see if you can discern any hidden message in the audio file. Did you hear anything? If not, you are once again in good company. While a handful of listeners—most likely those who came of age during the "satanic panic" of the 1980s—hear the word "Satan" or the number "666," most get an earful of gibberish. But now, click on the "Show/Hide Reverse Lyrics" tab and read the alleged verse that appears. Finally, play the song in reverse again, but now do so while reading the newly revealed lyrics. I guarantee that you will hear those words with such clarity that it will seem inconceivable that you were incapable of doing so just moments before. Truth be told, there is no backwards message in "Stairway to Heaven." Yet the fact that so many people believe otherwise illustrates the influence that expectation can have on perception. When we assume that we will perceive something, we tend to perceive it.[19]

And as supposed backwards messages in rock music go, so go allegations of media bias. When Democrats and Republicans expect to find

Figure 4-2: The image above—which was taken from jeffmilner.com/backmasking/stairway-to-heaven-backwards.html—includes a "Play Forward" function and "Forward" lyrics for a 24-second clip of Led Zeppelin's "Stairway to Heaven." The website enables one to click the play tab, listen to the clip, and follow along with the lyrics. Yet it also includes "Play in Reverse" and "Show/Hide Reverse Lyrics" tabs that allow one to listen to the same clip backwards and reveal an alleged backwards message (reproduced with permission).

partisan biases in the news, they tend to find them.[20] A study by Matthew A. Baum and Phil Gussin presented subjects with a transcript of a news report on the 2004 presidential election between Republican George W. Bush and Democrat John Kerry, and asked them to evaluate whether the material was favorable, neutral, or unfavorable toward either of the nominees. Each participant received an identical transcript that was painstakingly crafted to be balanced "in terms of positive, negative, and neutral references to the candidates."[21] The first section of the transcript, reproduced below, is a case in point (bracketed remarks are mine).

> Good evening. We start tonight with the presidential candidates on the attack [neutral]. Today with just 13 days left in the campaign, John Kerry was explaining why he believes the president does not understand the problems of ordinary people [anti–Bush] while, for President Bush, the message was mostly about why Senator Kerry's plans will leave Americans worse off [anti–Kerry].

But there was, of course, a twist. While the content of each transcript was the same, some subjects were told that the news report originated from CNN while others were informed that it came from Fox News. The result? Participants who believed that CNN was liberal concluded that the CNN version of the transcript favored John Kerry. Yet those who presumed that CNN was conservative thought that the CNN news report was partial to George Bush. Likewise, those who considered Fox News to be conservative, maintained that the Fox News version of the transcript favored Bush, while those who believed that Fox News was liberal concluded that their report privileged Kerry.[22] In a 2010 study, political scientist Jonathan Ladd similarly found that Democrats and Republicans were more likely to evaluate the media as biased when they were told that their party leaders believed that the media was "being too friendly with President Bush" or "being overtly critical of President Bush," respectively.[23] We see what we expect to see.

The scientific evidence belies the charge that the mainstream media is infused with a partisan bias. Unfortunately, when we're repeatedly told otherwise, we expect the media to be slanted and will discern it as such.[24] Thus, if we want to perceive the news media more clearly, we must first relieve ourselves of the expectation bias. For if we heed the scientific evidence—as opposed to the screeds of politicians or pundits—we might just start to see things a little differently.

Hostile Media Effect

Democrats and Republicans may also perceive balanced news as biased because of the *hostile media effect*. The hostile media effect is the tendency for partisans to judge media coverage that most nonpartisans find even-handed and objective, as biased against their own party or point of view.[25] The phenomenon was first studied experimentally when the Stanford psychologists Robert P. Vallone, Lee Ross, and Mark Lepper showed a group of pro–Arab and pro–Israeli students a series of television news broadcasts that debated Israel's responsibility for the 1982 Beirut Massacre, a tragic event that resulted in the deaths of many Palestinian civilians. Despite the fact that the students watched the same telecasts, the authors found that "each side saw the news segments as biased in favor of the other side." Pro-Arab subjects reported that while 42 percent of the news reports' references to Israel were favorable, only 26 percent were unfavorable. In contrast, pro–Israeli subjects reported that only 16 percent of the references to Israel were supportive, while 57 percent were derogatory.[26]

Vallone, Ross, and Lepper found that the hostile media effect permeates American politics as well. In an analysis of the 1980 presidential campaign, the three psychologists revealed that "among Jimmy Carter's supporters who thought that the media had favored one candidate over the other, 83% claimed that [Ronald] Reagan had been the favored candidate; conversely, among Reagan supporters who charged media partisanship, the consensus was even greater (96%) that it was Carter whom the media favored."[27] For example, when *Time* magazine published an article reviewing Reagan's campaign, accusations of media bias emanated from both sides of the political divide. One letter to the editor, written by someone seeing red, referred to the piece as a "slick hatchet job" and declared that the news magazine "ought to be ashamed of [itself] for printing [an article] disguised as an objective look at the man." Yet a second letter from a blue-seeing citizen wondered "Why didn't you just editorially endorse him?" and accused the author of "handily ... glossing over Reagan's fatal flaws."[28] The political scientists Russel Dalton, Paul Allen Beck, and Robert Huckfeldt found additional evidence of the hostile media effect when they examined voters' perceptions of partisan bias in newspaper coverage of the 1992 presidential election. While moderate voters concluded that the press did not exhibit a partisan bias, ardent Democrats and Republicans respectively maintained that the very same newspapers leaned toward the Republican nominee, George H.W. Bush, or the Democratic nominee, Bill Clinton.[29]

Recent research suggests that the hostile media effect operates through the medium of *selective categorization*. Selective categorization occurs when partisans classify neutral or even positive content as being biased against their point of view.[30] According to the professional norms of journalism, the press is encouraged to present opposing points of view in

Chapter 4. Perceiving Political Information 83

a fair and balanced manner.[31] As such, a political news report will generally contain equal proportions of pro-Democratic (PD), pro-Republican (PR), neutral (N), con-Democratic and (CD) and con-Republican (CR) content. Yet when a partisan perceives a fair-minded or favorable statement as antagonistic, a balanced news report will be transmogrified into an unbalanced hit job.[32]

Imagine that an evenhanded article, containing the content depicted in Figure 4-3, appeared in the newspaper during the 2016 presidential election between the Democratic Party's nominee Hillary Clinton and the Republican Party's nominee Donald Trump. On a positive note, the article states that Clinton devoted her life to public service while Trump made a name for himself in the private sector. On the negative side of the ledger, the report castigates Trump for making various vulgar and offensive comments and chastises Clinton for using her personal email to conduct public business, a practice at odds with federal rules and State Department guidelines.[33] To a nonpartisan observer, this article would appear to be balanced. Aside from the innocuous recognition of their nominations, the report makes one favorable and one unfavorable comment about each candidate.

| Clinton was Secretary of State (PD) | Clinton used private email for public business (CD) | Clinton and Trump won party nominations (N) | Trump has private sector experience (PR) | Trump says derogatory things (CR) |

Figure 4-3: An example of a balanced news report containing equal proportions of pro-Democratic (PD), con-Democratic (CD), neutral (N), pro-Republican (PR), and con-Republican (CR) content.

But to a partisan observer who engages in selective categorization, things appear quite differently. For instance, a Democrat might classify the favorable statement about Clinton's tenure as Secretary of State as unfavorable, believing that it undersells her experience by omitting the fact that she served as First Lady and was elected as a senator from the state of New York. Alternatively, a Republican might categorize the neutral statement about the Democratic nominee's primary victory as nauseatingly pro-Clinton, believing that it whitewashes Senator Bernie Sanders' allegation that Clinton and the Democratic National Committee conspired to "rig" the nomination against him.[34] In either case, selective categorization would ensure that the partisans would perceive the very same balanced article as more hostile to their point of view.

To paraphrase (with all due apologies) Shakespeare, the aforementioned research suggests that the fault of our partisan bias, dear citizen, is not in our mainstream media, but in ourselves. The press, on average, may not favor one political party over another, but the politically tribal do. Accordingly, the hostile media effect all but ensures that "even the most impartial mediators [will] face accusations of overt bias and hostile intent."[35] Therefore, when we perceive a partisan bias in the press, we should consider the possibility that the partiality isn't the media's, but rather our own. Fortunately, we can set ourselves apart from the hostile media effect by conducting an informal *content analysis* and compare our results with those of an acquaintance who is a member of the opposing party. A content analysis is a research method that involves coding and counting portions of content—such as a newspaper article or a nightly network news broadcast. For example, when social scientists study partisan bias in the news, they might analyze the amount of coverage that Democrats and Republicans receive by counting the number of paragraphs or minutes devoted to each party's policies, or they might evaluate the news' tone by tallying the number of positive and negative references to each party's candidate.[36] The critically thinking citizen should, from time to time, do the same. Consider the excerpt below:

> Iran Vows "Forceful Revenge" After U.S. Kills General
> *The New York Times*, January 3, 2020
> Iranian leaders issued strident calls on Friday for revenge against the United States after the killing of Maj. Gen. Qassim Suleimani in an overnight airstrike at the Baghdad airport. ... Iran's supreme leader, Ayatollah Ali Khamenei, called for retaliation and for three days of national mourning.
> On Friday, [President] Trump posted on Twitter about the strike, saying that General Suleimani "killed or badly wounded thousands of Americans over an extended period of time, and was plotting to kill many more but got caught!"
> ... [Democratic Speaker of the House Nancy] Pelosi said in a statement late Thursday evening [that the strike] "risks provoking further dangerous escalation of violence. America—and the world—cannot afford to have tensions escalate to the point of no return."
> ... Senator Marco Rubio, Republican of Florida, said on Twitter, that Mr. Trump had "exercised admirable restraint" and added that the Quds Force were "entirely to blame."
> Senator Tom Udall, Democrat of New Mexico, accused Mr. Trump of bringing the nation "to the brink of an illegal war with Iran."[37]

In this instance, we might deem the first paragraph as neutral and note that the report references the views of two Republicans and two Democrats. Perhaps we would also observe that Republican and Democratic views on the airstrike consume about five and a half lines of text each. Finally, we could ask a handful of friends with divergent political views to do the same and then discuss our results, paying particular attention to

Chapter 4. Perceiving Political Information

whether we classified neutral, pro, and con content in the same manner or if anyone engaged in selective categorization. At the very least, this practice will help us approach the matter of media bias in a more analytic and methodical manner. But it might also help us realize how often we're prisoners of our own perspective.

The Adversarial and Structural Biases of the News Media

Fervent Democrats and Republicans may also believe that the media is arrayed against their party because they mistakenly assume that the adversarial and structural biases of the press are partisan in nature. The *adversarial bias* refers to a journalist's tendency to be critical of people in power,[38] or—in the indelible words of Finley Peter Dunne—"to afflict the comfortable."[39] In the 1980s, S. Robert Lichter, Stanley Rothman, and Linda S. Lichter asked a group of journalists and business executives to write a fictional story about people depicted in ambiguous pictures, such as the "office scene" image in Figure 4-4. The exercise's underlying assumption—like that of the Rorschach ink-blot test—was that participant interpretations of the pictures would reveal something about their personalities and worldviews.[40] Sure enough, the

Figure 4-4: *In The Media Elite: America's New Powerbrokers*, Lichter, Rothman, and Lichter found that journalists were "consistently more likely than businessmen ... to criticize figures of authority" illustrated in ambiguous pictures such as the "office scene" above (Robert S. Lichter, Stanley Rothman, and Linda S. Lichter. 1986. *The Media Elite: America's New Power Brokers*. New York: Hastings House) (reproduced with permission).

authors found that journalists were "consistently more likely than businessmen to … criticize figures of authority"[41] and concluded that members of the media have an "urge to confront the powerful, to stand up to those in authority."[42]

Other scholars, however, contest that the adversarial bias is founded upon journalists' principles, not their personalities.[43] The Code of Ethics for the Society of Professional Journalists encourages reporters to "Be vigilant and courageous about holding those with power accountable" and "Recognize a special obligation to serve as watchdogs over public affairs and government."[44] It is, therefore, a journalist's job to point out the personal foibles and public failings of those who seek or hold government office.

Whatever its cause, the adversarial bias has made certain that the tone of coverage received by U.S. politicians has been more negative than positive.[45] A study from the Shorenstein Center on Media, Politics and Public Policy found that 87 percent of the news reports about Hillary Clinton's policy positions, leadership ability, and personal qualities during the 2016 presidential election were negative in tone.[46] A Democrat might interpret this unfavorable coverage as proof of the media's pro–Republican bias, but the evidence suggests otherwise. In fact, 87 percent of the news reports about Donald Trump's fitness for office were also negative. The real bias of the press is not partisan, the study concludes, but rather "a decided preference for the negative."[47] Mrs. Clinton and Mr. Trump didn't receive negative coverage because of their party allegiances; they suffered the slings and arrows of the press because they were running for president.

Structural bias, in contrast, derives from the pressures and incentives that operate within the news industry. The news industry is chiefly a commercial enterprise, and it is one that is becoming ever more competitive as an increasing number of media outlets compete for a decreasing number of consumers. As such, news organizations tend to prefer stories that are dramatic and scandalous because those are the types of stories that the press (correctly) believes the American people prefer.[48] In November 2017, a series of women accused Roy Moore, a Republican candidate for the U.S. Senate in Alabama, of sexual misconduct. Over the course of the next month, the scandal became a focal point of local and national media attention. Moore immediately categorized news coverage of the women's allegations as a political attack orchestrated by the "Obama-Clinton Machine's liberal media lapdogs." Steve Bannon, President Trump's former chief strategist and alt-right acolyte, similarly charged that the story was being pushed by a partisan media that was "part of the apparatus of the Democratic Party."[49] Of course, a sex scandal involving the Democratic President Bill Clinton and a twenty-two-year-old White House intern received

Chapter 4. Perceiving Political Information   87

an inordinate amount of the media's attention as well. In fact, the affair "received more coverage than any other story in 1998."⁵⁰ The media did not cover the allegations against Roy Moore or Bill Clinton because of some partisan bias. They devoted time to these stories because both charges were serious and salacious.

Devout Democrats and Republicans often interpret favorable news coverage of the opposing party and negative news coverage of their own, as evidence of a partisan bias. But the critical political thinker should alternatively assume that such coverage reflects an adversarial or structural bias, unless there is ample evidence to the contrary. If we are in the midst of consuming political news and begin to believe that it exhibits a partisan bias, we should ask ourselves, "Could this be an example of an adversarial or structural bias, instead?" If we are uncertain, we can ask ourselves, "Would this story have been published if its subject was a member of the opposing party?" For instance, reflect upon the following news reports:

Donald Trump Says John McCain Is No War Hero, Setting Off Another Storm
The New York Times, July 18, 2015
Donald J. Trump has made his name in politics with provocative statements, but it was not until Saturday, after the flamboyant businessman turned presidential candidate belittled Senator John McCain's war record, that many Republicans concluded that silence or equivocation about Mr. Trump's incendiary rhetoric was inadequate.
Mr. Trump upended a Republican presidential forum [in Iowa] ... by saying of the Arizona senator and former prisoner of war: "He's not a war hero. He's a war hero because he was captured. I like people who weren't captured." Mr. McCain, a naval aviator, was shot down during the Vietnam War and held prisoner for more than five years in Hanoi, refusing early release even after being repeatedly beaten.
From the Start, Signs of Trouble at Health Portal
The New York Times, October 12, 2013
In March, Henry Chao, the chief digital architect for the Obama administration's new online insurance marketplace, told industry executives that he was deeply worried about the Web site's debut. "Let's just make sure it's not a third-world experience," he told them.
Two weeks after the rollout, few would say his hopes were realized. For the past 12 days, a system costing more than $400 million and billed as a one-stop click-and-go hub for citizens seeking health insurance has thwarted the efforts of millions to simply log in.

While partisans might brand the first excerpt as biased in favor of the left, and the second example as partial to the right, it's more likely that the first article simply reflects the media's structural bias for conflict while the second displays its adversarial bias that revels in emphasizing the shortcomings of those in power. One would be hard-pressed to imagine that the news media would have ignored the attack on Senator McCain if it had been made by a Democrat, or disregarded any problems that arose while implementing a president's signature policy simply because that president was a Republican. While we might be justified in bemoaning the first article's obsession with conflict and the second's emphasis on the negative, it would be unwarranted to assume that they are partisan. For while the first two charges are supported by scientific evidence, the last one is not.

Opinion-Based Content and News Content

Partisans may also believe that the news media is biased against their party because they conflate the press's opinion-based content with its news content. In *Blur: How to Know What's True in the Age of Information Overload*, the media critics Bill Kovach and Tom Rosenstiel note that there are different kinds of material in the media, each with its own values and purposes.[51] For instance, news content emphasizes fact. It is assembled by reporters who—on account of their journalistic training, code of ethics, and job description—detail the day's events in an impartial manner. By contrast, opinion-based content is delivered by commentators who are paid to advocate for a particular point of view. As such, they generally interpret the day's events in a one-sided, partial fashion.[52] Consider the four excerpts below regarding a mass shooting that occurred in Las Vegas, Nevada, on October 1, 2017.

> Excerpt 1: At first, it sounded like fireworks—a loud, crackling noise. Then the awful realization began to spread, unevenly, through the crowd. ... By sunrise on Monday, the staggering toll at an outdoor country music festival on a cool desert night was becoming clear: at least 59 people killed, the police said, and 527 injured, either by gunfire or in the flight to safety. A lone gunman perched on the 32nd floor of the Mandalay Bay Resort and Casino had smashed the windows of his suite with a hammer, taken aim at a crowd of 22,000 people, and committed one of the deadliest mass shootings in American history. ... The police said they found 23 firearms in his suite ... and, according to Sheriff Joseph Lombardo of the Las Vegas Metropolitan Police Department, they also found ammonium nitrate, a fertilizer sometimes used in making bombs, in the gunman's car.[53]
>
> Source: Ken Belson, Jennifer Medina, and Richard Pérez-Peña. "A Burst of Gunfire, a Pause, Then Carnage in Las Vegas That Would Not Stop." *The New York Times*. October 2, 2017. Section A, Page 1.
>
> Excerpt 2: Good evening. ... The hearts of our nation ache tonight with a sickening familiarity, another mass murder, another taking of innocent lives on an unimaginable scale. Last night's attack here along the Vegas Strip is the

Chapter 4. Perceiving Political Information 89

worst US shooting in modern history. As of right now, at least 59 dead, hundreds injured. As we come on the air, a broken-out window on an upper floor of the Mandalay Bay Hotel, behind me, points to where hell was unleashed. A guest room, turned sniper's nest, where a 64-year-old man armed with more than a dozen weapons launched his withering rapid-fire gun attack, turning an open-air evening concert on the grounds just over my shoulder into an urban killing field.[54]

Source: "Las Vegas Mass Shooting." *NBC Nightly News with Lester Holt.* NBC. October 2, 2017.

Excerpt 3: After the horrific shooting in Las Vegas, the impulse of politicians is to lower flags, offer moments of silence, and lead somber tributes. But what we need most of all isn't mourning, but action to lower the toll of guns in America. ... [I]t is unconscionable for politicians to continue to empower killers at this scale. ... In every other sphere of life, we use safety regulations to try—however imperfectly—to reduce death and injury. ... Yet the federal government doesn't make a serious effort to reduce gun deaths. ... The gun lobby says that this isn't a time for politics. But if we can't learn lessons from tragedies, we're doomed to repeat them. ... So, let's mourn. But even more important, let's act.[55]

Source: Nicholas Kristof. "We Can Act Before the Next Mass Shooting." *The New York Times.* October 5, 2017. Section A, Page 23.

Excerpt 4: Now, while [President Trump] is trying to console the nation and offer support to the city of Las Vegas and the country, the media, Democrats, have rushed to politicize this tragedy in an absolutely despicable display. ... You know what, bodies weren't even in the morgue yet. Parents were at hospitals with their kids that are hanging onto life. None of this mattered to the left in this country. The impulse to politicize this tragedy as they do other tragedies is beyond the pale. They are using this tragedy, why? To score cheap political points and push a gun-control agenda. This is so shameful. ... Hillary Clinton, she took things further, going after the NRA. Here's what she tweeted. Quote, "Our grief isn't enough. We can and must put politics aside and stand up to the NRA and work together to try and stop all of this from happening again." Beyond disgusting, inappropriate and pathetic. ... Do they have any decency?[56]

Source: "Live Breaking News Edition of Hannity." *Hannity.* Fox News Channel. October 2, 2017.

The first two excerpts report the facts of the shooting in an unbiased manner. In essence, they exemplify the kind of straight news story typically found in the nation's major newspapers, like *The New York Times* and *The Wall Street Journal,* or on its television network newscasts, like *NBC Nightly News, CBS Evening News,* and *ABC World News Tonight.* Conversely, excerpts three and four are biased commentaries about the shooting. They demonstrate the opinion-based content regularly found in the op-ed section of the nation's major newspapers or on its evening cable news programs, like Fox News Channel's *Tucker Carlson Tonight* or MSNBC's *The Rachel Maddow Show*.

However, many Democrats and Republicans are incapable of differentiating between the two. In fact, nearly one-third of Americans admit that they don't understand the difference between news content and opinion-based content.[57] This is highly problematic. If partisans note the innate bias of opinion-based content but fail to note the difference between it and regular news content, they might incorrectly assume that the former's prejudices are shared by the latter. If *The New York Times* published a call for gun control on their back page, the thinking goes, then they must be anti-gun, and if they're anti-gun, then maybe they're exaggerating or even fabricating the details of the Las Vegas shooting printed on their front page. Yet the fact that Nicholas Kristof's op-ed in *The New York Times* exhibits a liberal point of view, does not mean that *The New York Times* has a liberal bias. Just because Sean Hannity expresses his personal perspective on Fox News's *Hannity*, does not mean that Chris Wallace will do so on Fox News's *Fox News Sunday with Chris Wallace*. News content and opinion-based content are drastically different—with the former being far less partisan than the latter.[58] We must recognize that difference, lest we unjustifiably dismiss a fact as an opinion. In an effort to differentiate between news content and opinion-based content, we should:

- Check for Labels: Oftentimes media outlets will explicitly label its opinion-based coverage. Newspapers will typically devote the second and third-to-last pages of each edition to opinion pieces written by the paper's editorial staff, syndicated columnists, and local residents. The editorial and op-ed ("opposite the editorial") pages are traditionally marked quite clearly. Labeling content on television and online is more challenging. Television news programs attempt to differentiate different kinds of content by distinguishing between different kinds of guests. A guest who was invited on the show to share news content will likely have been introduced as a journalist or reporter, whereas a guest who was called upon to share an opinion will be introduced as a commentator or contributor. Websites—such as foxnews.com and cnn.com—make an effort to separate its news content from its opinion-based content by placing the latter on a separate page which can be accessed by clicking on a tab labeled "opinion." Furthermore, any opinion pieces that do appear on the main page will generally be labeled as such.
- Check the Source: In the absence of labeling, we should use the

Internet to research the reputation and credentials of a media source and its contributors. As we have seen, the nation's network news broadcasts on NBC, CBS, ABC, and PBS do not exhibit an overall partisan bias. The same can be said for the main pages of the national newspapers, such as *The New York Times*, *The Washington Post*, *The Wall Street Journal*, and *USA Today*. But we will need to do some research when we immerse ourselves in the newspapers' opinion-based content. When we read the op-ed pages of *The New York Times*, it would behoove us to know that Nicholas Kristof is liberal and Bret Stephens is conservative. We should do the same for websites and cable news programs. A quick search will demonstrate that *Huffington Post* and *Daily Kos* are liberal websites while *The National Review* and *The Federalist* are conservative ones. Similarly, a search of Laura Ingraham and Lawrence O'Donnell will reveal that while the former favors the Republican Party, the latter is predisposed to the Democrats.

- Check the Tone: If the material is unlabeled and our research fails to yield any fruitful results, we can assess whether we're working with news content or opinion-based content by assessing its tone. News content generally expresses itself in a manner that is free of emotion. In contrast, opinion-based content is often designed to elicit a fervid response; it tends to be bombastic, hyperbolic, self-assured, and might contain invective as well. It's more performative than informative. For example, on January 3, 2020, *The Wall Street Journal* published, in part, the following news report:

> President Trump ordered a U.S. airstrike that killed Maj. Gen. Qassem Soleimani, leader of the foreign wing of Iran's Islamic Revolutionary Guard Corps, in an attack that is expected to stoke heightened tensions between Washington and Tehran and inflame frictions in the volatile Middle East.[59]

On Fox News, host Lou Dobbs praised Donald Trump's decision to launch the airstrike by suggesting that the president, "[who had] already set a standard [for presidents] that most mortals won't be able to meet, … is remarkably resourceful [and] bright [and] his judgement is second to none."[60] A panel of commentators on *The Young Turks*, a liberal program broadcast on Current TV, had a different take. Cenk Uygur called President Trump "an idiot" and intimated that the airstrike was "a really stupid idea."[61] The difference in tone between *The Wall Street Journal's* report and the commentary put forth by Dobbs and Uygur couldn't be any more stark.

Misinterpret Unfavorable Facts as Opinion

Finally, partisans may presume that a balanced news report is biased because they misperceive an unfavorable fact detailed therein as a hostile opinion. In 2018, the Pew Research Center asked a sample of U.S. adults to consider several statements and distinguish between those that were factual—or "could be proved or disproved based on objective evidence"—and those that were opinion because they "were based on the values and beliefs of the journalist or the source making the statement."[62] The results were discouraging. Only 26 percent of those surveyed were able to correctly classify all five of the following statements as factual.[63]

Factual Statements

- Spending on Social Security, Medicare, and Medicaid make up the largest portion of the U.S. federal budget.
- Health care costs per person in the U.S. are the highest in the developed world.
- Immigrants who are in the U.S. illegally have some rights under the Constitution
- President Barack Obama was born in the United States.
- ISIS lost a significant portion of its territory in Iraq and Syria in 2017.

What's more, the survey found that one's ability to discern between fact and opinion tended to be influenced by one's partisanship. When a factual statement threatened the sensitivities of the Democratic worldview, Democrats were more likely than Republicans to misidentify it as opinion. But when a fact was at odds with the tenets of the GOP, it was the Republicans rather than the Democrats who were most likely to mischaracterize it as an opinion. For instance, surveys at the time showed that Democrats were more critical than Republicans of President Trump's approach to the Islamic State of Iraq and Syria (ISIS).[64] Thus, it comes as no surprise that Democrats (34 percent) were more likely than Republicans (28 percent) to dismiss the factual statement "ISIS lost a significant portion of its territory … in 2017" as opinion.[65] Contemporary polling also revealed that Republicans were more inclined than Democrats to accept the demonstrably false notion that President Obama was born in Kenya.[66] Accordingly, Republicans (37 percent) were 26 percentage points more likely than Democrats (11 percent) to mischaracterize the fact "President Barack Obama was born in the United States" as opinion.[67]

In and of itself, the inability to distinguish between a fact and an

Chapter 4. Perceiving Political Information 93

opinion is troubling. Yet that problem may be compounded by its contribution to misperceptions of media bias. If Democrats watch a newscast that details the territorial losses of ISIS under President Trump, they may miscategorize that fact as an opinion. But they might also go one step further and dismiss the source providing that information altogether, believing that any program willing to air such an "opinion" must be imbued with a conservative bias. Alternatively, if Republicans read an article noting that President Obama is a natural born citizen, they may very well dismiss that factual statement as opinion and go on to conclude that it's just another example of the liberal media injecting its biases into the news. Yet, once again, that bias would truly be found in those consuming the news, not in those producing it. Therefore, when we engage with political information, we mustn't mistake fact for opinion. To avoid that error, we should ask ourselves: Can this statement be proved or disproved based on objective evidence? If it can, it is a fact. If it can't, then it's an opinion.[68] Consider the following excerpts from *The Washington Post* and *CBS News* regarding the U.S. economy:

> U.S. unemployment fell to 3.6 percent, lowest since 1969
> *The Washington Post*, May 3, 2019
>   The U.S. economy added 263,000 jobs in April, notching a record 103 straight months of job gains and signaling the current economic expansion shows little sign of stalling. The unemployment rate fell to 3.6 percent ... the lowest since 1969. The official unemployment rate has been at or below 4 percent for more than a year.[69]
>   Trump promised to eliminate the national debt. It has risen by $3 trillion
> *CBS News*, October 29, 2019
>   President Trump pledged to eliminate the national debt within eight years. Almost halfway to his self-imposed deadline, it has actually increased. The U.S. is $3 trillion more in debt than it was when Mr. Trump entered the White House. In nearly three years, it rose 15%—from $19.9 trillion to $22.9 trillion.[70]

Now, if we are loath to admit that the unemployment rate reached record lows during President Trump's first three years in office, we might be tempted to dismiss that fact as an opinion. But if we stop to ask ourselves whether that statement can be proved or disproved by objective evidence, the obvious answer is yes. We could search the unemployment data provided by the U.S. Bureau of Labor Statistics, note that it affirms *The Washington Post*'s reporting, and conclude that the paper is not in the pocket of President Trump. In the same way, if we're uneager to acknowledge that the national debt increased during President Trump's first three years in office, we might be inclined to mischaracterize that fact as conjecture. But if we stop to ask ourselves whether that statement can be proved or disproved by objective evidence, the answer, once again, is yes, and a quick inspection of the Treasury Department's data on the debt would verify CBS's reporting as well as their objectivity. Alas, politicians in our tribe will inevitably say stupid things, become embroiled in scandal, and preside over a myriad of policy failures. When they do, the press will undoubtedly be there to report it. But we mustn't misinterpret such unfavorable facts as hostile opinions, lest we wind up misinterpreting an objective source as biased. In these instances, it's not the media that is arrayed against our party, but reality itself.

Perceiving the Biased as Unbiased

Although major print and broadcast news outlets in the United States are, on balance, unbiased, there is biased media. Take Fox News and MSNBC. According to the political scientist Matthew Levendusky, the "existing evidence suggests Fox tilts to the Right, while MSNBC tilts to the Left."[71] He notes:

> When Fox and MSNBC discuss the same story.... Fox gives the conservative point of view, and MSNBC offers the liberal one.... Fox pays closer attention to stories consonant with conservative talking points, and MSNBC does the same for liberal ones.... To the extent that they present the other side's arguments, they typically do so in a derisive fashion, shooting down or mocking the opposing point of view.... Generally speaking, they spend a great deal of time criticizing the opposition ... in consistently negative terms. When these shows feature guests, they usually reinforce the host's viewpoint: one side is right, and the other side is wrong.[72]

Yet Democrats and Republicans aren't always willing to concede this point. Indeed, professor of communications Lauren Feldman found that partisans will often surrender to the *relative hostile media effect*, or "fail to fully recognize bias in the news that *is* biased, in instances when that bias is congruent with their views."[73] In other words, we readily acknowledge the partisan bias in our opponents' sources without heeding the one in our own. For example, a survey analysis by Natalie Stroud revealed that Democrats were 20 percentage points more likely to recognize the conservative bias of Fox News than the liberal bias of MSNBC, and Republicans were 40 percentage points more likely to recognize the liberal bias of MSNBC than the conservative bias of Fox News.[74] A host of experimental studies have similarly shown that Democrats and Republicans perceive less bias in news programs and news hosts that are slanted to support their view than their political opponents.[75]

Thus, while partisans agree that the media "tend to favor one side over the other" when covering political issues,[76] they disagree vehemently about which particular media is doing the favoring.⁷⁷ As press critic Tom Rosenstiel argues, Democrats and Republicans customarily make a distinction between "*the* media" which is biased and "*my* media" which is not.⁷⁸ But if we hope to be critical political thinkers, we must break that habit. We must not only guard against interpreting objective sources as biased (see sections above), we must also steer clear of interpreting biased sources as objective.

What We Can Do: Before we conclude that a news report is unbiased, we should ensure that we haven't (1) misinterpreted favorable opinions as fact or (2) succumbed to the trustworthy source effect.

Misinterpret Favorable Opinions as Fact

As noted above, a 2018 Pew Research Center survey revealed that Americans have difficulty identifying statements of fact. But the analysis made plain that they are incapable of diagnosing statements of opinion as well. In fact, only 35 percent of Americans were able to properly classify all five of the statements below as opinion.⁷⁹

Opinion Statements

- Increasing the federal minimum wage to $15 an hour is essential for the health of the U.S. economy.
- Abortion should be legal in most cases.
- Immigrants who are in the U.S. illegally are a very big problem for the country today.
- Democracy is the greatest form of government.
- Government is almost always wasteful and inefficient.

And as it was with statements of fact, the ability to accurately identify an opinion was contingent upon partisanship. While members of both parties correctly identified the opinion statements with which they disagreed as opinion, they incorrectly identified the opinion statements with which they agreed as fact. For example, recent polling has shown that Republicans have less favorable views of immigrants and immigration than Democrats.⁸⁰ Thus, it comes as no surprise that members of the GOP (50 percent) were more likely than Democrats (19 percent) to misidentify the opinion statement "Immigrants who are in the U.S.

illegally are a very big problem for the country today" as fact. Opinion polls also show that Democrats are more likely than Republicans to "strongly favor" raising the federal minimum wage.[81] Accordingly, Democrats (37 percent) were 20 percentage points more likely than Republicans (17 percent) to miscategorize the opinion statement "Increasing the federal minimum wage to $15 an hour is essential for the health of the U.S. economy" as fact.[82]

Of course, if Republicans were to hear that illegal immigrants are "a very big problem" in the United States on Fox News, and mischaracterize that statement as fact, they might go on to conclude that Fox News itself is unbiased. Equivalently, if Democrats were to mischaracterize an opinion about the benefits of raising the minimum wage they heard on MSNBC as fact, they too might wrongfully conclude that the source of that statement was objective as well. Hence, if we wish to avoid perceiving the biased as unbiased, we must first ensure that we don't mistake a favorable opinion for fact. To that end, before we accept any statement as true, we should ask ourselves if it can be proven to be so by objective evidence. If it can, it is a verifiable fact. If it can't, it is merely conjecture. For instance, recall that the unemployment rate had fallen to its lowest level in fifty years during President Trump's first term in office. In response to this fact, the Republican radio host Rush Limbaugh declared that "It happened because Donald Trump was elected president, and there aren't any two ways about this.... Had Hillary Clinton been elected, we wouldn't be talking about the economy this way."[83] Devout Republicans would most certainly agree, and some might conclude that this is a matter of fact. In truth, it is nothing more than Limbaugh's opinion. In comparison, recall that the national debt also increased by 15 percent during President Trump's first term in office. If a Democratic radio host responded to this fact by proclaiming "It happened because Donald Trump was elected president, and there aren't any two ways about this.... Had Hillary Clinton been elected, we wouldn't be talking about the economy this way," diehard Democrats might deem the statement fact, but they too would be wrong. There is simply no way to prove that the unemployment rate would be higher or that the deficit would be lower had Hillary Clinton had been elected president. To assume otherwise is to mistake an opinion for a fact.

Trustworthy Source Effect

Since partisans routinely judge attitude-consistent information as more factual than attitude-inconsistent information, it comes as no surprise that Democrats and Republicans may also fall prey to the *trustworthy source effect*, the proclivity to judge news outlets that report conciliatory information as more trustworthy than those reporting antagonistic material. In point of fact, a 2020 survey by *The Economist* and YouGov revealed that while 59 percent of Democrats deemed MSNBC as trustworthy, only 12 percent of Republicans agreed, and while 57 percent of Republicans found Fox News to be trustworthy, only 14 percent of Democrats did so.[84] As critical political thinkers, we must be willing to subject our preferred news sources to the same level of scrutiny that we apply to those from the other side. To that end, we should:

- Check the Source: Recall that while the nation's network news broadcasts and national newspapers do not exhibit a partisan bias, our favorite cable news programs and Internet websites probably do. In an effort to suss out whether our preferred sources exhibit a partisan bias, we can check their reputation online by simply searching the name of the source and "partisan bias."
- Check the Tone: Remember that opinion-based content is often designed to elicit an emotional response. Thus, if our favorite programs and postings are bombastic and self-assured, they're probably biased.
- Conduct a Content Analysis: We can also partner with an acquaintance from the other side of the aisle, conduct separate content analyses of our favorite source, and compare notes. For example, how much time or space did our source devote to an honest airing of both party's views? What stories did our source cover? And did our source treat each party's leaders and policies in an equally positive or negative manner? Of course, we don't have to abandon our favorite source if our comparative analyses indicate that it may be biased, but we should be open to that possibility and judge the information it supplies accordingly.

The U.S. news media surely has its shortcomings. But the present work isn't about how members of the media can become better journalists, it's about how we can become better citizens. As tribal Democrats and Republicans, we often see the unbiased as biased. In some instances, we will perceive a truly balanced report as unbalanced because of the expectation bias and hostile media effect. At other times, we will correctly perceive a bias against our favored party, but wrongfully conclude that it was of a partisan origin instead of an adversarial or structural one. Alternatively, we might conflate the biases of opinion-based content with news content, or presume that a partisan bias resides in a reporter rather than reality alone. And as tribal Democrats and Republicans, we often see the biased as unbiased as well, misconstruing favorable opinions as fact or placing faith in sources unworthy of our trust. Fortunately, if we take some of the aforementioned steps, we can improve our ability to distinguish between biased and unbiased political information and ensure that we don't end up dismissing what we should accept and accepting what we should dismiss.

source effect, the proclivity to judge news outlets that report conciliatory information as more trustworthy than those reporting antagonistic material. In point of fact, a 2020 survey by *The Economist* and YouGov revealed that while 59 percent of Democrats deemed MSNBC as trustworthy, only 12 percent of Republicans agreed, and while 57 percent of Republicans found Fox News to be trustworthy, only 14 percent of Democrats did so.[84] As critical political thinkers, we must be willing to subject our preferred news sources to the same level of scrutiny that we apply to those from the other side. To that end, we should:

- Check the Source: Recall that while the nation's network news broadcasts and national newspapers do not exhibit a partisan bias, our favorite cable news programs and Internet websites probably do. In an effort to suss out whether our preferred sources exhibit a partisan bias, we can check their reputation online by simply searching the name of the source and "partisan bias."
- Check the Tone: Remember that opinion-based content is often designed to elicit an emotional response. Thus, if our favorite programs and postings are bombastic and self-assured, they're probably biased.
- Conduct a Content Analysis: We can also partner with an acquaintance from the other side of the aisle, conduct separate content analyses of our favorite source, and compare notes. For example, how much time or space did our source devote to an honest airing of both party's views? What stories did our source cover? And did our source treat each party's leaders and policies in an equally positive or negative manner? Of course, we don't have to abandon our favorite source if our comparative analyses indicate that it may be biased, but we should be open to that possibility and judge the information it supplies accordingly.

The U.S. news media surely has its shortcomings. But the present work isn't about how members of the media can become better journalists, it's about how we can become better citizens. As tribal Democrats and Republicans, we often see the unbiased as biased. In some instances, we will perceive a truly balanced report as unbalanced because of the expectation bias and hostile media effect. At other times, we will correctly perceive a bias against our favored party, but wrongfully conclude that it was of a partisan origin instead of an adversarial or structural one. Alternatively, we might conflate the biases of opinion-based content with news content, or presume that a partisan bias resides in a reporter rather than reality alone. And as tribal Democrats and Republicans, we often see the biased as unbiased as well, misconstruing favorable opinions as fact or placing faith in sources unworthy of our trust. Fortunately, if we take some of the aforementioned steps, we can improve our ability to distinguish between biased and unbiased political information and ensure that we don't end up dismissing what we should accept and accepting what we should dismiss.

CHAPTER 5

Evaluating Political Information

> "The human understanding when it has once adopted an opinion (either as being the received opinion or as being agreeable to itself) draws all things else to support and agree with it. And though there be a greater number and weight of instances to be found on the other side, yet these it either neglects and despises, or else by some distinction sets aside and rejects, in order that by this great and pernicious predetermination the authority of its former conclusion must remain inviolate."[1]
>
> —Francis Bacon

The Problem: Political tribalism encourages Democrats and Republicans to subjectively evaluate information in order to arrive at a preferred conclusion.

In Part I of *The Autobiography*, Benjamin Franklin entertains his readers with an account of how he abandoned his vegetarian diet whilst on the open sea. The story is undoubtedly witty, but it's also exceptionally wise. He writes,

> I believe I have omitted mentioning that, in my first voyage from Boston, being becalmed off Block Island, our people set about catching cod, and hauled up a great many. Hitherto I had stuck to my resolution of not eating animal food and on this occasion, I considered ... the taking every fish as a kind of unprovoked murder, since none of them had, or ever could do us any injury that might justify the slaughter. All that seemed very reasonable. But I had formerly been a great lover of fish, and, when this came hot out of the frying pan, it smelled admirably well. I balanced some time between principle and inclination, till I recollected that, when the fish were opened,

I saw smaller fish taken out of their stomachs; then thought I, "If you eat one another, I don't see why we mayn't eat you." So, I dined upon cod very heartily.

In closing, the American polymath profoundly observed, "So convenient a thing it is to be a *reasonable creature*, since it enables one to find or make a reason for everything one has a mind to do."[2] Today, psychologists call this process *motivated reasoning*, a form of reasoning where people evaluate empirical evidence in a partial manner so as to endorse a preferred conclusion. In general, motivated reasoners exhibit a *confirmation bias*, in which they accept supportive evidence at face value, and a *disconfirmation bias*, in which they subject unsupportive evidence to hypercritical scrutiny.[3]

Motivated reasoning is ubiquitous in politics. A substantial body of evidence suggests that Democrats and Republicans will often accept information that favors their political preferences and identities, and summarily discredit information that does not.[4] In 1979, the psychologists Charles G. Lord, Lee Ross, and Mark R. Lepper created two purported studies on the death penalty and deterrence. Each study used a different method. One study analyzed the murder rate within a single state before and after it had adopted the death penalty ("before-after" study), and the other compared murder rates of neighboring states with different capital punishment laws ("adjacent states" study). Each study also arrived at a different conclusion. One found that the death penalty prevented additional crime, while the other concluded that it did not. Then, the trio mixed and matched the studies' methods and results, and presented them to two groups of subjects whose members included both proponents and opponents of capital punishment (Figure 5-1).[5]

Group A	
Before-After Study: Deterrent	**Adjacent States Study: No Deterrent**
Kroner and Phillips (1977) compared murder rates for the year before and the year after adoption of capital punishment in 14 states. In 11 of the 14 states, murder rates were *lower after* adoption of the death penalty. This research supports the deterrent effect of the death penalty.	Palmer and Crandall (1977) compared murder rates in 10 pairs of neighboring states with different capital punishment laws. In 8 of the 10 pairs, murder rates were *higher* in the state *with* capital punishment. This research opposes the deterrent effect of the death penalty.

Chapter 5. Evaluating Political Information

Group B	
Before-After Study: No Deterrent	**Adjacent States Study: Deterrent**
Kroner and Phillips (1977) compared murder rates for the year before and the year after adoption of capital punishment in 14 states. In 11 of the 14 states, murder rates were *higher after* adoption of the death penalty. This research opposes the deterrent effect of the death penalty.	Palmer and Crandall (1977) compared murder rates in 10 pairs of neighboring states with different capital punishment laws. In 8 of the 10 pairs, murder rates were *lower* in the state *with* capital punishment. This research supports the deterrent effect of the death penalty.

Figure 5-1: The table above displays the methods and summary results from a pair of studies that purportedly explored the deterrent effects of the death penalty. Note that the results for each pair of studies were swapped for Groups A and B (Source: Charles G. Lord, Lee Ross, and Mark R. Lepper. 1979. "Biased Assimilation and Attitude Polarization: The Effects of Prior Theories on Subsequently Considered Evidence." *Journal of Personality and Social Psychology*. Vol. 37, No. 11).

When the subjects were asked to judge "how well or poorly the study had been conducted ... and how convincing the study seemed as evidence on the deterrent efficacy of capital punishment," Lord, Ross, and Lepper found strong evidence of motivated reasoning.[6] In fact,

> Proponents [of the death penalty] found the prodeterrence study as significantly more convincing than the antideterrence study, ... regardless of whether it was the "before-after" design that suggested the efficacy of capital punishment and the "adjacent states" design that refuted it, or vice versa. Opponents, by contrast, regarded the prodeterrence study as significantly less convincing than the antideterrence study, ... again irrespective of which research design was purported to have produced which type of results. The same was true of the differences between ratings of how well done the two studies had been. ... As above, proponents found the prodeterrence study to have been better conducted than the antideterrence study, ... whereas opponents found the prodeterrence study to have been less well conducted.[7]

For example, proponents of the death penalty in Group A concluded that the "before-after" study was "well thought out" and that its authors had "gathered data properly," while the evidence derived from the "adjacent states" study was "relatively meaningless." Yet proponents in Group B came to the exact opposite conclusion. They suggested that the "before-after" study did not include enough data nor "cover a long enough period of time to prove that capital punishment is not a deterrent to murder." In addition, they praised the "adjacent states" study, claiming that the experiment was "accurate," and that the researchers were "careful in interpreting their results."

In contrast, opponents of the death penalty in Group A blasted the "before-after study," claiming that the study "should have taken data from at least 10 years before and as many years as possible after," while the "adjacent states" study contained "good evidence." Opponents in Group B, however, judged the studies very differently. Here they praised the "before-after" analysis because it compared "the same state to itself" and questioned the "adjacent states" study because "There might be very different circumstances between the sets of states, even though they were sharing a border." In short, individuals will dismiss and discount empirical evidence that contradicts their views, but they will accept the exact same evidence if it supports them.

In 2011, the political scientists Charles S. Taber and Milton Lodge similarly asked participants to rate the strength of four pro and four con arguments about gun control or affirmative action. They found that subjects who favored gun control or affirmative action rated congruent arguments as stronger than incongruent arguments, while those who were opposed rated the con arguments as stronger than the pro arguments.[8] What's more, Taber and Lodge's experiment revealed that subjects spent more time reading counter-attitudinal arguments than attitudinally congruent arguments because they were apparently "generating thoughts that denigrate or counter [those] arguments [so as to] bolster their prior convictions."[9] Evidently, citizens who are governed by political tribalism don't use reason to reach a conclusion, they use reason to justify a conclusion.

What We Can Do: As critical political thinkers, we should objectively evaluate political claims and draw our conclusions accordingly.

As critical political thinkers, we must try our best to repel the pull of partisan motivated reasoning and follow the evidence wherever it leads.[10] To that end, the next four chapters will furnish us with the tools we need to objectively evaluate false political information (Chapter 6), political statistics (Chapter 7), political arguments (Chapter 8), and political elections (Chapter 9). With these tools at the ready, we can begin the difficult work of holding ourselves and each other accountable when we behave as rationalizing—rather than rational—creatures.

CHAPTER 6

Evaluating False Political Information

"I don't think we can sustain a democratic society if citizens can't distinguish fact from fiction."[1]
—Emily Thorson

The Problem: Political tribalism inhibits the ability of Democrats and Republicans to differentiate between accurate and inaccurate political information.

On December 4, 2016, Edgar Maddison Welch entered a pizza shop in Washington, D.C. Armed with a rifle and revolver, the North Carolinian man was determined to liberate several youths who were allegedly ensnared in a sex-slave ring operating out of an underground chamber beneath the restaurant. But there was no dungeon, nor any children yearning to be freed. In fact, all he found was an ordinary pizzeria filled with families who were now fleeing for their lives. And although he was promptly arrested and eventually sentenced to four years in prison, the gunman left a host of traumatized employees and patrons in his wake.[2] All of this because Mr. Welch had fallen for a debunked conspiracy theory about Democratic politicians, pizzerias, and pedophilia. He had incorrectly identified false information as true, and the consequences were tragic.[3]

> **Types of False Information**
>
> False information, or misleading information, can take several forms. Four of the most common types of false information are the following:
>
> **Misinformation:** False information that is spread without the intent to mislead.
>
> **Disinformation:** False information that is spread with the intent to mislead.
>
> **Fake News:** False information that is designed to mimic credible news reports.
>
> **Satire:** False information that is designed to ridicule rather than mislead.

Figure 6-1: There are four major types of false information: misinformation, disinformation, fake news, and satire.

False information—that is, inaccurate information—has regrettably occupied a pride of place in American political history. Consider just a few examples. During the election of 1800, John Adams was cast as a monarchist who "planned to marry one of his sons to one of George III's daughters ... and reunite the United States and Britain."[4] In 1828, Andrew Jackson's mother was averred to have had a love child with an enslaved man, while in 1864 Abraham Lincoln was accused of plotting a national program of forced interracial marriage.[5] In the 1940s, opponents of Franklin Roosevelt claimed that he had had prior knowledge of the Japanese attack on Pearl Harbor, and in the 1950s supporters of Senator Joe McCarthy distributed a doctored photograph that appeared to show his chief foil, Senator Millard Tydings, in a conversation with the head of the American Communist Party.[6] More recently, it was purported that Pope Francis had endorsed Donald Trump for president and that his running mate Mike Pence had called Michelle Obama "the most vulgar first lady we've ever had."[7] Even fallacious videos, such as those featuring Barack Obama calling Mr. Trump "a dipshit" or Speaker of the House Nancy Pelosi slurring her speech in a drunken stupor, have begun to make an appearance.[8]

Unfortunately, a 2020 PBS *NewsHour*, NPR, and Marist Institute for Public Opinion poll found that 59 percent of Americans think "it is hard to tell the difference between what is fact and what is misleading information." In addition, more than half of those surveyed said that discerning deceptive stories "has become increasingly difficult."[9] This chapter will peg away at this predicament by describing several strategies that we can use to ferret out false headlines and articles, fabricated quotations, doctored photographs, and fake audio and video recordings.

Evaluating False Headlines and Articles

In 2019, the psychologists Craig A. Harper and Thom Baguley conducted a clever study. First, they created four fake news stories—each consisting of an image, a "breaking news" headline, and a 300-word article with a unique valence and target (as summarized in Figure 6-2). Then, the researchers randomly assigned one news report to each participant and asked them to categorize their article as either "true" or "fake news."[10]

Summary of Four Fake News Stories	
False Pro-Obama:	Barack Obama donated $50 million to charity
False Pro-Trump:	Donald Trump donated $50 million to charity
False Con-Obama:	Barack Obama committed voter fraud in the 2016 presidential election
False Con-Trump:	Donald Trump committed voter fraud in the 2016 presidential election

Figure 6-2: Harper and Baguley's 2019 study on fake news provided readers with one of four fake news articles and asked them to evaluate its veracity. Those articles—which are briefly summarized above—included information that was either favorable or unfavorable to President Obama or President Trump. The researchers found that while Democrats were more likely to deem the pro-Trump and anti-Obama stories as fake news and the pro-Obama and anti-Trump stories as true, Republicans were more likely to accept the pro-Trump and anti-Obama articles as true while dismissing the pro-Obama and anti-Trump stories to be fake news (Source: Craig A. Harper and Thom Baguley. 2019. "You are Fake News! Ideological (A)symmetries in Perceptions of Media Legitimacy." *PsyArXiv.* January 23).

The results revealed that a sizeable number of Democrats and Republicans were inclined to believe fake stories when those stories coincided with their political views. Democrats were more likely to place confidence in a fake news story about Barack Obama donating to charity or Donald Trump committing voter fraud than Republicans, and Republicans were more likely to give credence to a fake news story about Donald Trump donating to charity or Barack Obama committing voter fraud than Democrats.[11]

This is troubling. If political tribalism inhibits our ability to discern fact from fiction, and an inability to discern fact from fiction is a threat to democracy—as Emily Thorson contends in the epigraph above—then political tribalism is a threat to our democracy. As such, the responsibilities of citizenship demand that we put aside our partisan attachments and do our best to discern between accurate and inaccurate political news. Fortunately, we can drastically reduce our tendency to believe false information by adopting one skill: *lateral reading*. Most people read the news vertically, from the beginning of an article to the end. But critical political thinkers will read the news laterally—they will immediately move away from the original text, open up a tab in a web browser, and begin to investigate the source, the author, the author's sources, and other news sites for corroboration.

What We Can Do: When evaluating political headlines and articles, we should (1) search the source, (2) search the author, (3) search the author's sources, and (4) search for corroboration.

Search the Source

On October 29, 2016, abcnews.com.co posted an article under the headline: "Donald Trump Protestor Speaks Out: 'I Was Paid $3,500 To Protest Trump's Rally.'" The story, which alleges that the Hillary Clinton campaign paid actors to disrupt Donald Trump's public appearances, was retweeted by the Republican presidential nominee's campaign manager Kellyanne Conway as well as his son Eric, who proclaimed: "Finally the truth comes out! #CrookedHillary." The story, however, was a complete fabrication.[12] Before we even begin to read a news article, we should conduct an internet search of the source. If Conway or Trump had taken a moment to research abcnews.com.co, they would have discovered that while the webpage deftly mimics the name, logo, and URL of ABC News's abcnews.com, abcnews.com.co is an infamous fake-news forum.[13]

Search the Author

On March 6, 2017, NativeAmericansnews.com published an article suggesting that President Trump intended to sign an executive order that would "send around 3 million American Indians back to where they came from—India." The directive was deemed to be an essential component of the President's plan "to improve national security and combat illegal immigration."[14] Now, one would think that the reporter responsible for

Chapter 6. Evaluating False Political Information

breaking the story about Mr. Trump's ignorance of Native American history would want credit for his or her achievement. Yet the aforementioned article didn't include the name of its author, and our suspicions should be raised as a result. Other times, a false news report will include a byline. If that's the case, we should search the author's name, check the author's affiliations and credentials, consider whether the writer's area of expertise is relevant to the article's content, and judge accordingly. For instance, the article about protestors being paid to disrupt Trump rallies referenced in the previous section was allegedly written by Jimmy Rustling.[15] A quick internet search reveals that Jimmy Rustling is a term used to describe an occasion when strong emotions, particularly those of a sexual nature, are aroused. To be sure, Jimmy Rustling could have been a real reporter with cruel or clueless parents. But a simple search reveals that he was in fact a satirical fabrication of a fraud.[16]

Search the Author's Sources

On November 22, 2015, then-presidential candidate Donald Trump retweeted a racially charged graphic with the headline "USA Crime Statistics–2015." The image states that according to the Crime Statistics Bureau of San Francisco, 16 percent of "Whites [were] Killed by Whites" and 81 percent of "Whites [were] Killed by Blacks." When questioned about the tweet by Fox News host Bill O'Reilly the following day, Trump claimed that the graphic came from "sources that are very credible." Yet if the soon-to-be president had taken a brief moment to search his source's source, he would have found it to be very incredible. Indeed, there is no such thing as the Crime Statistics Bureau of San Francisco and the numbers presented in the graphic were grossly inaccurate.[17] In fact, the FBI's figures are the mirror image of those provided by Mr. Trump, with 81 percent of whites being killed by whites and 16 percent of whites being killed by blacks in 2015.[18]

Search for Corroboration

In January 2018, the so-called "Girther" controversy erupted online. Named after the "Birther" conspiracy that alleged former president Barack Obama had lied about his place of birth, Girthers averred that President Trump had lied about his weight. Soon after the White House published the results of a health exam listing Mr. Trump's weight as 239 pounds, the following tweet appeared on Twitter:

BREAKING NEWS from WSJ, leaked documents from Walter Reed Hospital shows @POTUS weight is 289 lbs., BP is 154/91, cholesterol is 237. Not quite the healthy person we were told. At 71, #Trump could drop dead any time.

If *The Wall Street Journal* (WSJ) had broken such a significant story, additional sources of prominence would surely have followed suit. Yet a search of other news outlets, including *The New York Times* and *The Washington Post*, reveals that no such report had been published.[19] In the eighteenth century, the Enlightenment philosopher Voltaire advised, "In the case of news, we should always wait for the sacrament of confirmation."[20] It was good advice then, and it is good advice now. If a seemingly important story is not being covered by most, if not all, of the major news outlets, we should be skeptical.

Evaluating Fabricated Quotations

Quotations are a common feature of rhetoric. A timely reference to the words of an esteemed figure can enhance a communicator's credibility by demonstrating his breadth of knowledge or by implying that the quoted authority agrees with her point of view. But the benefits that accrue to those who use quotations has lamentably incentivized some to abuse quotations. To be sure, a host of these offenses are quite benign. Sometimes an original utterance will be modified in a manner that is largely immaterial. On May 13, 1940, the British Prime Minister Winston Churchill declared, "I have nothing to offer but blood and toil, tears and sweat." Yet according to Paul F. Boller and John George, authors of *They Never Said It: A Book of Fake Quotes, Misquotes, and Misleading Attributions*, the somewhat awkward and redundant Churchillian remark was soon recast as, "I have nothing to offer but blood, sweat, and tears."[21] Other times, a misleading quotation will arise as the result of an honest mistake. In 1906, the English author Evelyn Beatrice Hall penned *The Friends of Voltaire*, a book in which she characterized the Enlightenment philosopher's response to a book-burning in his native France as thus: "'I disapprove of what you say, but I defend to the death your right to say it,' was his attitude now." In time, the author's eloquent turn of phrase was accredited to Voltaire himself. And while Boller and George point out that Hall "did not say that Voltaire either uttered or wrote the statement," and that "she simply summarized what she thought Voltaire's general attitude was and put it in quotes," the passage's widespread misattribution is unstartling given the ease with which it can be misread.[22]

Despite their imprecision, misquotes of this nature generally reflect the sentiments of those to whom they are ascribed. As such, they aren't necessarily a cause for concern. Of course, the same cannot be said for quotations that have been taken out of context or fabricated from whole cloth, for when one person attempts to misrepresent or manufacture the words of another, they undoubtedly do so with the intent to deceive. Thus, when we come upon a quote that paints our political party in a particularly positive light, or the opposing party in a notoriously negative one, we should be suspicious and immediately investigate. As Mark Twain (or was it Confucius? Or Einstein?) never said, if an utterance is too good (or bad) to be true, it probably is.

What We Can Do: When evaluating an alleged quotation, we should (1) attempt to locate the original source or (2) investigate whether reputable fact-checking organizations, such as Quote Investigator, Snopes, or PolitiFact, have analyzed the quotation's legitimacy.

Attempt to Locate the Original Source

On December 20, 1991, Oliver Stone's movie *JFK* opened in theaters across the country. The three-hour production was viewed by some 25 million people and grossed over 70 million dollars. But the blockbuster was also thoroughly misleading. For instance, the film repeatedly intimated that a cabal of powerful war mongers wanted to kill President Kennedy because he was intent on withdrawing U.S. military forces from Vietnam. In support of this claim, Stone included a segment of an interview in which Kennedy told Walter Cronkite of *CBS News*, "In the final analysis, it is their [South Vietnamese] war. They are the ones who have to win or lose it." Yet if one were to google "Kennedy-Cronkite Vietnam interview," one would find multiple links to the original broadcast, and if one were to listen to the recording in its entirety, one would find that Stone cherry-picked Kennedy's remarks to fit his narrative. In fact, in his very next breath the President said, "But these people who say we should withdraw from Vietnam are wholly wrong," and he reiterated that point several minutes later when he argued, "I don't agree with those who say we should withdraw. That would be a great mistake. That would be a great mistake."[23]

Similarly, ponder the oft-repeated aphorism attributed to Abraham Lincoln that "You can't build a little guy up by tearing the big guy down." Former president Ronald Reagan paraphrased the quotation at the 1992 Republican National Convention when he said, "[What Democrats] don't understand is the principle so eloquently stated by Abraham Lincoln: 'You cannot strengthen the weak by weakening the strong. You cannot help the poor by destroying the rich." Likewise, in 2015, the Republican governor of Ohio, John Kasich, appeared on *Fox News Sunday* and declared, "You can't build a little guy up by tearing the big guy down. Abraham Lincoln said it then, and he's right." Except Lincoln never said it.[24] Indeed, if one were to use the University of Michigan's online database to instantaneously comb through Lincoln's collected works, one would find that the aforementioned phrase yields zero results.[25] In truth, the idiom was coined by the Rev. William John Boetcker, an itinerant preacher and pamphleteer whose authorship has apparently been long since forgotten.[26] So, when we stumble upon a quotation, we should retype it in a search engine or online database and see if it can be verified. And if the results of our investigation are inconclusive, then we can take the next step and check with the fact-checkers.

Make Use of Reputable Fact-Checking Organizations

There are several reputable online resources, such as Quote Investigator, Snopes, or PolitiFact, that regularly authenticate quotations. For instance, during the presidential election of 2012, Republican nominee Mitt Romney's campaign aired a television ad that included a clip of the incumbent president, Democrat Barack Obama, saying: "If we keep talking about the economy, we're going to lose." Yet PolitiFact found that the quotation was taken out of context and selectively edited to give the impression that the sitting president was afraid to run on his economic record. Indeed, the Democrat's full remarks—"Senator McCain's campaign actually said, and I quote, 'If we keep talking about the economy, we're going to lose'"—tell a very different story. As the unedited quotation makes plain, then–Senator Obama made that statement while running for president against Republican nominee John McCain in 2008; not as the incumbent president seeking re-election versus Mitt Romney in 2012. Hence, Mr. Obama wasn't trying to obscure his own economic record; he was claiming that the GOP was attempting to hide theirs, as the pall of the Great Recession consumed the presidency of Republican George W. Bush.[27] Remarkably, when CBS News asked Romney advisor Tom Rath "whether it was unfair to lop off the top of Mr. Obama's comments, which would show the President was quoting the McCain camp," he feebly replied, "[Obama] did say the words. That's his voice."[28] Frankly speaking, that's undoubtedly true. But it's probably the only thing about the ad that is.

In 2016, the Democratic political action committee (PAC) Priorities USA Action produced an ad that featured ominous music and the voice of the Republican Party's presidential nominee, Donald Trump, saying, "This is the Trump theory on war. I'm really good at war. I love war, in a certain way ... including with nukes, yes, including with nukes." The thirty-second spot is powerful and unnerving, but it's also disingenuous. According to PolitiFact, "the ad uses two clips back-to-back of Trump speaking at events that were actually several months apart."[29] At a campaign rally in Iowa on November 12, 2015, the real estate mogul turned presidential hopeful criticized the United States for becoming embroiled in the Iraq War and said, "I love war, in a certain way, but only when we win." Five months later, Mr. Trump appeared on *Fox News Sunday with Chris Wallace* and said, "North Korea has nukes. Japan has a problem with that, I mean, they have a big problem with that. Maybe they would in fact be better off if they defend themselves from North Korea." When Wallace interjected and asked, "With nukes?," Trump replied, "Maybe they would be better off. Including with nukes, yes, including with nukes."[30] In sum, the Democratic PAC sliced and spliced Mr. Trump's words in order to create the impression that he loved nuclear war, an impression clearly unwarranted by the facts. Of course, the aforementioned utterances are just a drop in the sea of counterfeit quotations. Thus, the next time we happen upon a quote that is partisan in nature, don't trust, until you verify.

Evaluating Doctored Photographs

A few weeks after the terrorist attacks of September 11, 2001, an email containing a photograph from a camera allegedly found in the rubble remains of the twin towers began to circulate online. The snapshot, which featured an unsuspecting tourist posing for a picture on the roof of the World Trade Center as a hijacked airliner approached in the distance, was a fake—a crude forgery created by the photo's figure to morbidly amuse his friends.[31] Nevertheless, the haunting image was passed from inbox to inbox, reminding its recipients both of the horrors borne on that awful day and the power that altered pictures possess.

Photo manipulation is nothing new. Indeed, "the history of fakery in photography is as old as the medium itself."[32] Yet the quantity and quality of doctored images have undoubtedly increased with the passage of time.[33] According to Charles Seife, author of *Virtual Unreality: Just Because the Internet Told You, How Do You Know It's True?*, "Photo manipulation used to be a tricky business, requiring thousands of dollars in darkroom equipment, airbrushes, and some pretty specialized artistic talent to pull off properly." But now, thanks to image-processing software such as Adobe Photoshop, "anyone with a camera and a computer can attempt it, and with a little talent … can do a very credible job."[34] As a consequence, American politics has become flush with fake photographs. Consider just a few recent examples:

- In 2002, an altered image of George W. Bush depicted the President holding a children's book upside down while reading to a group of students at a charter school in Houston, Texas.[35]
- In 2008, a widely circulated email during the Democratic presidential primary included a doctored photograph of then–Senator Barack Obama holding a telephone upside down, and the statement: "When you are faking a pose for a camera photo opportunity, at least you can get the phone turned in the right direction! And he wants to be President???"[36]
- In 2012, an altered image of Mitt Romney—one of the wealthiest presidential candidates in U.S. history—appeared on Facebook. The photograph featured the Republican nominee posing with a line of children whose shirts spelled out the phrase "R-MONEY," instead of the well-heeled candidate's last name.[37]
- In 2017, a photoshopped image of President Donald Trump with a diarrhea stain down the back of his golf pants appeared online accompanied by the claim that Mr. Trump was incontinent.[38]
- Soon after Hurricane Florence hit the Carolinas in September 2018, a doctored photograph of President Trump reaching over the side of a raft to distribute a MAGA hat to a stranded flood victim began to make the rounds on Facebook.[39]
- In 2020, a photoshopped image showing former Vice President Joe Biden groping a female journalist went viral. The image was coupled with a report that Mr. Biden had "denied any impropriety, claiming that he was merely 'checking her sources.'"[40]
- In 2021, an altered image of President Joe Biden asleep at this desk in the Oval Office behind a pile of executive orders was posted on Facebook with the message: "AMERICA IN DECLINE: This decrepit old grifter works MAYBE five hours a day. We traded in a work horse, for someone that belonged out to pasture or sent to the glue factory a long time ago. Nothing says we threw in the towel better than this nauseating image, the 'commander in chief' can't even stay awake."[41]

But what's most disconcerting is the fact that fake images can have real effects. For instance, an analysis by Dario L.M. Sacchi, Franca Agnoli, and Elizabeth F. Loftus found that doctored photographs of the 1989 Tiananmen Square protest actually affected the way the study's participants remembered the event.[42] And a study led by Steven J. Frenda revealed that nearly half of those who were shown fake images of incidents that never occurred—such as President George W. Bush entertaining pitcher Roger Clemens at his ranch in Crawford, Texas, during Hurricane Katrina or President Obama shaking hands with Iranian President Mahmoud Ahmadinejad at the United Nations—"reported that they remembered the false event happening."[43] These results are sobering, and should serve as a clarion call to approach politically-tinged images with care. If not, we run the risk that fake photographs will reconstruct our old memories or even fabricate ones that are new.

What We Can Do: When evaluating a photograph, we should (1) investigate whether reputable fact-checking organizations, such as Snopes, PolitiFact, or FactCheck.org, have analyzed its legitimacy or (2) conduct a reverse image search using resources such as Tin Eye and Google Images.

Make Use of Reputable Fact-Checking Organizations

On August 29, 2008, the presumptive Republican presidential nominee John McCain announced Alaska Governor Sarah Palin as his vice-presidential candidate. Two days later, a photograph of Palin posing in an American flag bikini while holding a rifle began to spread online. By the following week, the image had become a topic of conversation on cable news, as a guest panelist on CNN wondered whether "people [will] say, yes, she looks good in a bikini clutching an AK-47, but is she equipped to run the country?"[44] Yet the photo was a fake. An investigation by FactCheck.org found that the image was the handiwork of a twenty-seven-year-old website editor in New York City who had simply Photoshopped Palin's head onto another woman's body and posted the composite on Facebook. And from there, the image was copied, shared, and spread like wildfire.[45] But we don't have to contribute to the conflagration. Instead, we can assess the authenticity of an image by checking in with the fact-checkers at Snopes, PolitiFact, and FactCheck.org. All we need to do is visit their websites, enter a few key words related to the image into the search bar, hit return, and read the results.

Conduct a Reverse Image Search

Of course, if we stumble upon an image that hasn't been investigated by a reputable fact-checking organization, we will have to verify it on our own. We can do so by performing a *reverse image search*, a process that allows a user to search for images rather than text. One simply uploads an image, or provides a link to an image that can be found online, and the search engine will find similar images on other websites. For instance, in 2017, NewsFeedObserver.com posted a story with a picture of a judge and the headline, "Muslim Federal Judge Rules Two Items of Sharia Law Legal." The article claimed that Judge Mahal al Alallaha-Smith issued a ruling that a Muslim man in America may "beat [his wife] in a non-life-threatening manner" and marry his first cousin because such actions are "prescribed by the Koran."[46] Yet when I left-clicked on the image, copied its URL, pasted it into the search bar on TinEye.com, and pressed return, my search yielded an identical picture from CNN's website, with one telling exception—the judge's nameplate. In truth, the photograph came from a news report about Los Angeles Superior Court judge Halim Dhanidina titled, "Being a Muslim judge in the age of Trump." NewsFeedObserver.com, which bills itself as a satirical website, lifted the photo from CNN and digitally manipulated the plaque by replacing Dhanidina's name with that of an imaginary federal judge.[47] Conducting a reverse image search is simple; fast; and, quite honestly, fun. And they are also extremely effective. As such, critical political thinkers should have this tool at the ready, and faithfully use it to expose any fake photos that might come their way.

Evaluating Fake Audio and Video Recordings

Unfortunately, advances in digital technology have also engendered the rise of *deepfakes*, manipulated audio and video files that make a person appear to say something he never said, or do something she never did. As of now, this technology is in its infancy. But as deepfakes become more sophisticated and widespread, our ability to distinguish between a real recording and a fake one will surely be tested.[48]

An audio deepfake occurs when a person's voice is "cloned" to produce synthetic audio that's indistinguishable from the original.[49] In 2016, the computer software company Adobe held its annual conference in San Diego, California. During the MAX Sneaks segment of the event, Adobe's Kim Chambers and the American actor, comedian, and filmmaker Jordan Peele introduced Adobe VoCo, an unreleased software prototype

Chapter 6. Evaluating False Political Information   115

with the ability to not only edit audio files but also use their phenomes to generate words from scratch. During the big reveal, Adobe research scientist Zeyu Jin pasted an audio clip—featuring Peele's friend and co-actor Keegan-Michael Key humorously recalling his reaction to being nominated for an Emmy—into the VoCo program. The file, which had been converted into an audio waveform and transcribed sentence, was projected onto the auditorium's silver screen. Jin pressed play, and the audience erupted in laughter as Key said, "I jumped on my bed and I kissed my dogs and my wife, in that order." Then, the research scientist proceeded to erase certain portions of the transcript and type out new phrases. Within seconds, VoCo altered the file and made Key say: "I kissed my wife and then my dogs," "I kissed Jordan and my dogs," and "I kissed Jordan three times."[50] It was both flawless and terrifying. One shudders to think of how this technology—dubbed "Photoshop-for-voice"—could be used for more nefarious purposes. Imagine an audio file from one of Barack Obama's audiobooks being transmogrified into a recording of the former president admitting that he was born outside of the United States, or an audio file from one of Donald Trump's campaign rallies being used to generate a confession that he worked closely with the Russians to hack ballot boxes in the 2016 election. Synthetic audio undoubtedly has its benefits. It gave the film critic Roger Ebert his voice back after cancer took it away. And let's be honest, audio deepfakes can be wildly entertaining—I mean, who wouldn't want to listen to a gaggle of former U.S. presidents rapping "F--- Tha Police" by N.W.A.?[51] But this technology also has its costs, and they might just be more than our politics can afford.

Similar fears have been aroused by the rise of deepfake visuals, "videos in which one person's face is swapped out for another, often so seamlessly that it can be difficult to tell that they have been altered."[52] As it stands, several computer software applications, such as DeepFaceLab and Zao, allow users to make altered videos and post them online. Some of the recordings are benign. For instance, one deepfake video swapped the face of actor Nicolas Cage with that of actress Amy Adams as she sang "I Will Survive" by Gloria Gaynor, while another showed actress Jennifer Lawrence speaking at the Golden Globes with the face of actor Steve Buscemi.[53] Yet others are downright disturbing—such as those that have swapped the faces of famous actresses, like Gal Gadot and Scarlett Johansson, onto the bodies of pornographic movie stars without their knowledge or consent.[54] What's more, consider the impact that deepfake videos could have on domestic politics and international affairs. What would happen, law professors Robert Chesney and Danielle Citron wonder, "if a fake video of a white police officer shouting racial slurs or a Black Lives Matter activist calling for violence" went viral? Or how many recruits and acts of terror could ISIS inspire if they created "a video depicting a U.S. soldier shooting civilians or discussing a plan to bomb a mosque?"[55] Or what about an altered video depicting "emergency officials 'announcing' an impending missile strike on Los Angeles or an emergent pandemic in New York City?"[56] As digital forensic expert Hany Farid notes, the fact that such "nightmare scenarios ... aren't out of the question ... should scare us."[57]

Yet the problem with deepfake technology isn't just its ability to present a lie as the truth, but also its capacity to provide cover for those seeking to dismiss the truth as a lie. When a public figure is accused of having said or done something inappropriate, and that allegation is supported by a genuine audio or video recording, he or she may try to cast doubt on the authenticity of that evidence by dismissing it as a deepfake. This phenomenon—which Chesney and Citron call the *liar's dividend*—is already rearing its ugly head in American politics.[58] In November 2016, *The Washington Post* released a recording of then-presidential candidate Donald Trump vulgarly bragging about groping women to an *Access Hollywood* correspondent on a hot mic in 2005. Although Trump publicly acceded to the authenticity of the tape and apologized for his comments in the final days of the campaign, he later claimed that it was not his voice on the tape after all.[59] Likewise, in the wake of an assault on the U.S. Capitol by hundreds of Trump supporters in January 2021, President Trump delivered an address in which he promised to punish the rioters and acknowledged President-elect Joe Biden's victory. Soon thereafter, however, a post appeared on Facebook claiming that the broadcast was fraudulent. "That's not real," the message exclaimed, "That's not real guys. Something's wrong with this video. This is a deep fake."[60] The post went viral.

What We Can Do: When evaluating an audio or video recording, we should (1) investigate whether reputable fact-checking organizations, such as Snopes, PolitiFact, or FactCheck.org, have analyzed its legitimacy. If not, we should (2) do our best to verify the recording on our own.

Although it's been possible to alter audio and video files for decades, doing so took time, skill, and a lot of money.[61] This is no longer the case. Fortunately, numerous efforts to develop deepfake-detecting software are currently underway. Yet these programs will never be foolproof. First, a deepfake that goes viral will likely be seen by millions of people before it's ever debunked by such software,[62] for as Jonathan Swift said, "Falsehood flies, and the Truth comes limping after it."[63] Second, researchers fear that these efforts will inevitably result in a sort of arms race, in which the methods used by those attempting to identify deepfakes will simply be incorporated and circumvented by those generating them. As such, the political scientist Brian Klass argues that "Ultimately, the solution lies with us.... If better forgers are coming, we, as citizens, need to ... become better detectives."[64] The tips described below will help us begin to do just that.

Make Use of Reputable Fact-Checking Organizations

In 2020, a video of then-Democratic presidential frontrunner Joe Biden lolling his tongue began to make the rounds on Facebook. The video wasn't realistic, nor technically even a deepfake.[65] Nonetheless, an investigation by PolitiFact offered definitive evidence of its fraudulent nature, including a link to the app which was used to doctor the video and a link to the original, unaltered recording. That same year, a video of President Trump appearing disoriented on the White House lawn appeared on Instagram. But PolitiFact once again proved that the twelve-second clip—which was accompanied by a message claiming that Trump was "deep into his degenerative neurological disease"—was a fake.[66] In short, the fact-checkers at Snopes, PolitiFact, and FactCheck.org do commendable work, and our efforts to verify suspicious recordings should begin with them.

Attempt to Verify a Recording on Your Own

However, if we stumble upon an audio or visual recording that has yet to be investigated by a reputable fact-checking group, we will have to do our best to verify it on our own.

- First, if a recording shows a politician in an unduly negative light, we should be skeptical. It's not a deal breaker—politicians say and do dumb things all the time. But, again, if it's too good (or bad) to be true, it probably is.
- Second, we should seek the source of the video. If one is lacking, that's a good indicator that it could be misleading.
- Third, we should paste the video's link into tools like Amnesty International's YouTube Dataviewer or the scanner at deepware.ai, and gather information on the recording's origins.
- Fourth, we should take a screenshot of the video, upload it to

Google or TinEye, and conduct a reverse image search to see if it appears elsewhere online, particularly in an unadulterated form.[67]
- Finally, we should make a habit of watching as many deepfake videos as possible, so we can learn how to discern a real recording from a fake one.[68] The differences can be hard to place, but the more we watch deepfake videos, the more we'll be able to detect slight movements of the mouth or the head that just don't seem quite right.[69]

Think Before We Share

As if all of this were not enough, there's still another matter with which we need to contend. In a 2021 study, Gordon Pennycook and his colleagues discovered that Democrats and Republicans were generally able to identify false information as "fake news." Lamentably, however, they also found that partisans were willing to share concordant fake news reports online even when they knew those reports were false. For instance, while 15.7 percent of Republicans rated the false headline "Over 500 'Migrant Caravanners' Arrested with Suicide Vests" as true, 51.1 percent of Republicans said that they would probably share it.[70] Likewise, while 7.5 percent of Democrats rated the fake headline "Michelle Obama Says She Plans to Run Against Trump in 2020—with Barack as Her V.P.!" as accurate, 41.3 percent of Democrats said they would consider sharing it.[71] Thus, our most pressing problem might not be discerning false information, but rather dispersing information we know to be false. Pennycook et al. argue that while we care about accuracy, we care about bolstering our partisan bona fides and earning the accolades of our online friends and followers a little more.[72] This is particularly true for "strong party identifiers" who have an "animus towards political opponents."[73] Many tribal partisans don't share false information because they think it's true. They share it because it's a signal of their tribal loyalty.[74]

Unfortunately, our social media sharing habits can exacerbate the *illusion of truth effect*, a cognitive bias that equates repetition with truth. Psychologists have found that when a claim is repeated, it becomes familiar, and when a claim is familiar, it's more likely to be perceived as accurate.[75] Thus, when we forward information we know to be false, it increases the odds that someone else will think that it's true. For example, Pennycook, Tyrone D. Cannon, and David G. Rand found that the more one is exposed to a fake news headline, the more likely one is to perceive that headline as true. When participants first read a false headline that claimed "BLM [Black Lives Matter] Thug Protests President Trump with Selfie....

Accidentally Shoots Himself in the Face," 11.7 percent of Democrats and 18.5 percent of Republicans rated it as true. But when the same participants were presented with the identical false headline a second time one week later, the number of those who judged the story as accurate significantly increased. Now, 17.9 percent of Democrats and 35.5 percent of Republicans rated the headline as true. Or consider the false headline: "Sarah Palin Calls to Boycott Mall of America Because Santa Was Always White in the Bible." On first exposure, 12.6 percent of Republicans and 24 percent of Democrats rated this header about the GOP's 2008 vice presidential nominee as accurate. Yet when they were exposed to the headline again, the percentage of gullible Republicans and Democrats jumped to 16.9 percent and 31.3 percent, respectively.[76]

While reading laterally, using reputable fact-checking sources, conducting reverse image searches, and familiarizing one's self with the digital tells of deepfakes are necessary to combat the spread of false information, they aren't sufficient. Of course, we need to identify false information. But we also have to resist the urge to knowingly pass it on for a laugh, a like, a retweet, or some partisan schadenfreude because those that receive it, might come to believe it. Happily, research has shown that when people are induced to think about accuracy, they're significantly less likely to consider sharing false headlines than those who are not.[77] Thus, to paraphrase the author Guy P. Harrison, we must think before we share.[78] When we ask ourselves, "Do I think this content is accurate or not?," we diminish the odds that we will spread false information. And as Pennycook et al. write: "Improving the quality of the content shared by one user improves the content that their followers see, and therefore improves the content that their followers share. This in turn improves what the followers' followers see and share," ad infinitum.[79]

In *Blur: How to Know What's True in the Age of Information Overload*, press critics Bill Kovach and Tom Rosenstiel argue that we'll increasingly have to rely on ourselves, rather than the press, to evaluate information.[80] We are our own editors, and we must take this responsibility seriously. As they write: "Democracy stakes everything on a continuing dialogue of informed citizens, and that dialogue rises or falls on whether the discussion is based on propaganda and deceit or facts and verification."[81] Hopefully, the tools provided in the pages above will improve our ability to distinguish fact from fiction, and thus contribute to the well-being of our democratic society.

CHAPTER 7

Evaluating Political Numbers

"The old saying is that figures will not lie, but a new saying is that liars will figure."[1]
—Carroll D. Wright

The Problem: Political tribalism hinders the ability of Democrats and Republicans to accurately evaluate political numbers.

On February 9, 1950, a relatively unknown member of the United States Senate approached the podium in the Colonnade Room of the McLure Hotel in Wheeling, West Virginia. "In my opinion," Joseph McCarthy said, "the State Department ... is thoroughly infested with communists." In fact, he is alleged to have continued, "I have here in my hand a list of 205 that were known to the Secretary of State as being members of the Communist Party and who, nevertheless, are still working and shaping policy in the State Department."[2] It was an explosive charge, and although McCarthy claimed that he'd been misquoted—and that his list was composed of just fifty-seven names—the tally's precise sum was beside the point. According to Charles Seife, author of *Proofiness: The Dark Arts of Mathematical Deception*, "It really didn't matter whether the list had 205 or 57 names. The very fact that McCarthy had attached a number to his accusations imbued them with an aura of truth. The numbers gave McCarthy's accusations heft [and] ... were too specific to ignore."[3] Indeed, those numbers made McCarthy a national figure and sparked an anticommunist campaign that would dominate American politics for the better part of a decade.

Numeric evidence has an almost magical quality, for its precision suggests a degree of certainty that appears almost incontrovertible. As a result, Democrats and Republicans will often use numeric evidence in the hopes of enhancing the legitimacy of their points of view. While some partisans will do so in an honest manner, others will not. Accordingly, we must improve our *numeracy*—or ability to understand and work with numbers—lest we be misled by the stewards of mathematical sophistry. To that end, this chapter will focus on five frequent sources of numerical bunk in politics: the dangling comparative, the meaning of "average," graphs, opinion polls, and the difference between absolute and relative change.

The Dangling Comparative

According to Brooks Jackson and Kathleen Hall Jamieson, authors of *UnSpun: Finding Facts in a World of Disinformation*, a dangling comparative "occurs when any term meant to compare two things—a word such as 'higher,' 'better,' 'faster,' 'more'—is left dangling without stating what is being compared."[4]

> **What We Can Do:** When politicians or political pundits tell us that something is "higher" or "lower" or "more" or "less," we should ask ourselves: What is actually being compared?

Consider the issue of arsenic. When present, elevated levels of the metalloid chemical in drinking water can cause serious health problems.[5] Therefore, in 1942 the U.S. Public Health Service stated that the amount of arsenic in public water systems shouldn't exceed 50 parts per billion. That level—which equates to 50 drops of water in an Olympic-size swimming pool—remained the nation's standard until Democratic President Bill Clinton recommended that it be reduced to 10 parts per billion in January 2001. Before that change could take effect, however, Republican President George W. Bush put off his predecessor's proposition and advised that the amount of arsenic in drinking water be reduced to 20 parts per billion instead.[6] Soon thereafter, the Democratic National Committee (DNC) produced a TV spot in which a little girl with an empty glass asked, "May I please have some more arsenic in my water, Mommy?" The message of the ad was clear: President Bush wanted to put "more arsenic" in drinking water. Except, of course, he didn't. When one compares President Bush's proposal to the level of arsenic in drinking water that existed at the time, one finds that the Republican wanted to reduce the amount of arsenic in drinking water by 30 parts per billion. Yet the DNC disingenuously decided to compare Bush's plan to that of President Clinton's, allowing them to reason that the Republican wanted "more arsenic" because his proposal (20 parts per billion) would have left more arsenic in the water than the Democratic plan (10 parts per billion), if the latter had ever been implemented. In short, the DNC had deceptively used the dangling comparative *"more"*—without ever answering the question: "More than what?"—so they could present President Bush's proposal to reduce the level of arsenic in drinking water by 60 percent as a call for "more arsenic."[7]

Of course, Democrats aren't the only ones who use the dangling comparative to obscure the facts. During the 2004 presidential election, several TV spots for George W. Bush declared that Senator "[John] Kerry supported higher taxes over 350 times."[8] At first blush, the ads seemed to suggest that the Democratic challenger had voted to increase taxes on hundreds of occasions as a member of Congress. Yet that impression is thoroughly misleading. To understand why, imagine a scenario in which John Kerry (1) voted against a Republican proposal to cut the top marginal income tax rate of 37 percent to 25 percent and (2) voted for a Democratic proposal to reduce that rate to 30 percent. In this instance, most reasonable observers would compare Kerry's votes to the current tax rate and conclude that he hadn't "supported higher taxes" at all. To be sure, the Democrat cast one vote for the status quo and another vote for a tax cut. But what if you wanted to portray Kerry in a less favorable light, as the Bush ads were wont to do? Well, if you compared Kerry's votes to the Republican proposal instead of the current tax rate, you could reason that the Democrat "supported higher taxes" because his votes for the status quo (37 percent) and the Democratic tax cut (30 percent) would have left taxes higher than the GOP's alternative had it have passed (25 percent). Here, the Bush campaign deceptively used the dangling comparative *"higher"*—without ever answering the question: "Higher than what?"—so they could categorize instances in which Kerry voted to maintain and even cut current tax rates as evidence of his support for higher taxes.

"In both cases," Jackson and Jamieson write, "the deceivers' central point may well have had a grain of merit." After all, President Bush did want "more" arsenic in drinking water than Democrats and Senator Kerry did want "higher" taxes than Republicans. "[B]ut rather than make an honest argument," the DNC and the Bush campaign "invited the public to accept gross exaggerations" with the dangling comparative.[9] Resultantly, the next time a politician, pundit, or partisan uses terms like "higher," "lower," "more," or "less," we must ask ourselves, "Compared to what?"

Chapter 7. Evaluating Political Numbers

The Misuse of Average

In 1954, Darrell Huff wrote the best-selling book *How to Lie with Statistics* in which he presented his readers with the following sketch (albeit with updated average incomes):

> You, I trust, are not a snob, and I certainly am not in the real-estate business. But let's say that you are and I am and that you are looking for property to buy along a road that is not far from the California valley in which I live. Having sized you up, I take pains to tell you that the average income in this neighborhood is some [$264,000] a year. Maybe that clinches your interest in living here; anyway, you buy and that handsome figure sticks in your mind. More than likely, since we have agreed that for the purposes of the moment you are a bit of a snob, you toss it in casually when telling your friends about where you live.
>
> A year or so later we meet again. As a member of some taxpayers' committee, I am circulating a petition to keep the tax rate down or assessments down or bus fare down. My plea is that we cannot afford the increase: After all, the average income in this neighborhood is only [$80,000 a year]. Perhaps you go

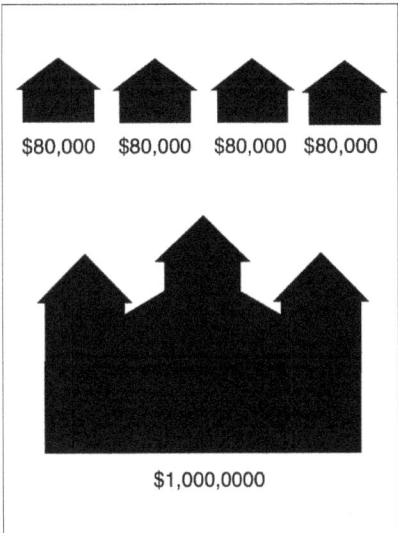

The Mean
The *mean* is the sum of a set of numbers divided by the quantity of numbers in the set.

Mean Annual Household Income
$80,000 + $80,000 + $80,000 + $80,000 + $1,000,000 = $1,320,000

$1,320,000 ÷ 5 = **$264,000**

The Median
The *median* is the middle value in a given set of data, arranged from lowest to highest.

Median Annual Household Income
$80,000, $80,000, **$80,000**, $80,000, $1,000,000

Figure 7-1: The mean and median are both arithmetic averages. But the mean can be skewed by an outlier to such an extent that it would be rendered—colloquially speaking—unaverage. As shown above, the mean annual household income ($264,000) of this neighborhood is distorted by a single $1,000,000 home. While the mean annual household income is mathematically average, it is not average in an everyday sense, as 80 percent of the households earns only $80,000 per year.

along with me and my committee in this—you're not only a snob, you're stingy too—but you can't help being surprised to hear about that measly [$80,000]. Am I lying now, or was I lying last year?

You can't pin it on me either time. That is the essential beauty of lying with statistics. Both those figures are legitimate averages, legally arrived at. Both represent the same data, the same people, the same incomes. All the same, it's obvious that at least one of them must be so misleading as to rival an out-and-out lie.[10]

Alas, Huff's trick is grounded in three common features of an arithmetic *average*, or number expressing the central value in a set of data. First, there are several distinct kinds of averages—including, most notably, the mean and the median. Second, a data set's mean and median can differ dramatically when its mean has been skewed by an *outlier*, a figure that is much larger or much smaller than most of the other values in a collection of data. Third, an average can be average in a mathematical sense but unaverage—that is, atypical or uncommon—in a colloquial one.

Sure enough, Huff used a distinct average for each sales pitch—his neighborhood's *mean* annual household income when enticing you to purchase a home, and his neighborhood's *median* annual household income when encouraging you to sign his petition. And even though these "legitimate averages" were "legally arrived at" and represented "the same data," Figure 7-1 illustrates how the former ($264,000) could be more than three times larger than the latter ($80,000) when it's skewed by an outlier—like a single household that earned $1,000,000 per year. Consequently, while both figures were average in an arithmetic sense, only the median annual household income was colloquially so. For in a neighborhood in which 80 percent of the households make $80,000 per year, an average annual household income of $264,000 is anything but typical or commonplace. So, Huff didn't "out-and-out lie." But his misleading use of the term "average" surely did rival one. Unfortunately, this little trick has found its way from the pages of our statistics books to the stages of our political campaigns.

What We Can Do: When a politician or political pundit uses the word "average," we should ask ourselves: Does average in this instance mean typical or commonplace?

In February 2003, Republican President George W. Bush claimed that American taxpayers would "receive an average tax cut of $1,083" under his new tax plan.[11] The President used the term "average" to describe his proposal's *mean* tax cut—a value that would indeed be in excess of $1,000. Yet while the mean tax cut was average in a mathematical sense, it was hardly average in a colloquial one. In fact, according to the Tax Policy Center, a non-partisan organization that attempts to provide independent analyses on matters of taxation, the median tax cut under Bush's plan was just $256. In fact, more than 80 percent of taxpayers would receive less than the $1,083 that President Bush had seemed to promise.[12] Why? Because the mean had been skewed by an outlier—an enormous $24,100 tax cut given to the top one percent of tax filers.[13] Accordingly, the "average" tax cut of which President Bush spoke was hardly typical or commonplace (Figure 7-2).

The Average Tax Cut?

Assume there are five taxpayers—four of whom will receive a tax cut of $250 and one who will receive a tax cut of $24,000.

$250 + $250 + $250 + $250 + $24,000 = $25,000

$25,000 ÷ 5 = $5,000

The mean tax cut is $5,000. Yet this is clearly not the typical tax cut. Indeed, 80 percent of the tax cuts are for $250.

Figure 7-2: In the example above, the mean tax cut ($25,000) is distorted by one large tax cut ($24,000) that is an outlier. While the mean tax cut is mathematically average, it is not average in an everyday sense, as 80 percent of the people will receive a tax cut of only $250.

Of course, Democrats play the numbers game, too. In 2015, former U.S. Senator and Secretary of State Hillary Clinton was seeking the Democratic Party's nomination for president. That June, her fundraising team emailed supporters imploring them to "Chip in $1 right now."[14] The solicitation—which obviously wasn't intent on raising vast sums of money—was in large part designed to reduce the mean contribution to the Clinton campaign.[15] According to the Center for Responsive Politics, 83 percent of Clinton's donations were large, or in excess of $200.[16] In contrast, about 70 percent of the money raised by her chief rival Bernie Sanders came from small donors. In fact, the Senator from Vermont's fondness for noting that the average contribution to his campaign was just $27 turned the figure into a punch line on *Saturday Night Live*.[17] Accordingly, Clinton feared that if her mean donation was some seven times larger than her opponent's, her campaign would be tagged as an elitist operation devoid of broad-based, grassroots support.[18] Thus, her campaign decided to use numbers to game the system. It solicited $1 contributions—outliers that would reduce the mean donation and give the appearance that her campaign wasn't beholden to big donors. Once again, while this average would be average in a mathematical sense, it wouldn't be typical or commonplace (Figure 7-3).

The Average Donation?

Assume there are fifteen donors—ten of whom contribute $500 each and five of whom contribute $1 each.

10 ($500) + 5 ($1) = $5,005

$5,005 ÷ 15 = $334

The mean donation is $334. Yet this is clearly not the typical donation. Indeed, 67 percent of the donations are for $500.

Figure 7-3: In the example above, the mean campaign donation ($334) is distorted by a handful of incredibly small contributions ($1). While the mean donation is mathematically average, it is not average in an everyday sense, as 67 percent of the contributions are for $500.

In sum, when a politician or pundit uses the term "average," we should ask ourselves: "Does average in this instance mean typical or commonplace? Or does it refer to a skewed arithmetic mean that is, colloquially speaking, unaverage?" We might resolve this line of inquiry by checking in with the fact checkers or even looking into the original data set on our own. But if an answer doesn't come forth, we should remain skeptical until one does. For in politics, an average is often anything but.

The Misuse of Graphs

A graph—or visual representation of data—can make vast amounts of complex statistical information comprehensible. Yet the medium may also be used to mislead. Therefore, we must do our level best to discern between accurate and inaccurate graphs. In *More Damned Lies and Statistics*, sociologist Joel Best writes that "the essential standard for judging graphs is remarkably simple: an accurate display should present visual proportions equivalent to the numeric proportions being represented."[19] This simple standard, however, is quite difficult to apply in practice because we often focus on a graph's visual content at the expense of its numerical information. Of course, we can't determine whether a graph's visual proportions are truly representative of its numeric proportions unless we give equal attention to both. Accordingly, when we encounter a graph, we should first and foremost focus on the numbers. Then, and

Chapter 7. Evaluating Political Numbers

only then, should we turn our attention to the graph's visuals to determine whether they faithfully represent its figures.

What We Can Do: When evaluating a graph, we should ask ourselves: Do the graph's visual proportions accurately reflect its numerical proportions?

Consider the following examples. On July 27, 1981, Republican President Ronald Reagan delivered a nationally televised address during which he compared the taxes that an American family would pay under his tax plan with those they would pay under a proposal put forth by Democrats in Congress. To help make his case, the GOP's standard-bearer presented a graph similar to the one in Figure 7-4 and suggested that the "space between the two lines is the tax money that will remain in your pockets if our bill passes and it's the amount that will leave your pockets if their tax bill is passed."[20] Yet Reagan's graph was gravely misleading, owing to the fact that it didn't include any numbers on its vertical axis. Hence, it's impossible to gauge whether the graph's visual proportions are equivalent to its numeric proportions because its numeric proportions are entirely absent.

In truth, a family making $20,000 in 1986 would have paid $2,385 in taxes under the Democrats' plan and $2,168 in taxes under the President's plan. Thus, the difference between the two proposals was $217—or 9

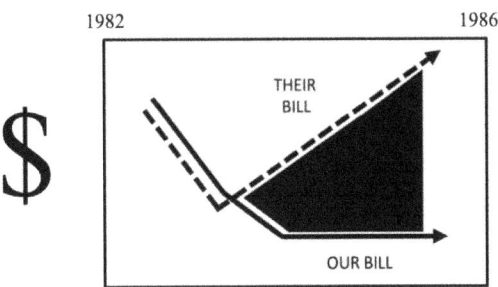

Figure 7-4: The image above is a misleading graph similar to the one used by President Ronald Reagan during a televised address in July 1981 to extol the virtues of his tax bill in comparison to the congressional Democrats' tax plan. The graph, however, is disingenuous. Since its vertical axis isn't labeled, voters were unable to determine the actual difference in taxes paid between the two proposals.

percent [$217 ÷ $2,385 = .09]. Yet according to the economist Gary Smith, the graph magnified "this 9 percent difference into 90 percent of the height of the line labeled 'their bill,' and the omission of numbers from the vertical axis prevents readers from detecting this misleading magnification."[21] Sure enough, when the graph's visual and numerical proportions are in concert—as they are in Figure 7-5—we're left with a drastically different impression. Afterwards, White House spokesman David Gergen tried to justify the administration's sleight-of-hand when he told reporters, "We tried it with numbers and found it was very hard to read on television, so we took them off. We were just trying to get a point across."[22] Well, color me skeptical. The Reagan team may have made its point, but it was a misleading one that was put forth in an underhanded manner.

In 2001, Republican President George W. Bush initiated a series of sweeping tax cuts that included a reduction in the highest marginal income tax rate from 39.6 percent to 35 percent. That tax cut, however, was temporary, and in 2012 a furious debate ensued over whether or not the tax cut should be renewed.[23] During its coverage of the dispute, Fox Business broadcast a graph analogous to the one in Figure 7-6. That graph, however, obscured the relationship between the size of its bars and the values they represented by omitting zero from its vertical axis. Accordingly, the cropped graph—whose right-hand bar was some six times higher than its left-hand bar—gave the impression that the highest marginal income tax rate would've increased by 600 percent if the Bush tax cut expired. But that's simply not true. The difference between a tax rate of 35 percent and

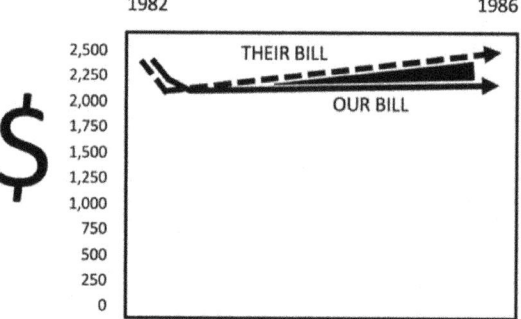

Figure 7-5: In contrast to Figure 7-4, the vertical axis of the graph here is labeled. As such, it provides a more accurate picture of what the average American family would pay in federal taxes under the Reagan plan versus the congressional Democrats' plan.

Chapter 7. Evaluating Political Numbers

one of 39.6 percent is 4.6 percentage points. Hence, "if the cuts expire," notes cognitive psychologist Daniel Levitin, "taxes will only increase 13 percent, not the 600 percent that is pictured (the 4.6 percentage point increase is 13 percent of 35 percent)" [.046 ÷ .35 = .13].[24] In other words, Fox Business portrayed the tax hike as some 46 times greater than it should've been. Of course, if Fox Business had depicted the data in an honest manner—as in Figure 7-7—it would've contradicted the channel's characterization of the looming tax hike as "Taxmageddon."[25]

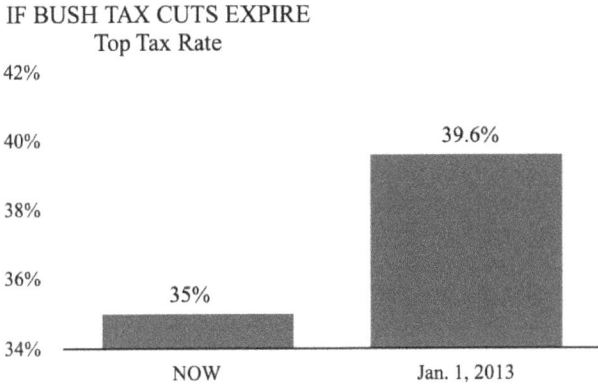

Figure 7-6: The image above is a misleading graph similar to the one broadcast on Fox Business in 2012 depicting the change in the highest marginal income tax rate if President George W. Bush's tax cut lapsed.

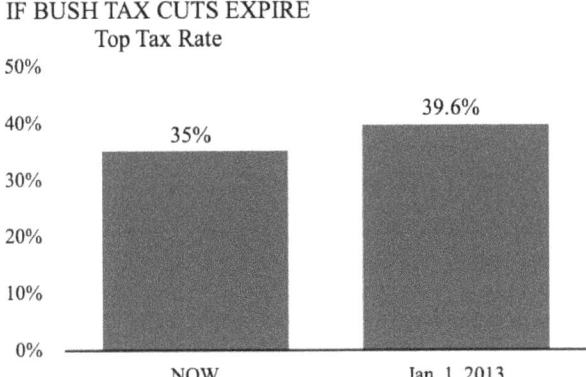

Figure 7-7: In contrast to Figure 7-6, the visual information of the graph here is proportional to its numerical information. As such, it provides a more accurate picture of how much the highest marginal income tax bracket would increase if the Bush tax cut expired.

On December 16, 2015, Democratic President Barack Obama's administration posted a graph on Twitter. The image—which was similar to the illustration in Figure 7-8—was accompanied by a message that declared: "Good news: America's high school graduation rate has increased to an all-time high."[26] Good news, indeed. Unfortunately, the same cannot be said for the tweet's incredibly misleading graph.

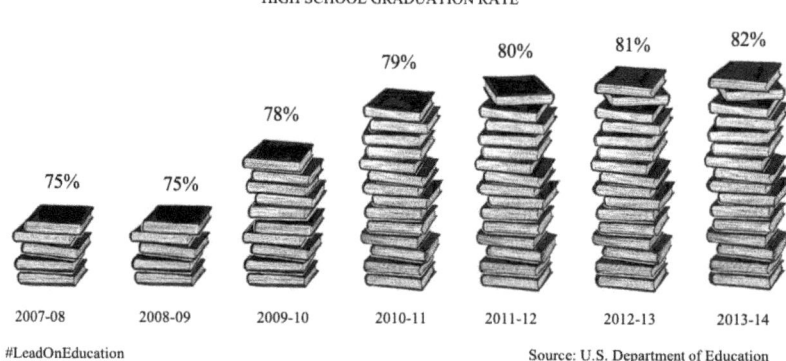

Figure 7-8: The illustration above is a misleading graph similar to one that the Obama administration posted on Twitter to herald an increase in the number of earned high school diplomas awarded during President Obama's tenure (illustration by E.S. Redmond).

If we adopt 2007–08 as our scale—that is, if we use five books to represent a 75 percent high school graduation rate—then the 82 percent high school graduation rate in 2013–14 should equate to five and one-half books (5/.75 = x/.82, .75x = 4.1, x = 5.5). Yet the Obama administration employed a whopping sixteen books to represent that milestone—almost three times more than is warranted by the data.[27] In fact, if the graph's visual proportions were equivalent to the numeric proportions being represented, they would've looked a lot more like the bars in Figure 7-9. While Democrats and Republicans might disagree about giving the Obama administration high marks for its educational policies, the conclusion that it deserves a failing grade for its graph should be a bipartisan one.

Finally, in 2018, *The New York Times Magazine* included a graph like the one in Figure 7-10 in an article exploring Republican President Donald Trump's influence on the federal courts.[28] To be sure, the nation's 45th

Chapter 7. Evaluating Political Numbers   131

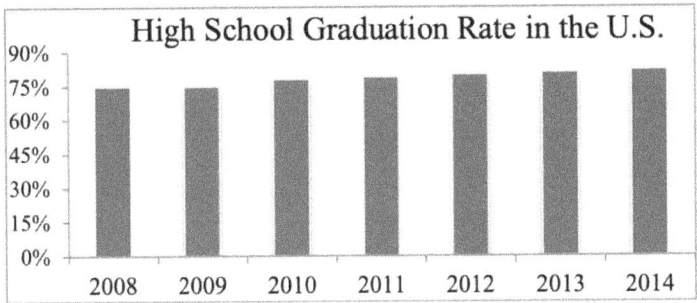

Figure 7-9: In contrast to Figure 7-8, the visual information of the graph here is proportional to its numerical information. Therefore, it accurately depicts the change in the number of earned high school diplomas under President Obama.

president reshaped the federal judiciary. Trump appointed more federal judges in four years (226) than any other one-term president, except Jimmy Carter (261).[29] Nevertheless, the magazine's graph is remarkably deceiving. If we use Barack Obama's gavel as our scale, we find that George W. Bush's gavel is almost one and one-third times too big, Bill Clinton and George H.W. Bush's gavels are two times too big, and Ronald Reagan's gavel is almost two and one-half times too big. And while President Trump appointed more appellate judges during the first congressional term than

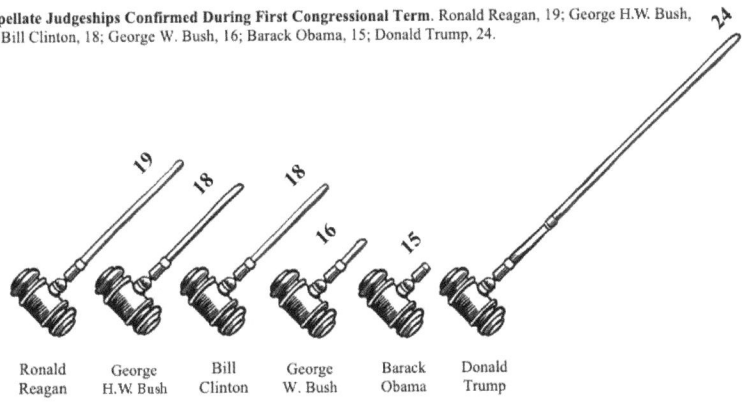

Figure 7-10: The illustration above is a misleading graph like the one used in a 2018 *New York Times Magazine* article to show the number of appellate judgeships confirmed during the first congressional term of the Ronald Reagan, George H.W. Bush, Bill Clinton, George W. Bush, Barack Obama, and Donald Trump presidencies (illustration by E.S. Redmond).

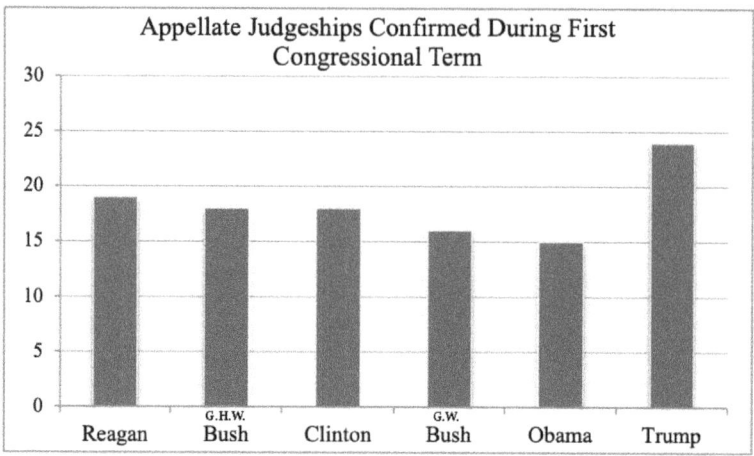

Figure 7-11: In contrast to Figure 7-10, the visual information of the graph here is proportional to its numerical information. As such, it accurately depicts the number of appellate judgeships confirmed during the first congressional term of the Ronald Reagan, George H.W. Bush, Bill Clinton, George W. Bush, Barack Obama, and Donald Trump presidencies.

his five predecessors,[30] his gavel in the graph is three and one-third times bigger than it should be. In fact, when the graph is adjusted to scale and the vertical axis is clearly labeled, we get a much more accurate picture of the data (Figure 7-11). Sure enough, Trump outpaced his predecessors in the matter at hand, but not nearly to the degree that *The New York Times Magazine* seemed to suggest.

In sum, critical political thinkers mustn't be seduced by the blocks and lines of a graph. Instead, they should carefully scrutinize the graph's numbers and then ask themselves: "Do the graph's visual proportions reflect its numerical proportions in an accurate manner?" Certainly, a graph—like a picture—is worth a thousand words. But the story it's spinning just might be a tall tale.

Public Opinion Polls

Public opinion polls—or surveys used to estimate the attitudes of a given population based on the views expressed by a sample of its members—are pervasive in American politics. Nary a day goes by without a poll being parsed by this pundit or that politician. As such, it's important that we know how to distinguish between a properly and improperly conducted poll.

Chapter 7. Evaluating Political Numbers

What We Can Do: When evaluating a political opinion poll, we should ask ourselves: (1) Is the poll's sample representative? (2) Are the poll's questions biased? And (3) have the poll's results been inappropriately aggregated?

First, we must ask ourselves: "Is the poll's sample representative?" A representative sample is one that accurately reflects the characteristics of the population from which it was drawn. Simply put, if 50 percent of the population is female, then 50 percent of the sample needs to be female. The same applies to characteristics like age, race, party affiliation, and other factors.[31] And the primary means of securing a representative sample is to select that sample in a random fashion, so that each member of the population has an equal chance of being chosen.[32] To illustrate, consider a large jar that contains a broad collection of beans that differ both in their color and proportion. If one were to randomly draw a sample of 100 beans from the urn, it would likely resemble the population. To be sure, there will be some variation, but the probability that the sample would deviate significantly from the population is quite low (Figure 7-12).

The table below contains the results of ten random samples of 100 beans. The samples were drawn from a population of 1,000 beans—of which 600 were white, 300 were green, and 100 were red. A perfectly representative sample of the population would consist of 60 white beans, 30 green beans, and 10 red beans. While none of the samples drawn were perfect, they were quite close. In fact, the average proportion of beans from the samples is almost identical to their proportion in the population. This is the power of probability and proper sampling.

Sample #	White (60)	Green (30)	Red (10)
1	54	31	15
2	53	40	7
3	64	25	11
4	61	29	10
5	58	31	11
6	60	26	14
7	58	34	8
8	66	22	12
9	66	25	9

Sample #	White (60)	Green (30)	Red (10)
10	56	31	13
Average	59.6	29.4	11

Figure 7-12: The table above displays the results of ten random samples of 100 beans—600 of which were white, 300 of which were green, and 100 of which were red. While no single sample is perfectly representative of the population, they all are quite close. What's more, the pooled mean for each color is nearly identical to its proportion of the population.

By contrast, non-random samples are more likely to include certain members of the population than others. Accordingly, they tend to be unrepresentative—and we can't infer anything about a population from an unrepresentative sample because the former isn't accurately reflected by the latter. Unfortunately, this proscription is often ignored in American politics. For instance, on September 26, 2016, Democrat Hillary Clinton and Republican Donald Trump participated in the first of three presidential debates. The next morning, Trump tweeted the results of more than half a dozen polls portraying him as the winner of the debate—some with a margin of victory greater than 50 percentage points.[33] But there's just one problem. The polls that Trump had played up on Twitter were informal online surveys that invited anyone to respond. As such, they were plagued by the *self-selection bias*, a distortion that often occurs when survey respondents are allowed to decide for themselves whether or not to participate in a poll. To make matters worse, the surveys' results were also distorted by the fact that respondents could vote multiple times, and, with the right software bot, perhaps even more than that.[34] Indeed, after the polls appeared online—at news websites ranging from Breitbart and Drudge to CNBC and TIME—a swath of Trump supporters took to the Internet, provided links to the polls on a handful of message boards, and instructed their followers on how to cast multiple votes for the billionaire businessman.[35] Sure enough, they voted … and voted … and voted again. In short, these surveys essentially asked a bunch of Trump supporters for their opinions, and they duly (and often repeatedly) provided them, with predictable results. The polls' samples weren't random or, as a consequence, representative. Hence, their results were meaningless. For as the polling analyst Ariel Edwards-Levy notes: "A poll that does not exert some measure of control over who takes it and how many times they do so is not a poll."[36]

As such, when we come upon a public opinion poll, we should evaluate its reliability by gauging whether or not its sample is random. To do so, we'll have to read beyond the survey's results. When a news source

Chapter 7. Evaluating Political Numbers 135

administers a poll with a random sample, they'll make that fact plain—even if it's in fine print under a graphic, buried in a press release, or accessed by a link to the survey's methods. For instance, the poll might explicitly state something like: "The results presented here are based on 1,500 completed telephone interviews conducted among a nationwide random sample of registered voters." Or it might provide the poll's *sampling error*—that is, "a calculation of how closely the results reflect the attitudes or characteristics of the full population that's been sampled."[37] And given the fact that a probability sample is a prerequisite of sampling error, the reporting of a sampling error indicates that a poll's sample was drawn in a random fashion (Figure 7-13).[38] Thus, if we scour a survey without finding any explicit or implicit evidence of random sampling, we should summarily dismiss its results.

Sampling Error
The metric used to relay the amount of sampling error is called the margin of error, and it will be stated as a plus or minus from the estimated statistic. Consider the following Gallup poll from October 2021:   Do you approve or disapprove of how Joe Biden is handling his job as president? 54% Approve 40% Disapprove   The poll's margin of sampling error was ± 4 percentage points. This means that the actual percentage of people who approve and disapprove of President Biden's performance is likely to be in the range of 50–58 percent (54 percent plus or minus 4 percentage points) and 36–44 percent (40 percent plus or minus 4 percentage points), respectively.

Figure 7-13: How to Apply the Margin of Error to a Political Opinion Poll—A Primer.

Unfortunately, a survey whose sample is random can still be rendered specious by a poorly constructed question. In *Thinking, Fast and Slow*, psychologist Daniel Kahneman recalls an experiment in which several Harvard Medical School physicians were given information on lung cancer surgery and asked whether they would recommend the procedure to their patients. There was, of course, a catch: some of the doctors were told that 90 percent of the patients who'd had the surgery survived, while others were informed that the procedure had a mortality rate of 10 percent. Note that the two descriptions are logically equivalent. Nevertheless, while 84 percent of the physicians in the "survival" group recommended surgery, only 50 percent of those in the "mortality" group followed suit.[39] They did so, Kahneman suspects, because of the *framing effect*, a cognitive bias in which people respond to a particular choice in different ways depending on how it is presented. In short, he wrote, the physicians concluded that "90% survival sounds encouraging" or that "10% mortality is frightening"—and chose accordingly. Hence, it's not just *what* one says that's important, but also *how* one says it.[40]

Evidence of the framing effect is widespread in public opinion polling.[41] Time and time again, the way in which a question is posed has proven to affect the answers that people provide.[42] Therefore, when we evaluate a public opinion poll, we must also ask ourselves: "Are the poll's questions biased?" For instance, consider the following possibilities:

- First, poll results can be swayed by the way that a question is phrased. In 1993, a now infamous Roper poll asked, "Does it seem possible or does it seem impossible to you that the Nazi extermination of the Jews never happened?" The survey found that an astounding 22 percent of Americans doubted that the Holocaust ever occurred. Yet it became evident that the query's double negative—is it "impossible" the Holocaust "never happened"—had simply befuddled many respondents.[43] In fact, once the question was rephrased in a grammatically appropriate manner, the number of people who denied the Holocaust fell to 1 percent.[44]
- Second, the results of a poll can be influenced by the options that it provides to its respondents. In 2018, a Quinnipiac poll asked, "Do you support or oppose the death penalty for persons convicted of murder?" The results showed that 58 percent of interviewees were in favor of capital punishment, while just 33 percent were opposed. Yet when they were presented with another alternative—life in prison with no chance of parole—the survey yielded drastically different results. Now, when asked, "Which punishment do you prefer for people convicted of murder: the death penalty or life in prison with no chance of parole?," support for the death penalty dropped to 37 percent, as 51 percent of those polled opted for life imprisonment.[45]
- Third, a poll's results can be dramatically altered when its questions include loaded language. A 2010 General Social Survey found that while 68 percent of respondents believed the government spent "too little" on "assistance to the poor," only 24 percent maintained that the government spent "too little" on "welfare." Although the terms "assistance to the poor" and "welfare" are largely synonymous, the latter has negative connotations for many Americans. Given that the term "welfare" often conjures up images of free riders amassing vast amounts of public assistance through manipulation and fraud, it's unsurprising that a greater percentage of Americans express support for those characterized by the less pejorative term "the poor."[46]

Or take the federal estate tax, "a tax levied on the net value of the estate of a deceased person before distribution to the heirs."[47] In 1992, the inheritors of the Mars candy and Gallo wine fortunes sought to engender public support for their efforts to repeal the levy by calling it a "death tax." As the political pundit and pollster Frank Luntz explained, "it is the same tax ... [but while] nobody really knows what an estate is ... they certainly know what it means to be taxed when you die."[48] As a consequence, the campaign proved to be remarkably effective. In a 2010 study, the political scientists Brian Schaffner and Mary Layton Atkinson found that the rhetorical shift increased the number of citizens who supported the tax by more than 34 percentage points.[49]

- Finally, a response to a well-written query can be skewed by a previous question. In March 2010, a Fox News poll asked: "Based on what you know about the health care reform legislation being considered right now, do you favor or oppose the plan?"[50] The question—which was perfectly fine—showed that 55 percent of registered voters opposed the Democrats' health care reform bill, versus just 33 percent in favor, for a difference of -22 percentage points.[51] By contrast, several other polls revealed a much smaller net score—typically around -2 percentage points.[52] So, how can an unbiased question produce such a biased result? According to the statistician Nate Silver, "the answer may have to do with the questions Fox asked *before* the question on health care."[53] Indeed, the questions that proceeded the health care query—such as, "Do you think Barack Obama's travel and speaking schedule makes him look more like he is a candidate on the campaign trail or more like he is the president of the United States?" or "Do you think President Obama apologizes too much to the rest of the world for past U.S. policies?"—reiterated Republican Party talking points that criticized the Democratic President for being the "Campaigner-in-Chief" and "Apologizer-in-Chief."[54] As such, they likely pushed some respondents to be more critical of President Obama and his health care plan than they otherwise would've been. For, as Silver notes, "When you ask biased questions *first*, they are infectious, potentially poisoning everything that comes below."[55]

All in all, it's imperative that we examine the complete wording and order of the questions posed in a poll. We should scroll down to the bottom of the article or press release that accompanies a survey, look for a hyperlink that says something like "Read entire poll results," "View complete question and responses," or "poll methodology," and click on it. Soon thereafter, we will be redirected to a separate webpage or PDF that will detail the poll's questions in full. If no such hyperlink exists, we should be suspicious and greet the poll's results with circumspection.

Lastly, when we evaluate a public opinion poll, we should ask ourselves: "Have politicos inappropriately aggregated a poll's results to make it appear as though the public holds an opinion that it truly doesn't possess?" In *How Not to Be Wrong: The Power of Mathematical Thinking*, mathematician Jordan Ellenberg asks his readers to imagine a survey in which "a third of the electorate thinks we should address the deficit by raising taxes without cutting spending; another third thinks we should cut defense spending; and the rest think we should cut Medicare benefits" (Figure 7-14). In this instance, a politician who supports spending cuts might use the poll as evidence that two-thirds of voters want to slash spending (cut defense + cut Medicare). Yet a politician who opposes spending cuts could use the very same survey as proof that two-thirds of voters don't want to slash spending for Medicare (raise taxes + cut defense) and defense (raise taxes + cut Medicare). Now, while both statements are technically true, they're also misleading. In each case, the politician disingenuously amalgamated the poll's results to make it appear as though the public shared his or her point of view, when, in fact, a majority of respondents neither supported nor opposed "spending cuts" on the whole.[56]

Or take the issue of abortion. In 2016, a Gallup poll found that 29 percent of Americans believed abortion should be legal under all circumstances, 50 percent believed it should be legal under certain circumstances, 19 percent believed it should be illegal under all circumstances, and 2 percent remained undecided (Figure 7-15).[57] Surely, a pro-choice interest group could amalgamate the results of this poll to suggest that 79 percent of the American people were pro-choice (always legal + sometimes legal); just

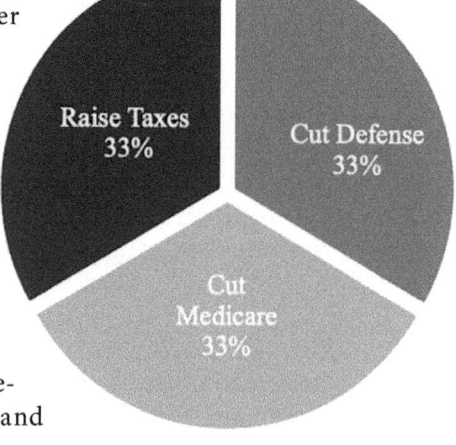

Figure 7-14: The image above contains the results of an imaginary poll in which one-third of those queried want to raise taxes, one-third want to cut defense spending, one-third want to cut Medicare (Jordan Ellenberg. 2014. *How Not to Be Wrong: The Power of Mathematical Thinking*. New York: The Penguin Press).

Chapter 7. Evaluating Political Numbers

as a pro-life interest group could combine the survey's results and posit that 69 percent of Americans were pro-life (never legal + sometimes legal). Once again, neither conclusion is wrong per se—that is, a majority of Americans could be pro-choice if the mother's life is at stake, and pro-life if a late-term abortion was administered for non-health reasons. Nevertheless, they falsely mask the fact that half of the respondents support abortion in some, but not all, cases.

Or consider the Affordable Care Act (ACA). According to Ellenberg, an October 2010 poll of likely voters found that 37 percent of respondents wanted to repeal Obamacare, while 36 percent hoped to expand it. In addition, 10 percent of those surveyed believed that the ACA should be weakened, while 15 percent thought that the law should remain unchanged (Figure 7-16).[58] Again, a conservative pundit could aggregate voters who wanted to "repeal," "weaken," and even

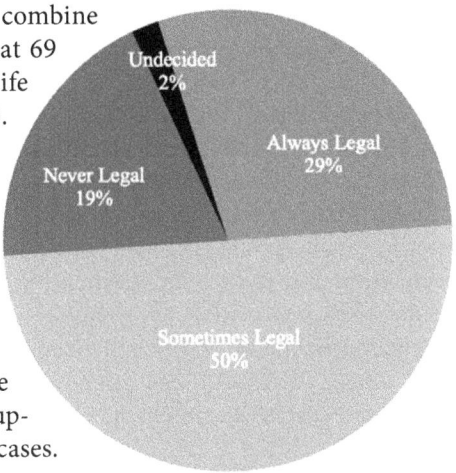

Figure 7-15: The image above—which contains the results of a 2016 Gallup poll on the issue of abortion—reveals that 29 percent of Americans believed abortion should be legal under all circumstances, 50 percent believed abortion should be legal under certain circumstances, 19 percent believed abortion should be illegal under all circumstances, and 2 percent remained undecided (Gallup. 2020. "Abortion." gallup.com).

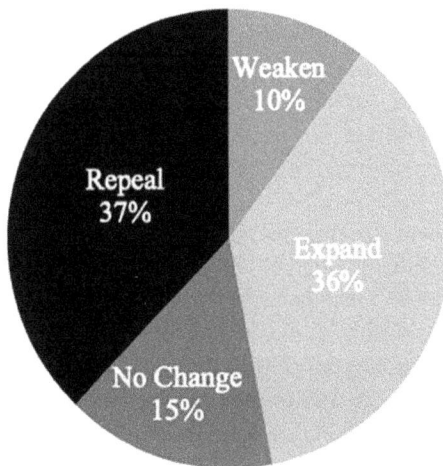

Figure 7-16: The image to the left—which displays the results of a poll on the Affordable Care Act—reveals that 37 percent of respondents believed the law should be repealed, 10 percent believed the law should be weakened, 15 percent believed that the law should remain unchanged, and 36 percent believed the law should be expanded (Jordan Ellenberg, 2014. *How Not to Be Wrong: The Power of Mathematical Thinking*. New York: The Penguin Press).

"expand" Obamacare to suggest that 83 percent of Americans opposed the Affordable Care Act, and a liberal pundit could combine the "expand," "no change," and even "weaken" voters to report that 61 percent of Americans supported the law.[59] Yet an honest analysis of the poll would have admitted that a majority of the American people neither supported nor opposed the divisive legislation. And any attempt to obscure that fact is misleading.[60]

Majority rule is a bedrock of democracy. As such, politicians and pundits long to profess that the public's views are aligned with their own—even when they're not. Thus, when partisans brandish a poll, we should be skeptical, track down the original survey, and make sure they haven't amalgamated the results in a misleading and self-serving manner. While Abraham Lincoln said "our government rests in public opinion," sometimes there just isn't a public opinion in which our government can rest.[61]

Absolute and Relative Change

Change—or the transformation from one state or condition to another—is a mainstay of American political discourse, and it is often expressed in numbers. Much ink has been spilt and many words have been spat debating changes in violent crime, the unemployment rate, or some other variable. Yet it's important to note that numeric changes can be described in absolute and relative terms, and that each of these measures can be misleading. Therefore, when partisans describe a numeric transformation in one thing or another, we must ask ourselves: "Is the change of which they speak absolute or relative?" Otherwise, we won't know when a purveyor of misinformation has portrayed a small turn as large or a large turn as small.

What We Can Do: When a politician or pundit describes a numeric change, we should ask ourselves: "Is the change of which they speak absolute or relative?"

Absolute change is the increase or decrease in the value of a variable, and it can be calculated by simply subtracting the old data from the new data. In contrast, *relative change*—that is, the percent increase or decrease in the value of a variable—is determined by dividing the absolute change by the old data and multiplying by 100 percent. For instance, if someone's salary increased from $40,000 per year to $60,000 per year, the absolute change in their annual salary would be $20,000, while the relative change would be 50 percent (Figure 7-17).[62]

Chapter 7. Evaluating Political Numbers

Absolute Change	Relative Change
New Data—Old Data	(New Data − Old Data) ÷ Old Data × 100%
Absolute Change in Annual Salary $60,000 − $40,000 = $20,000	Relative Change in Annual Salary ($60,000 − $40,000) ÷ $40,000 × 100% = 50%

Figure 7-17: The table above includes the formulas for calculating absolute change and relative change, as well as an example of the absolute and relative changes for a worker whose annual salary increased from $40,000 to $60,000.

That's all well and good, but here's the problem: sometimes absolute change can make a change seem less significant than it actually is. In 2011, Democrats in the Illinois state legislature increased the state's personal income tax rate from 3 percent to 5 percent. Of course, tax hikes tend to be unpopular. So, the measure's supporters downplayed the increase by noting that the absolute change to the tax rate was only two percentage points. Yet Republicans rightly pointed out that the relative change in the state income tax was a whopping 67 percent (Figure 7-18).[63] To be sure, if a family's annual household income was $40,000, it would go from paying $1,200 in taxes to coughing up $2,000, an increase of $800. According to Charles Wheelan, author of *Naked Statistics: Stripping the Dread from the Data*, the Democrats were trying to use absolute change to make a sizable tax increase appear quite modest.

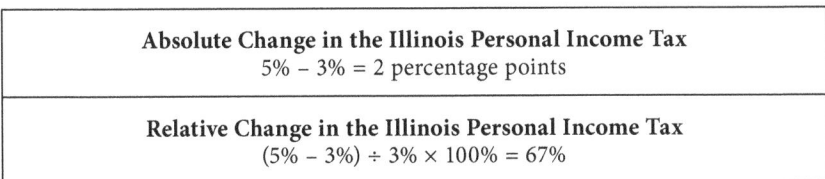

Figure 7-18: The table above presents the absolute and relative change in the Illinois personal income tax according to a proposal put forth by Democrats in the Illinois state legislature in 2011 and demonstrates how absolute change can make a change seem less significant than it actually is (Source: Charles Wheelan. 2013. *Naked Statistics: Stripping the Dread from the Data*. New York: W.W. Norton & Company).

At other times, relative change can make a change appear more significant than it really is. In April and May of 2018, the Trump administration announced that it had separated 1,995 children from their parents or guardians who were facing criminal prosecution for unlawfully crossing the border. In an effort to justify the controversial policy, Homeland Security

Secretary Kirstjen Nielsen suggested that a growing number of separations involved people posing as the parents of unrelated children. To wit, Nielsen argued that there had been a "314 percent increase in adults showing up with kids that are not a family unit. Those are traffickers, those are smugglers, ... those are criminals, those are abusers."[64] Yet, as Philip Bump of *The Washington Post* indicated, the number of so-called "fake family units" only increased from 46 in fiscal year 2017 to 191 in the first five months of 2018.[65] Hence, by choosing to report the relative change and not the absolute change in the number of fake family units seized at the border, the Trump administration gave the impression that an increase of 145 fake family unit cases was something far more substantial than it actually was (Figure 7-19).

Absolute Change in Fake Family Units at Southern Border 191 − 46 = 145 fake family units
Relative Change in Fake Family Units at Southern Border (191 − 46) ÷ 46 × 100% = 315%

Figure 7-19: The table above presents the absolute and relative change in the number of "fake family units" arriving at the U.S. southern border in the spring of 2018. The figures illustrate how a relative change can make a change appear more significant than it actually is (Source: Philip Bump. 2018. "How to mislead with statistics: DHS Secretary Nielsen edition." *The Washington Post.* January 18).

When a politico describes a numeric change, we should ascertain whether that change is absolute or relative. Then, we should calculate the type of change that wasn't used, compare it to the one that was, and determine whether absolute change or relative change is the most appropriate measure for the context at hand.

Political Tribalism and Numeracy

Numeracy is the antidote to pundits and politicians who use dangling comparatives, atypical averages, disproportionate graphs, maladministered polls, or misguided measures of change to mislead. Hence, it's important that we hone our mathematical skills and use them to evaluate statistical political information. Unfortunately, it appears as though some numerate Democrats and Republicans will forsake their ability to work with and understand numbers when those numbers challenge their cherished points of view.

In 2013, Dan Kahan led a now well-known study. First, the Yale

Chapter 7. Evaluating Political Numbers

psychologist and his colleagues gathered information on the partisan identities and mathematical abilities of over 1,000 U.S. subjects. Then, they randomly split this diverse array of numerate and innumerate Democrats and Republicans into two cohorts: a "medical group" that would evaluate the impact of a skin cream on rashes, and a "political group" that would assess the effect of concealed carry laws on crime rates. Finally, the researchers gave the participants one of the four tables shown in Figure 7-20, and asked them to interpret its contents. Members of the medical group—who received either Table A or Table B—were asked whether patients who used the skin cream were more likely to get better or worse than those who didn't. Members of the political group—who were given either Table C or Table D—were asked whether cities that banned the carrying of concealed handguns in public had higher or lower levels of crime than those that didn't. Unbeknownst to the participants, the numbers in each of the four tables were the same, but the labels at the top of the columns—"Rash Got Better" and "Rash Got Worse" for Tables A and B, and "Crime Increased" and "Crime Decreased" for Tables C and D—were switched.[66] The results, which one report dubbed the "Most Depressing Brain Finding Ever," were disheartening.[67]

Table A	Rash Got Better	Rash Got Worse
Patients who used the new skin cream	223	75
Patients who didn't use the new skin cream	107	21

Table B	Rash Got Worse	Rash Got Better
Patients who used the new skin cream	223	75
Patients who didn't use the new skin cream	107	21

Table C	Crime Increased	Crime Decreased
Cities that DID ban carrying concealed handguns in public	223	75
Cities that DID NOT ban carrying concealed handguns in public	107	21

Table D	Crime Decreased	Crime Increased
Cities that DID ban carrying concealed handguns in public	223	75
Cities that DID NOT ban carrying concealed handguns in public	107	21

Figure 7-20: Subjects in a 2013 study by Kahan, Peters, Dawson, and Slovic were randomly assigned one of the four tables above. Subjects who received either Table A or Table B were asked whether patients who used the skin cream at hand were more likely to get better or worse than those who did not. Subjects who received either Table C or Table D were asked whether cities that banned the carrying of concealed handguns in public had higher or lower levels of crime than those that did not (Source: Dan M. Kahan, Ellen Peters, Erica Dawson, and Paul Slovic. 2013. "Motivated Numeracy and Enlightened Self-Government." *Behavioral Public Policy*. Vol.1).

Properly interpreting the data in Tables A–D can be difficult. In fact, previous studies that have used a similar design found that most people incorrectly compare the absolute number of the various outcomes in the data instead of correctly computing and contrasting the ratios for each condition.[68] All else being equal, therefore, we would expect innumerate Democrats and Republicans in Kahan's study to inappropriately select the outcome that is associated with their table's largest absolute number, and their numerate counterparts to appropriately calculate their table's ratios—as presented in Figure 7-21—and answer accordingly.

Table A	Rash Got Better	Rash Got Worse	Table B	Rash Got Worse	Rash Got Better
Patients who used the new skin cream	223 + 75 = 298 223 ÷ 298 = .75 **75%**	223 + 75 = 298 75 ÷ 298 = .25 **25%**	Patients who used the new skin cream	223 + 75 = 298 223 ÷ 298 = .75 **75%**	223 + 75 = 298 75 ÷ 298 = .25 **25%**
Patients who didn't use the new skin cream	107 + 21 = 128 107 ÷ 128 = .84 **84%**	107 + 21 = 128 21 ÷ 128 = .16 **16%**	Patients who didn't use the new skin cream	107 + 21 = 128 107 ÷ 128 = .84 **84%**	107 + 21 = 128 21 ÷ 128 = .16 **16%**

Table C	Crime Increased	Crime Decreased	Table D	Crime Decreased	Crime Increased
Cities that DID ban carrying concealed handguns in public	223 + 75 = 298 223 ÷ 298 = .75 **75%**	223 + 75 = 298 75 ÷ 298 = .25 **25%**	Cities that DID ban carrying concealed handguns in public	223 + 75 = 298 223 ÷ 298 = .75 **75%**	223 + 75 = 298 75 ÷ 298 = .25 **25%**
Cities that DID NOT ban carrying concealed handguns in public	107 + 21 = 128 107 ÷ 128 = .84 **84%**	107 + 21 = 128 21 ÷ 128 = .16 **16%**	Cities that DID NOT ban carrying concealed handguns in public	107 + 21 = 128 107 ÷ 128 = .84 **84%**	107 + 21 = 128 21 ÷ 128 = .16 **16%**

Figure 7-21: If subjects in the 2013 study by Kahan, Peters, Dawson, and Slovic hoped to answer their assigned queries correctly, they would have had to calculate and compare the ratios for each experimental condition as shown in the tables above (Source: Dan M. Kahan, Ellen Peters, Erica Dawson, and Paul Slovic. 2013. "Motivated Numeracy and Enlightened Self-Government." Behavioral Public Policy. Vol.1).

On the whole, members of the medical group performed as expected. The study's results revealed that innumerate partisans were roughly two to two-and-a-half times less likely to provide the correct answer than their more numerate counterparts. Innumerate Democrats and Republicans who reviewed Table A tended to gravitate to the cell with the largest absolute number (223) and mistakenly conclude that people who used the skin cream were more likely to get better than those who didn't. Most innumerate partisans who received Table B incorrectly assumed that people who used the skin cream were more likely to get worse than those who didn't,

Chapter 7. Evaluating Political Numbers 145

for the very same reason (Figure 7-20). In contrast, numerate Democrats and Republicans who analyzed Table A tended to calculate and compare the ratios for each condition and correctly conclude that the rash was more likely to get worse among patients who used the skin cream (25 percent) than those who did not (16 percent). Similarly, most of the numerate partisans who received Table B correctly figured that the patients who used the skin cream were more likely to improve than those who didn't (Figure 7-21).[69] In short, whether or not the members of the medical group arrived at the right conclusion was contingent upon their mathematical ability, not their party.

The same, however, cannot be said about the political group. In comparison to their innumerate counterparts in the medical group, innumerate Democrats and Republicans in the political group were generally more likely to interpret the data correctly when they aligned with their political views and less likely to do so when they did not. What's more, this difference was even greater among the numerate. When the data violated any numerate partisans' beliefs, they suddenly responded as if they were innumerate. For instance:

- According to the data in Table C, crime decreased in 25 percent of the cities that banned the carrying of concealed handguns in public, but only in 16 percent of the cities that did not.[70] This conclusion—that gun control is correlated with less crime—aligns with the views of most Democrats and goes against the beliefs of most Republicans.[71] Here, while some 75 percent of numerate Democrats were able to interpret the data correctly, only 20 percent of numerate Republicans were able to do so, on average.
- According to the data in Table D, crime increased in 25 percent of the cities that banned the carrying of concealed handguns in public, but only in 16 percent of the cities that did not.[72] Here, the conclusion—that gun control is correlated with more crime—aligns with the views of most Republicans and contradicts the beliefs of most Democrats.[73] Now, while about 90 percent of numerate Republicans were able to interpret the data correctly, only 45 percent of numerate Democrats were able to do so, on average.

Kahan and his colleagues suggest that our first instinct is to jump to the wrong conclusion—the largest absolute number—in each of the four tables provided. The numerate, however, will often restrain that impulse, give the problem some thought, and ultimately interpret the data correctly. Unless, that is, the instinctual answer aligns with their partisan predilections. Then, the numerate won't override their hunch and they will misinterpret the data as a result.[74] Seeing red or blue seems to be more powerful than viewing what is numerically true.

According to Mark Twain, the nineteenth-century British statesman Benjamin Disraeli once quipped that "there are three kinds of lies; lies, damned lies, and statistics."[75] It is undoubtedly true that statistics can be used to mislead. Yet as the University of Texas at Austin's professor of mathematics Michael Starbird warns, "while it is easy to lie with statistics ... it is easier to lie without them."[76] Good statistics provide a means of analyzing large amounts of data which can be used to inform our decisions. But if our analyses are poisoned by our partisan biases, the benefits of statistics will be lost, and our decision-making will suffer as a result. Thus, we must be numerate. But we must also be numerate even when it's politically inconvenient to be so.

CHAPTER 8

Evaluating Political Arguments

"He that will not reason is a bigot; he that cannot reason is
a fool; and he that dares not reason is a slave."
— William Drummond[1]

The Problem: Political tribalism hinders the ability of
Democrats and Republicans to accurately evaluate arguments.

Arguments are ubiquitous in American politics. We see them when we read the newspaper, hear them when we watch the nightly news, and exchange them when we speak with family and friends. Yet our ability to honestly evaluate the quality of a political argument can be derailed by our partisan attachments. Take the subjects of offshore drilling and the DREAM Act (Figure 8-1):

Offshore Drilling
In March 2010, President Obama announced that the United States would expand drilling for oil and gas along the Atlantic coast and the eastern Gulf of Mexico. However, the Democratic President rescinded that order a few weeks later when the offshore drilling rig, Deepwater Horizon, exploded and spilled some 4.9 million barrels of oil into the Gulf of Mexico.
DREAM Act
In December 2010, the Senate failed to pass the Development, Relief, and Education for Alien Minors Act (DREAM Act). The legislation would have provided a pathway to citizenship for undocumented immigrants living in the United States—provided that they entered the country before the age of sixteen, earned a high school diploma, passed a criminal background check, and completed at least two years of college or served at least two years in the U.S. military.

Figure 8-1: During the time in which Druckman, Peterson, and Slothuus administered their study, offshore drilling and the DREAM Act were major political issues. The text box above provides some general background information on each issue (Source: John M. Broder. 2010. "Obama to Open Offshore Areas to Oil Drilling for First Time." *New York Times*. March 31; John M. Broder and Clifford Krauss. 2010. "U.S. Drops Bid to Explore Oil in Eastern Gulf." *New York Times*. December 2; David M. Herszenhorn. 2018. "Senate Blocks Bill for Young Illegal Immigrants." *New York Times*. December 18; Mauricio Cárdenas and Jeff Frank. 2010. "The Dream Act: A Bipartisan Opportunity." *Brookings*. December 6).

In 2013, the political scientists James N. Druckman, Erik Peterson, and Rune Slothuus presented a pair of arguments concerning these issues to a host of Democrats and Republicans and assessed the impact that those arguments had on the participants' policy views. The arguments, which are summarized in Figure 8-2, varied in both direction and strength—that is, some subjects received a strong-pro argument and a weak-con argument about offshore drilling, while others were given a weak-pro argument and a strong-con argument about the DREAM Act, and vice versa.[2] In the end, the analysis found that people's opinions can be swayed by a superior line of reasoning—unless they're told that the superior line of reasoning is aligned with the views of the opposing political party.

Offshore Drilling	Pro	Con
Strong	Increase the oil supply and lower gas prices	Dangerous for workers and maritime life
Weak	Lead to new technologies that may have applications beyond drilling	Overwhelms government regulators overseeing the drilling

The DREAM Act	Pro	Con
Strong	Provides young people an opportunity to contribute to American society	Encourages others to immigrate illegally to secure benefits for their children
Weak	Opinion polls suggest many Americans support the DREAM Act	The act is not well-designed and could be better

Figure 8-2: The table above includes the arguments that were randomly assigned to subjects in Druckman, Peterson, and Slothuus' 2013 study. These arguments include strong and weak arguments in favor of, and in opposition to, both offshore drilling and the DREAM Act (Source: James N. Druckman, Erik Peterson, and Rune Slothuus. 2013. "How Elite Partisan Polarization Affects Public Opinion Formation." *American Political Science Review*. Vol. 107, No. 1).

Chapter 8. Evaluating Political Arguments   149

Respondents of all political stripes tended to become more supportive of a policy after considering its strong-pro and weak-con arguments. When partisans read that offshore drilling would lower gas prices (strong) but overextend government regulators (weak), support for the practice increased by 18.8 percentage points among Democrats and 14 percentage points among Republicans. And when partisans read that the DREAM Act would provide young people with an opportunity to contribute to American society (strong) but was ill-designed (weak), support for the legislation rose among Democrats and Republicans by 14.8 and 17.4 percentage points, respectively. Likewise, respondents routinely became less supportive of a policy after considering its weak-pro and strong-con arguments. When partisans read that offshore drilling might result in new technologies (weak) but would endanger workers and the environment (strong), support for the policy decreased by 10.8 percentage points among Democrats and 10.4 percentage points among Republicans. And when partisans read that the DREAM Act polled well (weak) but would encourage illegal immigration (strong), support for the legislation declined among Democrats and Republicans by 14.0 and 20.1 percentage points, respectively. In sum, members of both parties found strong claims to be more persuasive than weak ones, and they willingly adjusted their opinions as a result. "Substance," Druckman, Peterson, and Slothuus wrote, "carried the day."[3]

But when the researchers presented a different group of participants with the same pair of arguments *and* a statement detailing the political parties' positions—that "Republicans in Congress tend to favor drilling and Democrats in Congress tend to oppose drilling," or "Democrats in Congress tend to favor the DREAM Act and Republicans in Congress tend to oppose the DREAM Act"—everything changed. Now, when Democrats received the strong-pro argument for offshore drilling that was endorsed by the Republican Party, and the weak-con argument that was endorsed by the Democratic Party, they found the weaker argument to be more persuasive. Accordingly, their support for the policy *decreased* by 12.8 percentage points. This is a 31.6 percentage point difference in opinion with their fellow Democrats who were exposed to the exact same set of arguments without any party cue (+18.8 percent to -12.8 percent). And when Republicans received the weak-pro argument for offshore drilling that was endorsed by the GOP and the strong-con argument that was endorsed by the Democrats, support for the policy *increased* by 11.8 percentage points—a 22.2 percentage point swing in opinion (-10.4 percent to +11.8 percent). Similarly, when Republicans received the strong-pro argument for the DREAM Act that was endorsed by the Democratic Party and the weak-con argument that was endorsed by the Republican Party, support for the legislation *decreased* by 19.2 percentage points. This was a 36.6 percentage point difference in opinion with their fellow Republicans who were exposed to the same set of arguments without any party cue (+17.4 percent to -19.2 percent). And when Democrats received the weak-pro argument for the DREAM Act that was endorsed by their party and the strong-con argument that was endorsed by the GOP, support for the legislation *increased* by 15.9 percentage points—a 29.9 percentage point swing in opinion (-14 percent to +15.9 percent). Here, Democrats and Republicans deemed weak arguments endorsed by their own side as more persuasive than strong arguments aligned with the views of the opposition. It was now party, instead of substance, that carried the day.

According to the seventeenth-century British author Thomas Fuller, "Logic is the armory of reason."[4] If so, it appears as though the depot has been captured by the forces of political tribalism. We have the capacity to acknowledge strong arguments, and even be swayed by them. But we often eschew that ability and follow our partisan shepherds instead. It's high time we make an effort to elevate logic over partisanship and restore reason to its rightful place.

Evaluating an Argument

An argument is a combination of statements. These statements include one or more premise(s) and a conclusion, with the former intended to establish the latter. An objective evaluation of an argument, therefore, requires that we determine whether or not the premises are accurate and whether or not they logically support the conclusion.

> **What We Can Do:** When we evaluate an argument, we should ask ourselves: (1) what evidence is given to support the conclusion, (2) is the evidence dependable, and (3) does the evidence logically support the conclusion?

Step One: Identifying Premises and Conclusions

The first step in evaluating an argument is to correctly identify its premise(s) and conclusion. In *How to Think About Weird Things: Critical Thinking for a New Age*, Theodore Schick and Lewis Vaughn suggest that we should, in a sense, jump to conclusions: "The easiest way to identify an argument is to find the conclusion first. If you first find the conclusion, locating the premises becomes much easier."[5] To find an argument's conclusion, the authors note that we should ask ourselves: "What claim is the speaker or writer trying to get us to accept?"[6] This claim can often be found at the beginning or end of an argument, and may be preceded by conclusion indicators such as *thus, hence, therefore, accordingly, consequently,* or *as a result*. Then, we should locate the argument's premises. We should ask ourselves: "What evidence does the speaker or writer provide in support of the conclusion?" This evidence may often be preceded by premise indicators such as *since, because, given that, inasmuch as, due to the fact that,* or *studies show*.[7]

Once we have identified an argument's premises and conclusion, we should create a diagram that outlines the argument's structure. The arguments found in newspaper editorials and on the nightly news can be lengthy, complex, and convoluted. A diagram—or map of an argument—will help organize a line of reasoning and thus make it easier to evaluate. To create a diagram, simply assign a number to each of the statements in an argument, and then draw arrows from the premises to the conclusion.[8] For instance, consider the following argument derived from Druckman et al.'s study detailed at the beginning of the chapter:

(1) We should not drill for more oil and gas off the Atlantic Coast and in the eastern Gulf of Mexico. (2) Offshore drilling is dangerous for workers and marine life and (3) the regulatory agencies responsible for overseeing offshore drilling are already overwhelmed by their current responsibilities.

The conclusion of this argument—or the claim that the writer is trying to get us to accept—is the first statement: "We should not drill for more oil and gas off the Atlantic Coast and in the eastern Gulf of Mexico." It's supported by two independent premises—statements two and three: "Offshore drilling is dangerous for workers and marine life," and "the regulatory agencies responsible for overseeing offshore drilling are already overwhelmed by their current responsibilities." As such, the argument can be diagrammed like so (Figure 8-3):

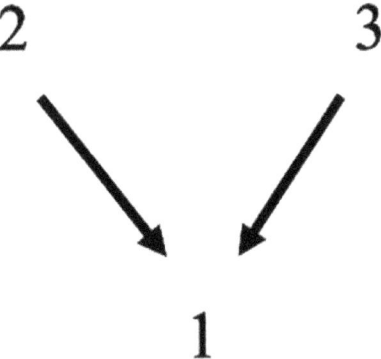

Figure 8-3: When diagramming an argument, one should organize the numbers assigned to each relevant statement by drawing one arrow from each premise—or cluster of premises—to the conclusion it supports. The illustration here, for example, diagrams an argument about drilling for oil and gas off the Atlantic Coast and in the eastern Gulf of Mexico.

In some instances, however, multiple premises may be dependent on one another in such a way that if one were omitted, the others would fail to provide enough support for the conclusion. These so-called conjoint premises can be depicted in a diagram with an addition sign. For instance, consider the following argument from Patrick J. Hurley's *A Concise Introduction to Logic*[9]:

> (1) Government mandates for zero-emission vehicles won't work because (2) only electric cars qualify as zero-sum emission vehicles, and (3) electric cars won't sell. (4) They are too expensive, (5) their range of operation is too limited, and (6) recharging facilities are not generally available.

This argument contains three premises (4, 5, and 6) that support a fourth premise (3) which, in turn, supports the conclusion (1) conjointly with a fifth premise (2). Its structure can be diagramed as follows (Figure 8-4):

Note that premises (4), (5), and (6) support premise (3) independently.

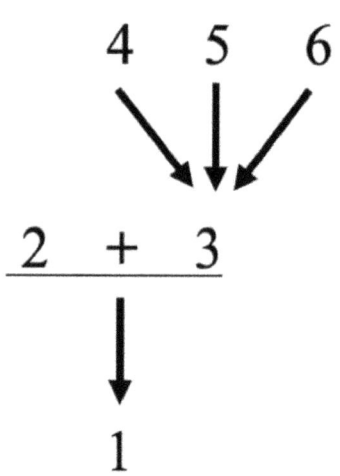

Figure 8-4: Some arguments can have a complex structure. For instance, the illustration above diagrams an argument regarding government mandates for electric cars which qualify as zero-sum emission vehicles. Here, three premises (4, 5 and 6) support a fourth premise (3) which, in turn, supports the conclusion (1) conjointly with a fifth premise (2).

In other words, if one or even two of premises 4–6 were false, the argument could still stand on the basis of the remaining premise(s). For instance, if electric cars had a large range of operation (5) and charging stations were readily available (6), the vehicles still might not sell (3) if they were too expensive (4). In contrast, premises (2) and (3) are conjoint—if one of them is undermined, so too will the other. To wit, the argument at hand claims that government mandates for zero-emission vehicles won't work because the only automobiles that meet that standard are electric, and electric vehicles won't sell. But if consumers did purchase electric cars (3), then it really wouldn't matter if they were the only zero-emission vehicle available. Conversely, if there was another option—say an efficient, popular, and affordable zero-emission solar-powered vehicle (2)—then it wouldn't matter if electric cars didn't sell because government mandates might work just fine for the solar-powered vehicles instead. To be sure, this argument is complex, but its evaluation can be significantly facilitated by mapping it out.

Therefore, when we come upon a political argument in a news broadcast, newspaper, or conversation, we should do our best to identify the conclusion and the premises, and organize them in a diagram. Then we can initiate the second step of evaluating an argument—determining whether the premises in a line of reasoning are dependable.

Step Two: Determining the Dependability of a Premise

In *Asking the Right Questions: A Guide to Critical Thinking*, M. Neil Browne and Stuart M. Keeley suggest that "it is extremely difficult, if not impossible, to establish the absolute truth or falsity of most [premises]." Hence, "rather than ask whether [the premises] are true, we prefer to ask whether they are dependable [and] the greater the quality and quantity of evidence supporting a [premise], the more we can depend on it."[10] Good sources are better than bad sources, and the more good sources we have, the better.

Quality evidence is information that comes from a reputable source. One might wonder if such sources still exist. The fact that media outlets—like Fox News and MSNBC—often provide politically slanted information, and social media networks—such as Facebook, Twitter, and YouTube—spread false political information is clearly a cause for concern.[11] Nonetheless, there are several sources that do provide dependable political information, including the Federal Statistical System of the United States, reputable research institutions, esteemed news organizations, and academic journals.

The Federal Statistical System of the United States is a decentralized network of federal agencies that produce data about the American people. Federal law mandates that this network process information in a mathematically sound and politically unbiased manner. The information it produces, therefore, tends to be very dependable. Thus, when a politician, pundit, or neighbor is trying to convince you of something that is at odds with one of the principal agencies of the Federal Statistical System listed in Figure 8-5, be skeptical.[12] For instance, during Democratic President Barack Obama's second term in office, the Bureau of Labor Statistics reported that the unemployment rate had fallen from 8.0 percent in 2013 to under 5.0 percent in 2016.[13] But Republican Donald Trump was having none of it. During his pursuit of the White House, the businessman repeatedly referred to the Bureau's official estimates of the unemployment rate as "phony," "total fiction," and "one of the biggest hoaxes in American modern politics."[14] Following his victory in the New Hampshire primary, the soon-to-be Republican presidential nominee told his supporters, "I am going to be the greatest jobs president that God ever created. Remember that. Don't believe those phony numbers when you hear 4.9 and 5% unemployment. The number's probably 28, 29, as high as 35. In fact, I even heard recently 42%."[15] After his first full month in office, however, President Trump was informed by the very same Bureau of Labor Statistics that the unemployment rate had dropped one-tenth of a percentage point, from 4.8% in January to 4.7% in February 2018. Now Mr. Trump sounded a different tune. His press secretary, Sean Spicer, told reporters, "I talked to the President ... and he said to quote him very clearly: '[The unemployment rate] may have been phony in the past, but it's very real now.'"[16] In truth, the information generated by the agencies within the Federal Statistical System is dependable. It was as dependable during the Obama administration as it was during the first month of the Trump administration. The only "phony" thing about this sordid scenario was Trump's disparagement of the data.

Bureau of Labor Statistics
Bureau of Census
National Center for Education Statistics
National Agricultural Statistics Service
Energy Information Administration
Bureau of Economic Analysis
Economic Research Service
Bureau of Justice Statistics
National Center for Health Statistics
National Science Foundation
Statistics of Income Division
Bureau of Transportation Statistics
Office of Research, Evaluation, and Statistics

Figure 8-5: Four major sources of dependable information are the Federal Statistical System of the United States, nonpartisan independent institutions, the mainstream media, and academic journals. The list here includes some of the federal agencies that produce reliable data as part of the Federal Statistical System of the United States.

Dependable political information can also be obtained from independent institutions that research and analyze a wide range of public policy issues. These organizations—which purposefully employ experts with diverse points of view—have well-earned reputations for being knowledgeable and nonpartisan. As such, the information provided by entities such as those listed in Figure 8-6 is likely to be of high quality. Consider the Annenberg Public Policy Center (APPC). The APPC, which is a hub for the study of public policy at the University of Pennsylvania, operates FactCheck.org—a project that monitors the factual accuracy of claims made by major political actors in the United States. For example, in May 2018, Senator Chuck Schumer held a press conference at a gas station in Washington, D.C. The Democratic Senator from New York blamed the "soaring" cost of gasoline on President Trump's "reckless decision" to back out of the Iran nuclear deal.[17] The nuclear framework, which had been negotiated during the Obama administration, required that Iran limit its nuclear activities in exchange for the lifting of economic sanctions and the release of frozen assets.[18] Upon becoming president, Trump withdrew the United States from the agreement based on his belief that it was "a horrible, one-sided deal that should have never, ever been made."[19] Of course, blaming the president for rising prices at the pump is a political pastime. But when the APPC fact-checked Senator Schumer's charge, they concluded that the effect of President Trump's decision to scrap the nuclear deal had a "relatively small impact" on the price of gasoline. Instead, the main reasons for rising prices at the pump were determined to be the decision by the Organization of the Petroleum Exporting Countries (OPEC) to curb its oil production in 2016, and a bustling economy.[20]

Annenberg Public Policy Center
Aspen Institute
Bipartisan Policy Center
Carnegie Endowment for International Peace
Council on Foreign Relations
Freedom House
James A. Baker III Institute for Public Policy
Kaiser Family Foundation
National Academies of Sciences, Engineering, and Medicine
National Bureau of Economic Research
Pew Research Center
RAND Corporation

Figure 8-6: Four major sources of dependable information are the Federal Statistical System of the United States, nonpartisan independent institutions, the mainstream media, and academic journals. The list here includes some of the nonpartisan independent institutions that research and analyze a wide range of public policy issues in an even-handed manner.

Dependable information can also come from news organizations that have a reputation for providing fact-based reporting and dispelling disinformation.[21] These organizations, such as those listed in Figure 8-7, are composed of journalists who are bound by a code of ethics that in part requires members of the press to take responsibility for the accuracy of their work and correct any mistakes in a forthright manner.[22] In April 2018, the Trump administration announced a "zero-tolerance" immigration policy that pledged to criminally convict anyone who crossed the U.S.–Mexican border unlawfully. Any child who crossed the border illegally with his or her parent or guardian would be immediately placed under the supervision of the U.S. Department of Health and Human Services and would remain separated from his or her parent or guardian until the latter was formally processed by the legal system. The following month, the former mayor of Los Angeles, Antonio Villaraigosa, took to social media to criticize President Trump's immigration policies. The Democrat tweeted a picture of two unidentified female detainees sleeping on a concrete floor in a steel-caged holding cell. The picture was accompanied by a message declaring: "Speechless. This is not who we are as a nation." Jon Favreau, a former speechwriter for President Obama, also took to Twitter to express his dismay:

> Jon Favreau @jonfavs—Look at these pictures. This is happening right now, and the only debate that matters is how we force our government to get these kids back to their families as fast as humanly possible: azc.cc/1imLTBb via @azcentral

Soon thereafter, however, the Associated Press issued a report detailing that the photograph tweeted by Villaraigosa and Favreau had actually been taken by the AP's Ross D. Franklin in 2014. Thus, the image depicted the status of immigrant children during the administration of President Obama, not that of President Trump.[23] The photo depicted two of the hundreds of unaccompanied children who had been apprehended while crossing the border illegally, and were being held in a makeshift detention center in Nogales, Arizona, until they could be placed with relatives already in the country to await their day in immigration court.[24] Villaraigosa and Favreau have since deleted their tweets.[25]

Associated Press (AP)	The New York Times
Bloomberg News	The Wall Street Journal
British Broadcasting Corp. (BBC)	The Washington Post
Foreign Affairs	PBS NewsHour
The Economist	Reuters

Figure 8-7: Four major sources of dependable information are the Federal Statistical System of the United States, nonpartisan independent institutions,

Chapter 8. Evaluating Political Arguments

the mainstream media, and academic journals. The list here includes some of the generally reputable news sources governed by a journalistic code of ethics which demands accuracy.

Finally, dependable information can often be found in academic journals which publish articles written by scholars in a particular field of study. Material published in such journals must survive the *peer review* process in which a panel of impartial experts—who specialize in the subject matter at hand—analyze the study's methodology, logic, and conclusions, and attest to their validity.[26] Thus, when a politician or pundit contradicts the conclusion of a study published in a reputable academic journal, such as those listed in Figure 8-8, the critically-thinking should be skeptical. For example, in February 2015, Jim Inhofe of Oklahoma took to the floor of the U.S. Senate in Washington, D.C., to express his doubts about climate change. "We keep hearing that 2014 has been the warmest year on record," the Republican Senator said, "[but] do you know what this is?" Inhofe reached into a plastic bag, removed an object, and held it aloft. "It's a snowball from just outside here," he continued, "so it's very, very cold out, very unseasonable." But the findings of a 2008 study published in *Science*, for instance, were at odds with Inhofe's theatrics. In fact, the authors note that "it is likely that there has been significant anthropogenic warming over the past 50 years," and that this human-caused climate change "is having a significant impact on physical and biological systems" across the globe.[27] In this instance, we should abide by the evidence published by a group of climatologists rather than the rantings of a senator who doesn't even appear to understand the difference between climate and weather.

American Journal of Psychology
American Political Science Review
Annual Review of Astronomy and Astrophysics
Cultural Anthropology
Journal of Finance
Journal of Political Economy
Journal of the American Medical Association
Nature
Science
The New England Journal of Medicine
The Quarterly Journal of Economics

Figure 8-8: Four major sources of dependable information are the Federal Statistical System of the United States, nonpartisan independent institutions, the mainstream media, and academic journals. The list here includes just a few examples of the hundreds of highly reputable academic journals.

Of course, none of the sources detailed above are perfect. Limited budgets can impinge upon the Federal Statistical System's ability to gather accurate data.[28] An increase in the number of well-funded, partisan research organizations has restricted the ability of nonpartisan institutions to attract and retain scholars to conduct in-depth analyses.[29] Reputable news organizations are often driven by a profit motive that can skew their coverage toward the dramatic and the personal which can distort reality, and provide only a caricature of complex situations.[30] And while peer reviewers ensure that a study's experiments were properly designed, and that the data supports the author's conclusions, they do not re-create the study's experiments, review the raw data, or check the author's calculations.[31] To do so would simply be too time consuming for reviewers who are already overworked and undercompensated, if they're paid at all.[32]

Accordingly, we should temper our confidence in the dependability of any information that is derived from even a reputable source, until that information is independently verified by other well-regarded sources. For while the quality of evidence is critically important, so too is its quantity. The answer to the age-old question: "Quality or Quantity?" is "Both!"

Let's say that you and ninety-nine of your closest friends set out to determine whether a particular coin is fair. Imagine that you flip the coin ten times, record the number of heads tossed, and pass it on to another participant who will follow suit. Finally, you plot the results by placing an X in the column associated with the number of heads tossed by each participant. Assume that the results are as follows:

0	1	2	3	4	5	6	7	8	9	10
					XX					
					XX					
					XX					
				XX	XX	X				
				XX	XX	XX				
				XX	XX	XX				
				XX	XX	XX				
				XX	XX	XX	X			
				XX	XX	XX	XX			
		XX	XX	XX	XX	XX	XX			
		XX	XX	XX	XX	XX	XX	XX		
		XX	XX	XX	XX	XX	XX	XX		
		XX	XX	XX	XX	XX	XX	XX	XX	

Number of Heads

Figure 8-9: Given enough opportunities, the probability that an uncertain event will occur is almost certain. For example, the illustration above contains the number of heads tossed out of ten attempts during 100 trials using the coin-flipping simulator on random.org. Even though the probability of tossing nine heads is very low (1 percent), it occurred twice in this instance.

Chapter 8. Evaluating Political Arguments 159

Would you declare the coin to be fair? If one tosses a coin ten times, the probability of flipping five heads (24.6 percent) is greater than the probability of flipping either four or six heads (20.5 percent) which, in turn, is greater than the probability of flipping either three or seven heads (11.7 percent) et cetera. Those odds are largely satisfied by the results above—results that I received while using the coin-flipping simulator on random.org. Hence, you would be well advised to conclude that the coin is fair. Note, however, that while flipping either a very low number of heads or a very high number of heads is improbable, it's not impossible. To be sure, the probability that any single participant would toss either one head or nine heads are low (1.0 percent). But that also means that the odds of at least one of the one hundred participants achieving such a result is very real. Indeed, it happened twice in the experiment above. Improbable things happen all the time, and if you and your ninety-nine friends hadn't compiled the results of each experiment, the two participants who tossed nine heads may very well have incorrectly concluded that the coin was unfair. But their results were just outliers and if they had never bothered to evaluate more than one data point, they never would have known just how unrepresentative that particular data point was.

Just as we should not deem a coin to be unfair based on a single set of tosses, neither should we determine whether a premise is dependable based on one statistic, one study, one news report, or one article in an academic journal. On occasion, even the best sources may include information that is biased, mistaken, or even fraudulent. The chance that several reputable sources would simultaneously encounter the same problem, however, is far less likely.[33] As such, we should follow the Enlightenment philosopher David Hume's advice and proportion our beliefs to the evidence.[34] When the number of high-quality sources that support a premise increase, so too should our support for that premise, and as the number of high-quality sources that oppose a premise increase, so too should our level of skepticism.

Consider the high-quality sources detailed above. While the Bureau of Labor Statistics' official estimate of the unemployment rate is a dependable measure of the state of the economy, it's only one measure. Thus, we can further evaluate the disagreement concerning the unemployment rate between Mr. Trump and the Bureau of Labor by considering other economic indicators. To be sure, these other measures—such as the Gross Domestic Product (+1.6 percent), consumer spending (+2.5 percent), wages (+2.5 percent) and the stock market (+11.5 percent)—were more indicative of an economy with an unemployment rate of 5 percent than 42 percent.[35] We have good reason to believe, therefore, that the Bureau of Labor Statistics was right, and Mr. Trump was wrong. Similarly, the Annenberg Public

Policy Center's conclusion that oil prices were determined by a myriad of factors beyond the Trump administration's decision to withdraw from the Iran nuclear deal was echoed by an analysis done by another respected research institution: the Council on Foreign Relations.[36] The importance of quantity also manifests itself among esteemed news organizations. In addition to the Associated Press, *The New York Times* also reported that the picture of young immigrants in steel cages being circulated by Democrats on social media was taken when Barack Obama was president, not Donald Trump.[37] Similarly, a single study published in an academic journal is not sufficient grounds to draw any conclusions on the reality of anthropogenic climate change. But a 2013 study published in *Environmental Research Letters*—which analyzed 4,014 peer-reviewed articles that took a position on the issue of anthropogenic climate change and found that 3,894, or 97 percent, of the papers concluded that the earth's climate is warming and human activity is the most likely cause—is very convincing.[38] In many aspects of life, less may be more. But when it comes to evaluating the evidence offered in support of an argument's premises, two high-quality sources are better than one, three high-quality sources are better than two, and so on.

Step Three: Assessing the Logic of an Argument's Structure

The final step in evaluating an argument is to determine whether or not an argument's premises logically support its conclusion. A line of reasoning may include a dependable premise that is supported by a large quantity of high-quality evidence, but if that premise doesn't infer the conclusion, the argument is built upon a *logical fallacy*—or error in reasoning that makes the argument unsound or uncogent.[39] For example, consider the following:

> (1) Barack Obama was re-elected president in November 2012 and the (2) Sandy Hook Elementary School shooting took place on December 14, 2012. (3) Therefore, President Obama is responsible for the shooting.

Note that the two premises are dependable statements. Nevertheless, they do not logically support the conclusion. This argument is based on a logical error—known as the *post hoc ergo propter hoc fallacy*—in which one wrongly assumes that since Y followed X, then X must have caused Y. Surely, just because Barack Obama was president when the Sandy Hook shooting occurred does not mean that he was responsible for the tragedy. There are many contributing factors to school shootings—including mental illness, access to guns, peer relationships, and familial neglect or abuse, et cetera.[40] Of course, one could try to make the case that President Obama should've pushed for gun control legislation during his first term and so on, but there's no guarantee that those measures would've been approved by Congress, and even if they had, it's unlikely that they would've been able to prevent the massacre at Sandy Hook.[41] There are simply too many variables involved to place the blame on one person, even if that person is the president of the United States.

A good argument needs both dependable premises and valid or strong logic. Unfortunately, fallacious logic can often seem incredibly persuasive. But as the columnist Burton Hillis observed, "there's a mighty big difference between good, sound reasons and reasons that sound good."[42] Familiarizing ourselves with the logical fallacies described below will go a long way in helping us identify that difference.

1. **Equivocation:** The fallacy of equivocation occurs when the same term or phrase is used with one meaning in one part of an argument, and a different meaning in another part. For instance, during the 2016 Republican presidential primary election, Senator Ted Cruz's campaign produced a television ad attacking Donald Trump's views on Planned Parenthood, a nonprofit organization that provides reproductive health care. After the ad's narrator condemned how "Planned Parenthood treats the unborn," it cut to an interview in which Mr. Trump told Fox News's Sean Hannity that "Planned Parenthood serves a good function."[43] The ad failed to mention, however, that Mr. Trump also said, "Let's say there is two Planned Parenthoods in a way. You have it as an abortion clinic. Now that's actually a fairly small part of what they do, but it's a brutal part and I'm totally against it. They also, however, service women."[44] By equating Planned Parenthood with abortion and including a sound bite of Mr. Trump stating that the organization "serves a good function," the ad implied that Trump was pro-choice. Yet it's clear that Mr. Trump was equating Planned Parenthood with its other services—such as prenatal care, breast exams, and cervical cancer screenings. The Cruz campaign, in this sense, called two different things by the same name, and thus engaged in the fallacy of equivocation.

2. **Red Herring:** The red-herring fallacy occurs when an individual introduces an irrelevant issue in an effort to divert attention from the matter at hand. During the 2016 presidential campaign, a decade-old recording surfaced of Donald Trump saying, "You know, I'm automatically attracted to beautiful [women], I just start kissing them. It's like a magnet. Just kiss. I don't even wait. And when you're a star they let you do it. You can do anything. Grab them by the pussy.

You can do anything."⁴⁵ Soon thereafter, Anderson Cooper asked Mr. Trump about the offensive recording during a presidential debate. "You bragged that you have sexually assaulted women," the CNN anchorman said. "Do you understand that?" The Republican nominee replied, "No, I didn't say that at all. I don't think you understood what was—this was locker room talk. I'm not proud of it. I apologize to my family. I apologize to the American people. … Yes, I'm embarrassed by it. I hate it. But it is locker room talk, and it's one of those things. I will knock the hell out of ISIS. We're going to defeat ISIS." Cooper pressed the issue: "Just for the record though, are you saying that … you did not actually kiss women without consent or grope women without consent?" "No, I have not.," Mr. Trump said, "And I will tell you something, we are going to make our country safe."⁴⁶ It is no surprise that Mr. Trump would want to change the subject. But given that ISIS— the Islamic State of Iraq and Syria—had little to do with the question that was asked, the candidate's tough talk on the terrorist organization was nothing more than a red herring.

3. **Appeal to Tradition:** The appeal to tradition fallacy occurs when an individual argues that something must be true or good because it's part of an established tradition. On February 28, 2011, President Barack Obama addressed the National Governors Association. During his remarks, Mr. Obama argued that "we need to invest in our infrastructure, everything from new roads and bridges to high-speed rail and high-speed Internet." He continued, "Lincoln laid the rails during the course of a civil war. Eisenhower built the Interstate Highway System. We don't have third-rate airports and third-rate bridges and third-rate highways. That's not who we are."⁴⁷ Yet as Schick Jr. and Vaughn note, traditions can be wrong. "The fact that people have always done or believed something is no reason for thinking that we should continue to do or believe something."⁴⁸ Enslaving people was once a tradition. So too was sacrificing innocent people to the gods. Thus, while invoking the memory of the founding fathers and renowned presidents is a pastime of American politics, it's not the stuff of which good arguments are made. President Obama may or may not have made a good point about investing in infrastructure, but he most certainly did not make a good argument.

4. **Cherry Picking:** Cherry picking—or the fallacy of incomplete evidence—is the act of acknowledging data that confirms a particular position while ignoring data that contradicts that point of view. In July 2016, Donald Trump delivered his acceptance speech at the Republican Party's presidential nominating convention. During his remarks, the party's standard-bearer stated, "Decades of progress made in bringing

down crime are now being reversed by [the Obama] administration's rollback of criminal enforcement." In support of this claim, Mr. Trump noted that "Homicides last year increased by 17 percent in America's 50 largest cities."[49] In one sense, Mr. Trump was correct. The number of homicides had increased in 2015. Yet by cherry picking the data from 2015 alone, Mr. Trump obscured the fact that the number of homicides had repeatedly hit record lows during much of Mr. Obama's time in office. In fact, according to FBI statistics the mean number of homicides during President Obama's time in office (15,157)[50] was lower than that during the George W. Bush (16,573), Bill Clinton (19,424), George H.W. Bush (23,350), Ronald Reagan (20,236), and Jimmy Carter (20,795) administrations.[51]

5. **Hasty Generalization:** The hasty generalization fallacy occurs when one offers an anecdote as evidence to support a claim. An anecdote is "an account of a particular incident or event."[52] Evidence, however, is defined as the "the available body of facts or information indicating whether a belief or proposition is true or valid."[53] Hence, an anecdote cannot be proffered as evidence because a "particular incident" is not the equivalent of a "body of facts." Anecdotes are, by definition, limited in number. They cannot demonstrate, in and of themselves, that a given event is typical or probable. As such, evidence requires that one examine a representative sample of, if not all of, the relevant cases. Anecdotes have been a common feature of the debate surrounding the Affordable Care Act (ACA), or Obamacare. In its effort to provide Americans with access to affordable health care, the ACA expanded the Medicaid assistance program and provided federal subsidies in an effort to make health care more affordable.[54] In 2014, President Obama delivered remarks on the ACA which included several personal testimonials. For instance, he referred to a California man, whose annual healthcare premiums plunged "from over $30,000 to under $9,000." He also took note of a "bartender from Pennsylvania" who was able to secure health insurance due to the ACA and, as a result, was receiving treatment for ovarian cancer.[55] In 2015, House Republicans similarly shared personal testimonials about people's experiences with Obamacare. Not surprisingly, they offered a different perspective. For example, one man from California described how his monthly premium "doubled from $650 to $1300," while a widow from Georgia wrote that she had "lost [her] insurance coverage" entirely.[56] Of course, none of these testimonials alone are evidence of the success or failure of the Affordable Care Act. They are anecdotes, and without the context of a much larger sample size there is simply no way of knowing which stories are representative and which are anomalous.

Anecdotes may be a powerful rhetorical device that can simplify and personalize even the most complex and abstract issues, but we should never confuse a story with a statistic.

6. **Ad hominem:** The ad-hominem fallacy occurs when an individual attacks the person making an argument rather than the argument itself. In 2010, President Obama pledged that the United States would not use nuclear weapons against any nation that signed and abided by the Nuclear Non-Proliferation Treaty, a treaty in which nuclear-weapon states committed to seeking nuclear disarmament and non-nuclear-weapon states agreed to forgo developing or acquiring nuclear weapons. The then-Republican governor of Alaska, Sarah Palin, argued that such a pledge was an act of unilateral disarmament akin to telling bullies on a playground that if you "punch me in the face…. I'm not going to retaliate." When asked to address Palin's criticism, President Obama simply said, "the last I checked Sarah Palin is not much of an expert on nuclear issues."[57] President Obama could have responded by noting that his position placed no restrictions on the use of conventional weaponry or even a nuclear response if an adversarial nation violated the provisions of the treaty. Instead, he chose to challenge Sarah Palin's intelligence rather than the evidence or logic of her claim. What matters most, however, is the quality of the argument, not the qualities of the person making the argument.

7. **Slippery Slope:** The slippery-slope fallacy assumes that if a particular position is accepted, extreme versions of that position must also be approved. This line of thinking is legitimate if there is good reason to believe that the alleged chain of events will unfold. It is a fallacy, however, when such an event is unlikely.[58] For instance, in response to the Supreme Court's decision to legalize gay marriage in 2015, televangelist Pat Robertson predicted that since "they have said homosexual marriage is a constitutional right … love affairs between men and animals are going to be absolutely permitted."[59] But the acceptance of a moderate position does not necessarily demand the acquiescence to a more extreme one. There is an enormous difference between sanctioning a relationship between two consenting adult human beings and sanctioning one involving a non-human animal. Certainly, the recognition of gay marriage does not require the acknowledgment of "love affairs between men and animals."

8. **Appeal to Popularity:** The appeal-to-popularity fallacy assumes that a claim is justified because it is favored by a large group. In 2013, President Obama criticized the U.S. Senate for failing to pass a measure that would have expanded background checks to most gun sales in the aftermath of the mass shooting at Sandy Hook Elementary

Chapter 8. Evaluating Political Arguments 165

that took twenty-seven lives, including those of twenty children. That bill, the President said, would have protected "more of our people from gun violence" but "it's not going to happen because…. Republicans in the Senate just voted against the idea" despite the fact that "90 percent of the American people support universal background checks that make it harder for a dangerous person to buy a gun."[60] Mr. Obama was correct. A Quinnipiac University poll just prior to the Sandy Hook shooting found that 91 percent of Americans supported background checks on all gun sales.[61] But that fact alone does nothing to support his argument that background checks would reduce gun violence. Just because a majority of people believe something to be true doesn't make it so. The issue at hand is whether background checks reduce gun violence, not whether they are popular.

    9. **Either-Or Fallacy:** The either-or fallacy assumes that there are only two alternatives when, in fact, there are more than two. When the either-or fallacy is committed accidentally, it shows a lack of imagination. However, when it is done intentionally, it's designed to force people into supporting an alternative they might otherwise have not supported simply because the only other alternative presented is untenable. For instance, supporters of the United States' effort to confront communism in Southeast Asia would often greet opponents of the Vietnam War with the refrain, "America, love it or leave it!" In other words, if you oppose the war, then you must hate America, and if you hate America, then you should move elsewhere.[62] Yet the implication that either people support the war and love their country or oppose the war and hate their country is a false dilemma. People can speak out against a war and love their country, simultaneously. Indeed, it may very well be their love of country that inspires them to oppose a war they believe to be antithetical to the nation's values or interests.

    10. **Appeal to Emotion:** The appeal-to-emotion fallacy occurs when one attempts to cynically manipulate the feelings of another in an effort to illicit the latter's endorsement of a particular conclusion. And perhaps no feeling is more powerful than fear. In 2004, the George W. Bush campaign produced a television ad featuring a pack of wolves. As the predators prowled through the forest an ominous voice stated, "After the first terrorist attack on America, John Kerry … voted to slash America's intelligence spending by six billion dollars." The narrator went on to suggest that such drastic cuts "would have weakened America's defenses" and attracted "those who are waiting to do America harm." While this dire warning was being issued, the wolves ran directly toward the camera and seemingly into living rooms across the country.[63] According to Brooks Jackson and Kathleen Hall

Jamieson, the effect of the Wolves ad was extraordinary. Indeed, a majority of Americans came to believe that Kerry had voted to cut intelligence spending after the terrorist attacks of September 11, 2001. In fact, Kerry voted to increase intelligence spending after 9-11. Upon closer inspection one realizes that the commercial never claimed that Senator Kerry voted to cut intelligence spending following 9-11 as it wasn't even mentioned. Rather, it argued that Kerry voted to reduce intelligence spending after "the first terrorist attack on America." According to the Bush campaign, this attack was the truck bomb that exploded in the parking garage under the World Trade Center in 1993. In this sense the Wolves advertisement did not lie—Senator Kerry did, in fact, propose a bill to cut intelligence spending by 3.7 percent in 1994. It did, however, mislead. Jackson and Jamieson suggest that "many viewers who heard 'terrorist attack' automatically thought of September 11, 2001, a terrifying event still vivid in voters' memories" and drew their conclusion accordingly.[64]

In 2011, Congressman Paul Ryan introduced a bill in the House of Representatives to overhaul Medicare. Soon thereafter a liberal group called the Agenda Project produced an advertisement criticizing the plan. The ad featured the song "America the Beautiful" and a figure, representing Mr. Ryan, pushing a smiling grandmother in a wheelchair. The congressman, however, veered off the path and up a cliff. The grandmother attempted to stop the wheelchair, but her efforts were futile. As Ryan pushed the grandmother over the precipice, text appeared on the screen and asked, "Is America beautiful without Medicare?"[65] The ad was misleading. While the Republican plan did seek to privatize Medicare, the popular program would have still received government subsidies. More important, the changes would have had no impact on people fifty-five years and older. Thus, the changes would not affect individuals currently on Medicare or those who would be joining the program over the next decade. Grandma would not have been thrown off a cliff. Yet, according to PolitiFact, the ad "preyed on seniors' worries about whether they could afford health care."[66]

The use of fear in political advertising is particularly troubling because that emotion is processed in the amygdala, a mass of cells located in the temporal lobes of the brain. Stimulation of that area of the brain can temper activity in the prefrontal cortex, the part of the brain affiliated with self-control and complex thought and thus significantly impair our ability to "think, decide, and solve problems."[67] This, of course, is often the purpose of fear mongering. If a politician can unnerve the electorate, he or she can obscure the facts, and if a politician can obscure the facts, he or she may be able to mobilize the public to support policies that the latter will come to regret. For as the English poet Samuel Taylor Coleridge noted, "In politics, what begins in fear usually ends up in folly."[68]

Thomas Jefferson believed that "in a republican nation, whose citizens are to be led by persuasion and not by force, the art of reasoning becomes of first importance."[69] Unfortunately, our ability to reason is often compromised by political tribalism. If you are a Democrat, your party attachment may very well lead you to incorrectly conclude that a bad Democratic argument is good or a good Republican argument is bad. Likewise, if you are a Republican, your partisan commitment may lead you to incorrectly decide that a bad Republican argument is good or a good Democratic argument is bad. As such, we must make a concerted effort to identify and diagram an argument's premises and conclusion, and ensure that the former aren't only dependable but that they also support the latter in a logical manner. Evaluating an argument takes a lot of work. Yet it is well worth the undertaking. Bad arguments can engender bad decisions, and bad decisions can doom the fate of nations.

CHAPTER 9

Evaluating Political Elections

"The alternate domination of one faction over another, sharpened by the spirit of revenge, natural to party dissension, ... has perpetrated the most horrid enormities."
—George Washington[1]

The Problem: Political tribalism hinders the ability of Democrats and Republicans to accurately evaluate political elections.

The lessons relayed in ancient Greek mythology are timeless. Take the ill-fated destinies of the descendants of Tantalus—the arrogant and wicked king who boiled his son Pelops in a stew that he attempted to serve to the gods for dinner. As punishment, Zeus placed Tantalus in a pool of water beneath a bountiful grove of fruit trees; inflicted him with an insatiable appetite; and ensured that whenever the filicidal father stooped in his desire to drink or grasped in his eagerness to eat, the pool's water would drain and the trees' fruit would sway just beyond his reach. And there Tantalus stood, wanting in the midst of plenty, eternally tantalized.[2]

In the meantime, the gods resurrected Pelops and the formerly scorned scion went on to become a king and sire several sons of his own, including Atreus and Thyestes. The two brothers, however, became bitter enemies when Thyestes had an affair with Atreus's wife and outmaneuvered him to become king. In response, Atreus drove Thyestes from the throne and had his three young nephews—Aglaus, Orchomenus, and Collileon—cut into pieces, boiled, and fed to their unsuspecting father. An enraged Thyestes beget another son, Aegisthus, who slayed Atreus and reclaimed the crown. Aegisthus's reign, however, was short-lived as he was duly overthrown and replaced by Atreus's son, Agamemnon.[3] As king,

Chapter 9. Evaluating Political Elections

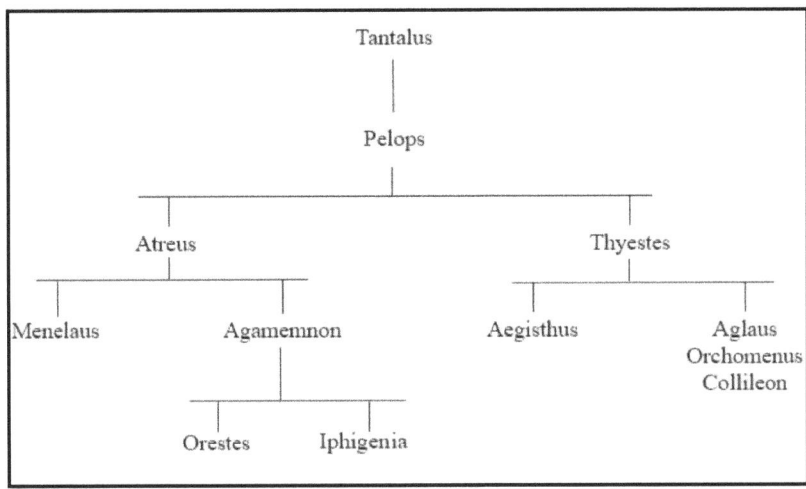

Figure 9-1: The illustration above is a partial family tree of the House of Atreus, the descendants of the cursed king Tantalus in ancient Greek mythology.

Agamemnon was renowned for his role in the Trojan War—it was he who sacrificed his eldest daughter, Iphigenia, in order to propitiate the gods and obtain the favorable winds that blew his soldiers towards Troy, and it was he who, after ten years of fighting, captained the Greeks to victory.[4] But even the mighty Agamemnon could not escape the cycle of vengeance that plagued his family.

According to the *Oresteia*—a tragedy composed by the Ancient Greek playwright Aeschylus in the 5th century BCE—Agamemnon's triumphant return home from Troy was mired in tragedy. In his absence, the king's wife, Clytemnestra, had become lovers with his cousin and nemesis, Aegisthus. The amorous pair had exiled Agamemnon's son and heir, Orestes, and pledged to kill the king upon his return. So, on the evening of his homecoming, the Queen ensnared Agamemnon in a net while he was taking a bath and plunged her dagger into his chest.[5] Yet the intergenerational cycle of violence continued when Orestes returned from exile and slayed Aegisthus. Then, bestride the lifeless body of his first cousin once removed, the expatriated prince turned his attention and ire toward his mother:

> **ORESTES:** Come here. I want to kill you by his side, and, since you thought he was, in life, a better man than my father, you must sleep with him in death.
> **CLYTEMNESTRA:** Easy, my son, take pity.... I bore you, reared you. Let me grow old with you!
> **ORESTES:** No, you gave me birth, then threw me out.... You did wrong, killing; now suffer wrong and die!

To his mind, Orestes had avenged the death of his father by killing his mother. But before he could even wipe her blood from his blade, the Erinyes appeared. The terrifying goddesses of vengeance—whose coal-black bodies were adorned with blood-shot eyes, bat wings, and snakes for hair—had arrived to "hound [the] mother-killer from his home."[6] And so they did. The Erinyes pursued Orestes across the Greek world until he finally arrived in Athens and called upon Athena—the goddess of wisdom—for help. "Queen Athena," Orestes prayed, "Receive me graciously, a cursed, hounded man. I've come at last, goddess, here to your house, waiting for justice to be fulfilled."[7]

When Athena arose, she pledged to "deal with this matter fairly, once and for all." The goddess of wisdom selected a group of the city's "ablest citizens" to serve as "a panel of judges," and instructed the litigants to "call your witnesses, prepare your proofs, and bring forth whatever evidence you have that best supports your case."[8] The Erinyes argued that Orestes had to be punished because he had killed his mother. In turn, Orestes asserted that he killed his mother because she had murdered his father. Then, the jurors deliberated and cast their ballots. Athena stepped forward and asked the parties if they were willing to accept the panel's decision. "Yes," the Erinyes replied. "We pay you the respect you pay to us." Orestes, too, consented: "It's all up to you now to decide. However the case turns out, I will accept your ruling."[9] And with that, Athena announced that Orestes had been acquitted by a single vote.

Despite their previous pledge to the contrary, the Erinyes now refused to accept the verdict. "Enraged [and] aggrieved," the goddesses of vengeance claimed to have been "wronged, mocked, [and] spit on by the citizens!" In response, Athena delivered a sermon truly worthy of her moniker. "Let me persuade you not to shoulder such a burden of grief," the goddess of wisdom said. "You haven't been disgraced. So don't be angry … and incite bloodshed throughout my land. Don't infuse in my people a war lust they'll turn inward on each other." She continued, "I swear wholeheartedly to you … that you will have your seat … in this land of justice, and there you will sit on gleaming thrones beside your sacred altars, forever honored by my citizens." Incredulous, the Erinyes asked, "You'd make us as powerful as that?" Yes, Athena assured them, "We will swell the fortunes of your followers." Immediately, the Erinyes noted that their "anger [was] easing" and they pledged to abide by the verdict and "accept a home here."[10] Athens was at peace.

The *Oresteia* is a chilling tale that continues to transcend space and time, as the advice that Aeschylus imparts in his masterpiece is as relevant to partisans in the United States today as it was to those in Ancient Athens. In particular, Democrats and Republicans would be wise to ponder its lesson on the importance of the winners' magnanimity and the losers' consent to a democratic society.

The Problem: Political tribalism encourages Democrats and Republicans to revel in favorable political elections and withhold their consent from unfavorable ones.

In most analyses, we are told that the horrific intergenerational cycle of violence—a sequence in which the House of Atreus both literally and figuratively ate its own—was finally brought to an end by the creation of the state (represented by the "panel of judges" composed of Athens' "ablest citizens").[11] Indeed, according to Daniel Breyer, an associate professor of philosophy at Illinois State University, "The most straightforward reading of [the *Oresteia*] ... is that we move from an honor culture in which the offended take responsibility for avenging wrongs to an institutionalized culture in which a formal legal system handles such things."[12] However, a deeper reading of the trilogy reveals that it was not the state, per se, that ended the bloodshed. Rather, it was the fact that the Erinyes agreed to accept the verdict produced by that state that truly brought peace, and the Erinyes did not accept that ruling until Athena promised that they would be respected despite their loss.[13] Hence, the state may be necessary for a just peace, but it is not sufficient. As Aeschylus so profoundly suggests, democracy will only succeed when its citizens are gracious in victory and yielding in defeat.

Reveling in Victory

The acquittal of Orestes was a bitterly contested affair. Nevertheless, Athena struck a conciliatory—rather than a triumphal—chord in its wake. Again, the goddess of wisdom assured the Erinyes that they weren't "disgraced" by their loss and promised that they would be "forever honored ... in this land of justice." Athena understood that a democratic society could not survive unless the winning party was willing and able to ameliorate the losing party's loss. But if Athena is right—if democracy's very survival depends upon the magnanimity of the majority—then we may have some dark days ahead.

Democrats and Republicans increasingly appear to have little interest in assuaging the political disappointments of their partisan opponents. Rather, they relish them. In the aptly titled article "Liberal Schadenfreude

Is Out of Control: Why gloating after the election is nastier than ever," journalist Katherine Goldstein noted:

> When the TV networks declared that Obama won his second term [in 2012], I whooped with glee, did a little dance and posted a few social media updates including, "Proud to be an American tonight. 4 MORE YEARS." I was so incredibly happy.... But I began to notice, both in media coverage and in social media networks, that Obama supporters were not just thrilled that our guy won—folks were insanely, morbidly happy that all Republicans were miserable.[14]

Indeed, one blogger wrote, "So please know, my fervid conservative friends, that I am temporarily suspending the empathic sensibility that generally informs most of us on the left ... [and] am laughing at you." Another boasted, "I am just 99% completely fucking delighted by every single weepy right-wing temper tantrum.... So, fuck being gracious."[15] In the aftermath of the 2016 presidential election, some Republicans gleefully shared a meme that featured a picture of a dejected Hillary Clinton supporter overlain with text deriding her for not knowing "how to lose."[16] Even Donald Trump got into the act. In December 2016, the then-President-elect embarked on a self-described "thank you tour," during which he mocked a newscaster who supposedly cried upon learning of his victory and taunted protesters by joking that someone "should remind them that Clinton lost."[17] Later that month, he continued to rub salt into the collective wounds of his opponents when he incorrectly claimed that the Democratic Party had "suffered one of the greatest defeats in the history of politics in this country."[18] Republicans across the country could even purchase a coffee mug emblazoned with the phrase "Liberal Tears."[19]

Withholding Consent in Defeat

Democracy, however, demands more than a conciliatory majority. Yes, Aeschylus's Athena was a model of magnanimity. But it was the Erinyes's "easing" anger and willingness to "accept [Athens as] a home" that ultimately secured the democratic state. In *Losers' Consent: Elections and Democratic Legitimacy*, Christopher J. Anderson, André Blais, Shaun Bowler, Todd Donovan, and Ola Listhaug note that what ultimately "makes democracy work ... is the restraint of the losers." Democracy will not succeed, they write, unless its losers are willing to "accept both a distasteful outcome and the process that produced it."[20] Unfortunately, many Democrats and Republicans appear unready to do just that.

For instance, it has become increasingly common for members of the losing party to question the legitimacy of the democratic process by

Chapter 9. Evaluating Political Elections   173

alleging election fraud. A 2012 Fairleigh Dickinson survey found that 37 percent of Democrats believed that Republicans committed voter fraud to win the presidency in 2004, and 36 percent of Republicans believed that Democrats did the same to keep the White House in 2012.[21] In *Election Meltdown: Dirty Tricks, Distrust, and the Threat to American Democracy*, legal scholar Richard L. Hasen notes that "American election litigation has nearly tripled since 2000, from an average of 94 cases per year before [that year] to an average of 270 cases after." In 2016 alone, election litigation was up 23 percent compared to 2012.[22] This is hardly surprising given some of the charges that were leveled in the midst of the campaign. As early as August 2016, Republican Donald Trump began alleging that the election would be rigged in favor of his opponent Democrat Hillary Clinton. In an appearance on Fox News's *Hannity*, Trump suggested,

> I've been hearing about it for a long time. And I know last time [in the 2012 election], there were—you had precincts where there were practically nobody voting for the Republican. And I think that's wrong. I think that was unfair frankly.... How is that possible? And I've been hearing about it for a long time. And I just hope that there's really—I hope the Republicans get out there and watch very closely because I think we are going to win this election, but if it's rigged.... I'm telling you. November 8th, we'd better be careful because that election is going to be rigged. And I hope the Republicans are watching closely if it's going to be taken away from us.[23]

At a campaign rally in Pennsylvania on October 10, 2016, the GOP's presidential nominee bellowed,

> So, this year, we have an election coming up on November 8th. So important that you get out and vote. So important that you watch other communities, because we don't want this election stolen from us. We don't want this election stolen from us. We do not want this election stolen.[24]

One week later, Trump tweeted "Of course there is large scale voter fraud happening on and before election day."[25] Later that day, at a rally in Wisconsin, he claimed,

> People that have died 10 years ago are still voting.... More than 1.8 million deceased individuals, right now, are listed as voters. Oh, that's wonderful. Well, if they're gonna vote for me, we'll think about it, right? But I have a feeling they're not gonna vote for me. Of the 1.8 million, 1.8 million is voting for someone else.... Then there's the issue of illegal immigrants voting.... They even want to try to rig the election at the polling booths. And believe me, there's a lot going on. People that have died ten years ago are still voting. Illegal immigrants are voting. I mean ... voter fraud is very, very common.[26]

There was no evidence whatsoever to support any of Trump's charges. Nevertheless, his allegations of a rigged election system resonated with members of the GOP. Indeed, a Politico poll found that 73 percent of Republicans believed that the election could be stolen from Trump. "In other words," the political scientists Steven Levitsky and Daniel Ziblatt note, "three out of four Republicans were no longer certain that they were living under a democratic system with free elections."[27]

Unfortunately, the dramatic and controversial outcome of the 2016 presidential election failed to temper such fears. While Clinton received about 2.9 million more popular votes nationwide, Trump secured a victory in the Electoral College, winning 30 states and a majority of the electoral vote.[28] This afforded both sides the opportunity to question the democratic process. In an interview on May 31, 2017, Hillary Clinton claimed that "the best estimate is that 200,000 people in Wisconsin were either denied or chilled in their efforts to vote." On March 3, 2019, Clinton suggested that "the best studies that have been done said somewhere between 40,000 and 80,000 people were turned away from the polls [in Wisconsin in 2016] because of the color of their skin, because of their age, because of whatever excuse could be made up to stop a fellow American citizen from voting." Despite such claims, however, PolitiFact rated the former Democratic presidential nominee's claims as "mostly false" and "pants on fire," respectively.[29] Nevertheless, a 2018 *Economist*/YouGov poll found that 66 percent of Democrats continued to believe that the false allegations of election fraud in 2016 were "Definitely true" or "somewhat true."[30] For his part, Donald Trump suggested that Hillary Clinton won the popular vote because some 3 million illegal votes had been cast.[31] The claim began when Gregg Phillips, a conservative activist, tweeted on November 13, 2016, that he had "verified more than three million votes cast by non-citizens." Although Phillips pledged to "release everything to the public," he never did.[32] Nonetheless, Alex Jones's conspiracy theory–laden website Infowars published an article the following day under the headline, "Report: 3 million votes in presidential election cast by illegal aliens."[33] On November 27, President-elect Trump took to Twitter and claimed that he "won the popular vote if you deduct the millions of people who voted illegally" and that "serious voter fraud" had been uncovered in "Virginia, New Hampshire, and California." Although PolitiFact gave these baseless charges a "pants on fire" rating, a July 2017 Morning Consult/Politico poll revealed that 47 percent of Republicans believed that Trump won the popular vote, compared to 40 percent who believed that Clinton won.[34] This is, to say the least, troubling. According to Hasen, "our democracy depends on confidence in the fairness of the vote."[35] As such, "leaders on both sides of the aisle" need to reject "unsupported claims of stolen or rigged elections."[36]

It has also become common for members of the losing party to reject unfavorable democratic outcomes by questioning the legitimacy of a sitting president. In 2016, an NBC News/Survey Monkey poll found that 72 percent of GOP voters believed that Barack Obama was born outside of the United States and was thus ineligible to be president.[37] Even prominent Republican leaders expressed their doubts. Former Republican Arkansas governor Mike Huckabee said, "I would love to know more [about Obama's birth]. What I know is troubling enough," and Joe Arpaio—the controversial Republican Sheriff of Maricopa County, Arizona—asserted that the president's birth certificate was "definitely fraudulent."[38] Fox News' Sean Hannity declared that President Obama was "not my president" on a special edition of his show *Hannity*.[39] Donald Trump himself tweeted that "An 'extremely credible source' has called my office and told me that @BarackObama's birth certificate is a fraud."[40] Democrats have invoked the "not my president" shibboleth as well. In 2016, a Gallup poll revealed that 23 percent of those who voted for Hillary Clinton in that year's election were unwilling to accept Donald Trump as the legitimate president.[41] A similar survey found that 57 percent of young adults viewed "Trump's presidency as illegitimate."[42] On Presidents' Day in 2017, tens of thousands of people attended a series of "Not My President's Day" rallies in dozens of cities throughout the United States to express their disfavor with President Trump.[43] In response to these developments, the Republican Party activist and commentator Erich Reimer wrote,

> the fact is that President Trump won on November 8th and is the 45th president of the United States and of all Americans, no matter who we voted for, our approval of him, or our political beliefs. The "Not My President" movement nonetheless continues with the outrageous and dangerous notion that President Trump is somehow less than a legitimately-sanctioned president. Not only is this sentiment extraordinarily disrespectful to the leader of our nation, it sets a dangerous political precedent that all Americans should be hesitant to encourage ... [W]e as Americans have to accept the results of the election ... despite what a tense election it had been.[44]

Unfortunately, Reimer's advice went unheeded. As early as July 2020, President Trump was hedging on whether he would accept to outcome of the forthcoming election and suggesting that it was going to be rigged. After his Democratic opponent, Joe Biden, was declared the winner on November 7, 2020, Trump refused to concede and falsely claimed that the Democrats had engaged in voter fraud, and that he had won the election. Biased conservative news outlets—such as Fox News, Newsmax, and One America News Network—echoed the president's conspiracy theories as did Republican leaders like Senator Lindsey Graham (R-SC) who said, "They can all go to hell as far as I'm concerned—I've had it with these people. Let's fight back. We lose elections because they cheat us."[45] Throughout November and December, Trump and his allies filed and lost over eighty lawsuits contesting the election, harassed countless Republican state officials who Trump supporters accused of complicity in covering up alleged voter fraud, and even created alternate slates of electors who met and cast their votes for Trump.[46] Given all of this, it is hardly surprising that a 2020 Politico/Morning Consult poll found that 70 percent of Republicans erroneously believed that the 2020 election wasn't "free and fair."[47] Then on January 6, 2021, a group of Trump's supporters stormed the Capitol in an effort to stop Congress from certifying the electoral vote and overturn the results of a free and fair election. Members of Congress were forced to shelter in place while rioters smashed windows and forced their way into lawmakers' offices. Five people, including a Capitol police officer, died during the insurrection. All of this because some losers chose not to consent.[48] George Washington was right: horrid enormities, indeed.

What We Can Do: When we evaluate political elections, we should be magnanimous in victory and accepting of defeat.

According to Anderson and his colleagues, "the democratic bargain calls for winners who are willing to ensure that losers are not too unhappy and for losers, in exchange, to extend their consent to the winners' right to rule."[49] Levitsky and Ziblatt similarly note that each party "must refrain from either incapacitating the other [party] or antagonizing them ... [by] eschewing dirty tricks or hardball tactics in the name of civility and fair play."[50] Thus, if we intend to keep our republic, we should be magnanimous and willingly share power in victory and be accepting and sufficiently deferential in defeat.

Magnanimous in Victory

First, when our party wins an election, we should—to borrow a phrase from the nineteenth-century Austrian diplomat Klemens von Metternich—"avoid the appearance of victory."[51] For example, in *Thirteen Days: A Memoir of the Cuban Missile Crisis*, Robert F. Kennedy wrote,

> What guided all [President John F. Kennedy's] deliberations [during the Cuban Missile Crisis] was an effort not to disgrace [Soviet Premier] Khrushchev, not to humiliate the Soviet Union.... After it was finished, he made no statement attempting to take credit for himself or for the Administration for what had occurred. He instructed all members of the ... government that no interview should be given, no statement made, which would claim any kind of victory.[52]

Martin Luther King, Jr., similarly called for magnanimity after an agreement was reached to desegregate public facilities in Birmingham, Alabama, in May 1963. According to Jonathan Rieder's *Gospel of Freedom: Martin Luther King, Jr.'s Letter from Birmingham Jail and the Struggle that Changed a Nation,*

> King called for "calm dignity and wise restraint." ... The victory was not a "victory for the Negro" over the white man. It was a victory "for democracy and the whole citizenry of Birmingham, Negro and white." King warned against gloating. When they returned to the integrated public facilities, they must avoid being "haughty in spirit." And don't forget to step into the shoes "of those who have opposed us." Appreciate "the new adjustments" that integration "pose for them. We must be loving enough to turn an enemy into a friend."[53]

In short, we can relish our political party's victory without taking pleasure in the opposing party's defeat. Once the election is over, we should put away our campaign hats and signs, and remove the Trump flags from our homes or the Biden bumper stickers from our cars. We should also stop creating or sharing mean-spirited content online. Now is the time for graciousness, not gloating. We must remember what it's like to be on the losing end of a hard-fought political campaign—the incredulity, the disappointment, the tears, and the outright fear—and reassure those on the other side of aisle that a victory for our party is not necessarily a loss for theirs, and that the end of a campaign is not the end of the world.

Second, when our political party wins an election, we should encourage its leaders to share power with the losing side. In *Why We're Polarized*, Ezra Klein notes that Democrats and Republicans "both represent huge swaths of Americans." As such, "the fact that one [party] has the majority does not mean the other [party] should be deprived of a voice."[54] The majority party should negotiate with the minority party in good faith and be willing to compromise. Likewise, research in political science has shown that political institutions which enable rival parties to control different levels or branches of government can significantly attenuate the negative effects of losing. As such, we should acknowledge the importance of a federalist system that allows voters to offset a loss at the national level with a victory at the state level, even if we disagree with the policies emanating from that state. And we should appreciate the importance of midterm elections that enable the loser of yesteryear's presidential election to become the winner of today's congressional one, even if the divided government that results will make life more difficult for our own party.[55] If we want the losers to consent, we must ensure that they are not "mocked, [and] spit on" and that they have a "seat ... in this land of justice."

Accepting of Defeat

Of course, when our party loses an election, we have to accept that result. As the Roman rhetorician Quintilian said, "When defeat is inevitable, it is wisest to yield."[56] In 1788, over 150 delegates met in Richmond, Virginia, to ratify or reject the U.S. Constitution. According to the American writer Catherine Drinker Bowen, it was "the ablest of all the ratification conventions and the best prepared, a gathering studded with stars, with names and faces known throughout the state and beyond."[57] And chief among these were James Madison, a Federalist who supported the Constitution, and Patrick Henry, an Antifederalist who did not. The two were a study in contrasts—Madison quietly reading a fastidious argument from his notes while Henry extemporaneously shouted his points as he twirled his wig on a fist held high above his head. Yet in his closing remarks, the bombastic Virginian said that "If he should find himself in the minority, he would have ... those painful sensations which arise from a conviction of being overpowered in a good cause. But he would be a peaceful citizen."[58] Sure enough, when the Constitution was approved by an eighty-nine to seventy-nine vote, Henry stayed true to his word. That very night, an angry group of Antifederalists held a mass meeting to hash out how they would resist the new government. Talk of revolution was in the air, but then Henry stood to address them. According to Bowen, Henry told his wrathful colleagues that he had done his best against the Constitution "in the proper place [at the convention]." The question, he said, was now settled; "as true and faithful republicans you had all better go home."[59] And so, they did.

The United States knows all too well the awful price that is paid when the losing side withholds its consent. In November 1860, Abraham Lincoln was elected president. Yet eleven southern states rejected the legitimacy of his victory and inaugurated a civil war that would kill some 750,000 Americans.[60] Though we aren't in danger of another civil war as of yet, we are trending in the wrong direction. Flippant talk of civil war and succession are becoming more commonplace. On Townhall.com, a Trump supporter published an article titled: "Why Democrats Would Lose the Second Civil War, too."[61] A recent essay in *The New Republic* declared "Dear Red-State Trump voter, we're done.... It's time for blue states and cities to effectively abandon the American national enterprise, as it is currently constituted. You go your way, we'll go ours. In short, we'll take our arrogant, cosmopolitan, liberal-elite football—wait, make that *soccer* ball—and go home."[62] Yet these sentiments aren't just confined to the pages of partisan websites and magazines. In fact, a 2018 Rasmussen poll revealed that 37 percent of Democrats and 32 percent of Republicans said that they think "it's likely that the United States will experience a second civil war sometime in the next five years."[63] Another recent study found that 18 percent of Democrats and 13 percent of Republicans were willing to agree that violence would be justified if the opposing party won the 2020 election.[64] In light of these numbers, the insurrection of January 2021 isn't all that surprising.

In addition, when our party loses an election, we also have to accept the consequences. After Barack Obama and the Democrats won a sweeping victory in 2008—securing not only the White House but also both chambers of Congress—several prominent House Republicans like Paul Ryan (R–WI) and Kevin McCarthy (R–CA) pledged that the GOP would be the "Party of No." Senate Minority Leader Mitch McConnell similarly declared that the "single most important thing we want to achieve [in the Senate] is for President Obama to be a one-term president."[65] Then, the Republican Congress proceeded to pursue its policy of obstruction to an extent unparalleled in American history.[66] When the Republicans secured control of the White House and both chambers of Congress in the 2016 election, Democrats were more than willing to return the favor. In fact, even before Trump took the oath of office, Representative Jerry Nadler (D–NY) argued that Democrats "must do everything we can to stop Trump and his extreme agenda now … by [w]aging fierce battles against every regressive action he takes—from personnel appointments to his legislative program—in order to thwart or at least slow them down." He promised that he would use whatever "parliamentary tools [are] available to us" because "this is a fight we must not lose."[67] And as the party's leaders go, so go the party's rank and file. A 2018 Pew Research Center poll found that just 44 percent of Republicans and 46 percent of Democrats—who historically had been much more supportive of working across the aisle than the GOP—said "they liked elected officials who make compromises with people they disagree with."[68] Another survey found that "about six-in-ten of those in both parties think … political compromise means their party gets more."[69] As of late, losers in America have ignored Athena's advice and have "infuse[d] in [our] people a war lust" and "turn[ed] inward on each other." In January 2021, they even "incite[d] bloodshed throughout [this] land."

We all have to do better. We should abide by the words of the Republican Party's 2008 presidential nominee John McCain, who, during his concession speech, said: "I urge all Americans who supported me to join me in not just congratulating [Barack Obama but offering him] our goodwill and earnest effort to find ways to come together ... it is natural tonight to feel some disappointment, but tomorrow we must move beyond it and work together.... I wish Godspeed to the man who was my former opponent and will be my President."[70] If we hope to keep our republic, Democrats and Republicans are going to have to emulate the magnanimity of Athena and the consent of the Erinyes. If we don't, we'll surely follow in the footsteps of the House of Atreus and eat our own.

Conclusion
Keeping the Republic

"In the end, however, there is only one group of people who must bear the ultimate responsibility for the current state of affairs, and only one that can change any of it: the citizens of the United States of America."[1]
—Tom Nichols

Human beings are tribal beings, and in the United States today few tribes loom larger than one's political party. Unfortunately, political tribalism's toxic blend of in-party affinity (partisanship) and out-party antipathy (negative partisanship) makes the difficult task of keeping a republic all the more daunting. According to the folk theory of democracy, citizens should process political information in an objective manner and ensure that the outputs of that effort inform their political opinions and party attachments. Unfortunately, many Americans adhere to the tribal theory of democracy instead—that is, they first and foremost identify with a political party, and then allow that attachment to influence their political opinions and the manner in which they acquire, perceive, and evaluate political information. Yet this approach has created a citizenry that's more hostile, extreme, and susceptible to shoddy thinking, as well as a government that is unresponsive and thus ultimately undemocratic.

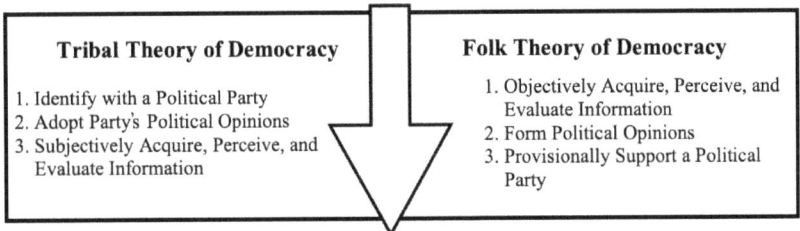

Figure C-1: The Folk and Tribal Theories of Democracy.

Conclusion

Summary of Solutions

If we intend to keep our republic, we must do better. Although we can't eliminate the cognitive and psychosocial causes of political tribalism, we can endeavor to control their pernicious effects. As a means of explanation, consider Homer's *The Odyssey*. In Book Twelve of the ancient Greek epic poem, Circe warns Odysseus of the perils he'll face in an upcoming encounter with the Sirens—creatures whose enchanted singing lured nearby sailors to shipwreck and ruin on the rocky shoals of their island. To ensure his safe passage, the goddess famously advised the weary king:

> Steer wide; keep well to seaward; plug your oarsmen's ears with beeswax kneaded soft; none of the rest should hear that song. But if you wish to listen, let the men tie you in the lugger, hand and foot, back to the mast, lashed to the mast, so you may hear those harpies' thrilling voices; shout as you will, begging to be untied, your crew must only ... keep their stroke up, till the singers fade.[2]

Odysseus—who was known in part for his intelligence—sagely followed Circe's instructions and survived as a result. He had the humility to acknowledge his impulses, as well as the wisdom and will to restrain them. We would do well to follow his example. Too many of us have succumbed to the siren song of political tribalism and have thus had a hand in steering the ship of state on its current perilous course. But like Odysseus, we can recognize our cognitive and psychosocial vulnerabilities and do our best to inhibit them by applying the prescriptions described herein. When we implement the strategies detailed in the pages above—and recapped in the pages below—we can bind ourselves to the mast of critical thinking, avoid the lure of political tribalism, and set sail for the more tranquil waters of the democratic ideal. To that end, critically thinking citizens should do their best to seek, perceive, and evaluate political information in an honest and even-handed manner and update their opinions and party attachments accordingly. In summary, we should:

Chapter 1

Recognize the role that political tribalism plays in our lives: We must honestly evaluate our personal proclivity to succumb to political tribalism—or to assume the best of our political party, and the worst of the opposing one. We must pay attention to how we feel and behave when we talk or think about politics. Politics is incredibly important. Emotions will—and often should—run high. But if we've become fervidly invested in the daily, hyperbolic pseudo-partisan squabbles that tend to populate social media feeds and cable news programs, we may need to reevaluate the role that politics plays in our lives.

Focus on what unites, rather than what divides, cross-partisans: We should actively identify and cultivate any interests, values, and beliefs that we share with members of the opposing party. These similarities can be the bridges that will span the moats that have come between us.

Cultivate relationships with members of the other party: We shouldn't stereotype, discriminate against, dehumanize, or aggress counter-partisans. Instead, we should make a concerted effort to become friends with a reasonable colleague or neighbor on the opposing side of the political aisle. If we want to reduce the amount of tribalism in our politics, we should start by giving "the other" a name and a face.

Chapter 2

Assess whether our political opinions are truly our own: We need to think hard about public issues before deciding where we stand. Prior to taking a position, we should complete a t-chart that not only details *how* a policy works but also *how* we know that our viewpoint is justified. This is difficult, time-consuming work. If we're too busy with our families, jobs, and other commitments to become well-informed on the issues, so be it. But we should at least be honest with ourselves and with others, and not behave as though we know more than we do.

Assume the Cognitive and Psychosocial Responsibilities of Citizenship: We should make an effort to objectively process political information, but we should also ensure—so long as it's safe—that our efforts bear fruit. For most of us, most of the time, it will be a question of resolve—whether or not we have the dedication to think critically about matters of public import and the firmness of purpose to hold a position at odds with our political tribe. Self-government depends upon the people's ability to govern themselves. Of course, this is true in a collective sense—by way of the principles of popular sovereignty and majority rule et cetera. But it is also true in a personal sense—if we can't govern our tribal instincts, they will surely govern us.

Chapter 3

Assess the role that selective exposure plays in our lives: Each day we should count the number of liberal and conservative editorials we read, or the number of minutes we spend watching MSNBC or Fox News, or the number of left-leaning and right-leaning accounts that we follow on Twitter, or the number of Democrats and Republicans with whom we discussed politics that day. If we find a persistent imbalance, then we need to engage our curiosity, seek out contrary points of view, and deliberate with those with whom we disagree.

Engage our curiosity: Citizens who abide by the tribal theory of democracy rarely ask questions because they routinely believe that they have all the answers. By contrast, citizens who subscribe to the folk theory of democracy recognize the gaps in their knowledge and aspire to fill them.

Seek out contrary points of view: We should seek content from reasonable counter-partisan sources. And remember—if a contrary columnist or pundit doesn't broaden our understanding of the other side, we should keep looking for one that will.

Deliberate with those with whom we disagree: We should find a reasonable friend or colleague with whom we can have political conversations, and we should remind ourselves that the point of these parleys is to pursue understanding, not victory. To that end, we should focus on sources and epistemology, and, above all, listen.

Chapter 4

Avoid the expectation bias: We should stop assuming that the mainstream news media exhibits a partisan bias. If we expect a political news source to be biased, we will likely find it to be so, even when it's not.

Be on guard against the hostile media effect: In fact, the scientific evidence suggests that most partisan biases reside within ourselves, rather than the mainstream media. So, before we conclude that a particular paper or channel is a biased source, let's make sure we aren't actually the source of the bias. We should make a regular habit of conducting informal content analyses on news articles or programs we believe to be biased, comparing our results with friends or colleagues from the opposing party, and assessing whether we selectively miscategorized any neutral or favorable material as hostile to our point of view.

Avoid miscategorizing adversarial and structural biases as a partisan bias: We should remember that political news coverage tends to be hostile and dramatic. Hence, when we consume content that appears to have a partisan bias, we should entertain the possibility that it might be an adversarial or structural bias instead. Ask ourselves: Would this story have been reported if its subject was a member of the opposing party or have similar stories been reported in the past about members of the opposing party? If so, the media might be exhibiting a bias, but it probably isn't a partisan one.

Distinguish between news content and opinion content: We must remember that some political news coverage is designed to be biased. Therefore, we should check whether print content is labeled as opinion and broadcast content is delivered by commentators or contributors (rather than journalists or reporters). In the absence of labels, we should research whether the source has a reputation of being objective or partisan. If we are still in doubt, we should assess the tone of the content. If it's hyperbolic and self-assured, we are likely dealing with opinion.

Beware of unfavorable facts: Before we conclude that a particular statement in the news reveals a partisan bias, we should make sure that we haven't mischaracterized a fact—or something that can be proved or disproved based on objective evidence—as an opinion. We should remind ourselves that a factual statement that reflects positively on the opposing party, or negatively on our own, is not in and of itself evidence of a partisan bias.

Beware of favorable opinions: Before we conclude that a news report is objective, we should make sure that we haven't mistaken an opinion for a fact. A news report that reflects negatively on the opposing party, or positively on our own, is not necessarily unbiased. If the statement can't be proved or disproved by objective evidence, it is an opinion and therefore might evince a partisan bias.

Be on guard against the trustworthy source effect: Democrats and Republicans tend to find sources that report favorable information about their political tribe as more trustworthy than those that report antagonistic material. To avoid this error, we should check the source's reputation for objectivity, check its tone, and even conduct our own informal analysis of its content. If scientific studies deem the source to be biased, we should be wary. And compare notes with a reasonable counter-partisan—do they find the source to be as balanced as you? If not, why? And do they have a point?

Chapter 6

Read laterally: To better assess the accuracy of an article or headline that we encounter online, we should research the source, the author, and the source's sources. In addition, we should check to ensure that its claims are being corroborated by other major news outlets.

Verify political quotations: When we happen upon a quote that makes members of our party look particularly good or members of the opposing party especially bad, we should try to locate the original source using an Internet search engine or online database, or investigate whether it has been verified by a reputable fact checker such as Quote investigator, Snopes, PolitiFact, or FactCheck.org.

Verify political photographs: When we encounter a photograph that makes a member of our party look markedly good or a member of the opposing party unusually bad, we should investigate whether it has been verified by a reputable fact checker or conduct a reverse image search to ensure that the image has not been doctored.

Verify political videos: When we chance upon an audio or video recording that makes a member of our party look notably good or a member of the opposing party decidedly bad, we should investigate whether it has been verified by a reputable fact checker. If that is unfruitful, we should use a resource like Deepware's Scanner to assess the video's veracity, or TinEye to conduct a reverse image search of a screenshot of the video.

Think before we share: Lastly, if your research finds that an article, headline, quotation, photograph, or video is false, don't share it with others. It may seem as though it's an innocuous way to burnish your tribal bona fides, get a few likes, or enjoy some schadenfreude at the opposing party's expense, but many of those with whom you share it might just believe it to be true, particularly if they have already seen it on multiple occasions.

Chapter 7

Beware of dangling comparatives: When politicians or political pundits tell us that something is "higher" or "lower" or "more" or "less," we should ask ourselves what is actually being compared.

Be on the lookout for the misleading use of the word "average": When a politician or political pundit uses the word "average," we should assess whether average in this instance means typical or commonplace, or whether it refers to a skewed arithmetic mean that is, colloquially speaking, unaverage.

Assess the accuracy of graphs: When evaluating a graph, we should assess whether its visual proportions accurately reflect its numerical proportions. First, assess a graph's numbers and then determine whether or not those numbers are rightly portrayed by the graph's visual information. If a graph doesn't have numbers or the graph's numbers aren't proportionate to its visual data, the graph should be ignored.

Assess the accuracy of opinion polls: When evaluating any political opinion poll, we should assess whether the poll's results are skewed by an unrepresentative sample, biased questions, or inappropriate combinations. We should ask ourselves: Does the poll explicitly state that it used a random sample or include a margin of error? Can I access the poll's questions and, if so, is their wording, option offerings, and order unbiased? Have the poll's results been aggregated in a misleading and self-serving manner?

Avoid conflating absolute and relative change: When a politician or pundit talks about change, we should assess whether that change is absolute (new data—old data) or relative (new data—old data / old data × 100%). Then, we should calculate the type of change that wasn't used, compare it to the one that was, and determine which measure of change is most appropriate for the situation at hand.

Chapter 8

Deconstruct an argument: When we come upon an argument, we should identify the argument's premises and conclusion, organize them in a diagram, determine whether the argument's premises are dependable by assessing the quality and quantity of evidence that support them, and reckon whether the argument incorporates one or more logical fallacies.

Chapter 9

Be yielding in defeat and magnanimous in victory: We should always be gracious to our political opponents following an electoral victory and—in the absence of clear evidence of voter suppression or fraud—consent to an electoral defeat. We need to put away our political signs and hats after an election, eschew the "not-my-president" rhetoric, and realize that politics need not be a zero-sum endeavor.

Keeping the Republic

According to the author Ezra Klein, "our identities are manifold. 'Republican' is an identity, as is 'Democrat.' But so is 'fair-minded,' or … 'curious,' … [and these] can be as much an identity … as to be a member of a political party."[3] In similar fashion, the political scientist Eric Groenendyk argues that Democrats and Republicans have dual—and often dueling—identities: the loyal partisan and the good citizen.[4] Therefore, the essential question is this: which of these identities will we seek to activate—the party apparatchik or the critical political thinker?

Fortunately, Groenendyk found that when people are reminded that it is a responsibility of citizenship to "consider all available information—not just those ideas espoused by their fellow partisans—and to hold government accountable," they largely choose to activate their folk identity instead of their tribal one. What's more, Klein notes that "Like a muscle or neural pathway, the identities we use most grow strongest, [while] the ones that lie fallow weaken."[5] In other words, when we are reminded to be a folk citizen, we often act like a folk citizen. And the more we act like a folk citizen, the easier it becomes. Hence, Groenendyk concludes that "the promotion of ... overcoming one's biases and acting with an open mind ... is vital if we want partisans to act like good citizens."[6] It has been the guiding purpose of this book to make a contribution—however small—to that effort.

Of course, trying to adhere to the folk theory of democracy will be difficult. Being a critical political thinker can be taxing, time-consuming, and downright disquieting. What's more, the fruits of our labor can seem fleeting and inconsequential. One might ask: If someone resists the urge to retweet a misleading graph today but succumbs to sharing a false image tomorrow, what's the point? Or if someone stopped watching cable news and started mapping arguments or making policy graphic organizers et cetera, what impact could that possibly have on the body politic en masse? In response, I would argue that every paddle stroke we take toward the democratic ideal is a paddle stroke we didn't take toward the realm of political tribalism. After all, even "one paddle stroke forward and two paddle strokes back" are better than the alternative of three paddle strokes back. And while one's solitary pursuit of the democratic ideal can't chart the course of a nation; it can help change the direction of the ship of state when its stroke is added to the strokes of other folk citizens. As Russ Roberts writes in his book, *How Adam Smith Can Change Your Life: An Unexpected Guide to Human Nature and Happiness*: "You alone make very little difference. But you make a contribution. And when you join in with others, you make all the difference."[7] So, set your sights on the democratic ideal and make your contribution. Each and every one of us must possess the humility to acknowledge our partisan biases and lack of political knowledge, as well as the courage to listen to opposing points of view, ground our political opinions in the evidence, and challenge our fellow citizens when they do not. For it is only together that we can keep the republic.

Chapter Notes

Preface

1. Shenkman, Rick. 2008. *Just How Stupid Are We? Facing the Truth About the American Voter*. New York: Basic Books. 37.
2. Anishanslin, Zara. 2019. "What We Get Wrong About Ben Franklin's 'a republic, if you can keep it'." *The Washington Post*. October 29.
3. Delli Carpini, Michael X, and Scott Keeter. 1989. *What Americans Know About Politics and Why It Matters*. New Haven: Yale University Press.
4. Rozansky, Michael. 2017. "Americans Are Poorly Informed about Basic Constitutional Provisions." *Annenberg Public Policy Center*. September 12.
5. Doyle, Gerry. 2006. "About Those First Amendment Rights, Doh!" *Chicago Tribune*. March 1.
6. Achen, Christopher H., and Larry M. Bartels. 2016. *Democracy for Realists: Why Elections Do Not Produce Responsive Government*. Princeton: Princeton University Press.
7. Lombrozo, Tania. 2016. "Is the Mind's Approach More Like a Scientist or a Trial Lawyer?" *NPR*. April 11.
8. Benen, Steve. 2019. "45 Years Later, Republicans Borrow a Page from Earl Landgrebe." *MSNBC*. December 12.
9. Stanovich, Keith E. 2009. *What Intelligence Tests Miss: The Psychology of Rational Thought*. New Haven: Yale University Press. Butler, Heather A., Christopher Pentoney, and Mabelle R. Bong. 2017. "Predicting Real-world Outcomes: Critical Thinking Ability Is a Better Predictor of Life Decisions than Intelligence." *Thinking Skills and Creativity*. Vol. 25. 38–46. Stanovich, Keith E., Richard F. West, and Maggie E. Toplak. 2013. "Myside Bias, Rational Thinking, and Intelligence." *Current Directions in Psychological Science*. Vol. 22, No. 4. 259–264. Jardina, Ashley, and Michael Traugott. 2018. "The Genesis of the Birther Rumor: Partisanship, Racial Attitudes, and Political Knowledge." *Journal of Race, Ethnicity, and Politics*. Vol. 4, Issue 1. 60–80.
10. Finkel, Eli J., Christopher A. Bail, Mina Cikara, Peter H. Ditto, Shanto Iyengar, Samara Klar, Lilliana Mason, Mary C. McGrath, Brendan Nyhan, David G. Rand, Linda J. Skitka, Joshua A. Tucker, Jay J. Van Bavel, Cynthia S. Wang, and James N. Druckman. 2020. "Political Sectarianism in America." *Science*. Vol. 370, Issue 6516.
11. Kalmoe, Nathan. 2021. Personal Communication. April 1. Kiley, Jocelyn. 2014. "In Search of Libertarians." *Pew Research Center*. August 25.
12. Boxell, Levi, Matthew Gentzkow, and Jesse M. Shapiro. 2020. "Cross-Country Trends in Affective Polarization." *National Bureau of Economic Research*. June. 1–43.
13. Aldrich, John H. 1995. *Why Parties? The Origin and Transformation of Political Parties in America*. Chicago: The University of Chicago Press.
14. Mutz, Diana C. 2006. *Hearing the Other Side: Deliberative versus Participatory Democracy*. Cambridge: Cambridge University Press.
15. Marietta, Morgan, and David C. Barker. 2019. *One Nation, Two Realities: Dueling Facts in American Democracy*. New York: Oxford University Press. Ditto, Peter H., Brittany S. Liu, Cory J. Clark,

Sean P. Wojcik, Eric E. Chen, Rebecca H. Grady, Jared B. Celniker, and Joanne F. Zinger. 2018. "At Least Bias Is Bipartisan: A Meta-Analytic Comparison of Partisan Bias in Liberals and Conservatives. *Perspectives on Psychological Science*. Vol. 14, No. 2. 273–291.

Chapter 1

1. Rowling, J.K. 2000. *Harry Potter and the Goblet of Fire*. New York: Scholastic Press. 176.
2. Berreby, David. 2005. *Us and Them: The Science of Identity*. Chicago: The University of Chicago Press.
3. Mason, Lilliana. 2018. *Uncivil Agreement: How Politics Became Our Identity*. Chicago: The University of Chicago Press.
4. Berreby, David. 2005. *Us and Them: The Science of Identity*. Chicago: The University of Chicago Press. 173.
5. Hippel, William von. 2018. *The Social Leap: The New Evolutionary Science of Who We Are, Where We Come From, and What Makes Us Happy*. New York: Harper Wave.
6. LeBlanc, Steven A. 2003. *Constant Battles: The Myth of the Peaceful Noble Savage*. New York: St. Martin's Press. 69–70, 113.
7. Kinder, Donald R., and Cindy D. Kam. 2009. *Us Against Them: Ethnocentric Foundations of American Opinion*. Chicago: The University of Chicago Press. 8.
8. Moffett, Mark W. 2019. *The Human Swarm: How Our Societies Arise, Thrive, and Fall*. New York: Basic Books.
9. Ibid.
10. Ibid., 86 and 92.
11. Willets, Megan. 2014. "How to Order a Beer Like a True German." *Business Insider*. March 31.
12. Moffett, Mark W. 2019. *The Human Swarm: How Our Societies Arise, Thrive, and Fall*. New York: Basic Books. 82.
13. Tarantino, Quentin, director. *Inglourious Basterds*. Universal Pictures, 2009.
14. Martin, James. 2008. "Catholics Will No Longer Recite 'And Also with You.'" *NPR*. April 11.
15. White, Matthew. *The Great Big Book of Horrible Things: The Definitive Chronicle of History's 100 Worst Atrocities*. New York: W.W. Norton. 2012.
16. Ghose, Tia. 2012. "Why We Care About Our Ancestry." *Live Science*. October 26.
17. Roos, Dave. 2018. "Human Sacrifice: Why the Aztecs Practiced This Gory Ritual." *History*. October 11.
18. Thomas, Hugh. 1997. *The Slave Trade: The Story of the Atlantic Slave Trade, 1440-1870*. New York: Touchstone.
19. Balakian, Peter. 2003. *The Burning Tigris: The Armenian Genocide and America's Response*. New York: HarperCollins. 166.
20. Hitler, Adolf. 1999. *Mein Kampf*. Boston: Houghton Mifflin Company. 306–307.
21. Chang, Iris. 1997. *The Rape of Nanking: The Forgotten Holocaust of World War II*. New York: Basic Books. 6 and 219.
22. Power, Samantha. 2002. *A Problem from Hell: America and the Age of Genocide*. New York: Basic Books. 119.
23. White, Kenneth R. 2007. "Scourge of Racism: Genocide in Rwanda." *Journal of Black Studies*. Vol. 39. No. 3. 471–481.
24. Brown, Dee. 1970. *Bury My Heart at Wounded Knee: An Indian History of the American West*. New York: Holt, Rinehart, and Winston. Davis, James F. 1991. *Who Is Black? One Nation's Definition*. University Park: Penn State University Press.
25. Orkent, Daniel. 2019. *The Guarded Gate: Bigotry, Eugenics, and the Law That Kept Two Generations of Jews, Italians, and Other European Immigrants Out of America*. New York: Scribner. 55 and 276–311.
26. Frail, T.A. 2017. "The Injustice of Japanese-American Internment Camps Resonates Strongly to This Day." *Smithsonian Magazine*. January.
27. Rutherford, Adam. 2020. *How to Argue with a Racist: History, Science, Race, and Reality*. London: Weidenfeld & Nicolson. 101–105.
28. Taylor, Adam. 2017. "How Do People Define Their National Identity? By Speaking the Language, Study Says." *The Washington Post*. February 1.
29. Moffett, Mark W. 2019. *The Human Swarm: How Our Societies Arise, Thrive, and Fall*. New York: Basic Books. 86.
30. Asimov, Isaac. 1981. *Asimov's Guide to the Bible: The Old and New Testaments*. New York: Avenel Books. 248.
31. Green, Alfred, director. *Invasion, U.S.A.* American Pictures Corp. 1952.

32. Jaksa, Kari L. 2011. "Sports and Collective Identity: The Effects of Athletics on National Unity." *SAIS Review of International Affairs.* Vol. 31 No. 1. 39–41.

33. Pampuro, Amanda. 2019. "Wearing Your Candidate on Your Sleeve: Merchandising the 2020 Race." *Courthouse News Service.* September 13. Enda, Jodi. 2012. "When Republicans Were Blue and Democrats Were Red." *Smithsonian Magazine.* October 31. Arn, Jackson. 2018. "Why Democrats Are donkeys and Republicans Are elephants." *CNN.com.* November 6.

34. Reeve, Elspeth. 2012. "People Celebrating Obama's Re-Election Through Tattoos." *The Atlantic.* November 8.

35. Zuppello, Suzanne. 2019. "When Tattoos Become Political Statements." *Inside Out.* July 5. Fink, Jenni. 2018. "National Tattoo Day: Donald Trump Has Become a Popular Inspiration, For Both Supporters and Critics." *Newsweek.* July 17.

36. Abadi, Mark. 2017. "Democrats and Republicans Speak Different Languages—and It Helps Explain Why We're so Divided." *Business Insider.* August 11.

37. Mason, Lilliana. 2018. *Uncivil Agreement: How Politics Became Our Identity.* Chicago: The University of Chicago Press.

38. *Ibid.*, 35.

39. Pew Research Center. 2018. "Trends in Party Affiliation Among Demographic Groups." *Pew Research Center.* March 20.

40. *Ibid.*

41. Hetherington, Marc, and Jonathan Weiler. 2018. *Prius or Pickup: How the Answers to Four Simple Questions Explain America's Great Divide.* Boston: Houghton Mifflin Harcourt. 89–121. Katz, Josh. 2016. "Duck Dynasty vs. Modern Family: 50 Maps of the U.S. Cultural Divide." *The New York Times.* December 27.

42. Mason, Lilliana. 2018. *Uncivil Agreement: How Politics Became Our Identity.* Chicago: The University of Chicago Press. 14.

43. Iyengar, Shanto, Gaurav Sood, and Yphtach Lelkes. 2012. "Affect Not Ideology: A Social Identity Perspective on Polarization." *Public Opinion Quarterly.* Vol. 76, Issue 3. 405–431.

44. Doherty, Carroll, Jocelyn Kiley, and Bridget Jameson. 2016. "Partisanship and Political Animosity in 2016." *Pew Research Center.* June 22.

45. Kiley, Jocelyn, and Shiva Maniam. 2016. "Lesbian, Gay, and Bisexual Voters Remain a Solidly Democratic Bloc." *Pew Research Center.* October 25.

46. Pew Research Center. 2016. "Party Affiliation Among Voters, 1992–2016." *Pew Research Center.* September 13.

47. Ahler, Douglas J., and Gaurav Sood. 2018. "The Parties in Our Heads: Misperceptions About Party Composition and Their Consequences." *The Journal of Politics.* Vol. 80, No. 3.

48. Sherman, David K., Leif D. Nelson, and Lee D. Ross. 2003. "Naïve Realism and Affirmative Action: Adversaries Are More Similar Than They Think." *Basic and Applied Social Psychology.* Vol. 25, No. 4. Ahler, Douglas J. and Gaurav Sood. 2018. "The Parties in Our Heads: Misperceptions About Party Composition and Their Consequences." *The Journal of Politics.* Vol. 80, No. 3.

49. Mounk, Yascha. 2019. "Republicans Don't Understand Democrats—And Democrats Don't Understand Republicans." *The Atlantic.* June 23.

50. Parker, Victoria A., Matthew Feinberg, Alexa Tullett, and Anne E. Wilson. 2021. "The Ties That Blind: Misperceptions of the Opponent Fringe and the Miscalibration of Political Contempt." *ResearchGate.* September 9.

51. Mason, Lilliana. 2018. *Uncivil Agreement: How Politics Became Our Identity.* Chicago: The University of Chicago Press. 4.

52. Pew Research Center. 2016. "Partisanship and Political Animosity in 2016." *Pew Research Center.* June 22.

53. *Ibid.*

54. Kalmoe, Nathan P., and Lilliana Mason. 2019. *Lethal Mass Partisanship: Prevalence, Correlates, and Electoral Contingencies.* National Capital Area Political Science Association Meeting.

55. Edsall, Thomas B. 2019. "No Hate Left Behind." *The New York Times.* March 13.

56. Iyengar, Shanto, and Sean J. Westwood. 2015. "Fear and Loathing Across Party Lines: New Evidence of Group Polarization." *American Journal of Political Science.* Vol. 59, No. 3. 690–707.

57. Balliet, Daniel, Joshua M. Tybur, Junhui Wu, Christian Antonellis, and Paul A. M. Van Lange. 2018. "Political Ideology,

Trust, and Cooperation: In-Group Favoritism among Republicans and Democrats During a U.S. National Election." *Journal of Conflict Resolution*. Vol. 62, No. 4.

58. Marks, Joseph, Eloise Copland, Eleanor Loh, Cass R. Sunstein, and Tali Sharot. 2018. "Epistemic Spillovers: Learning Others' Political Views Reduces the Ability to Assess and Use Their Expertise in Nonpolitical Domains." *Cognition*. Vol. 188. 74–84.

59. Grunwald, Michael. 2016. "The Victory of 'No.'" *Politico*. December 4.

60. Chiu, Allyson. 2019. "'I'm friends with George Bush': Ellen DeGeneres Defends Watching Football with Former GOP President." *The Washington Post*. October 8.

61. Hetherington, Marc, and Jonathan Weiler. 2018. *Prius or Pickup: How the Answers to Four Simple Questions Explain America's Great Divide*. Boston: Houghton Mifflin Harcourt. 89.

62. Mason, Lilliana. 2018. *Uncivil Agreement: How Politics Became Our Identity*. Chicago: The University of Chicago Press. 55.

63. *Ibid*.

64. Pew Research Center. 2016. "Partisanship and Political Animosity in 2016." *Pew Research Center*. June 22.

65. Smith, David Livingstone. 2011. *Less Than Human: Why We Demean, Enslave, and Exterminate Others*. New York: St. Martin's Press. 26.

66. *Ibid*.

67. *Ibid*., 83.

68. *Ibid*., 13–25.

69. Brown, Brené. 2018. "Dehumanizing Always Starts with Language." brenebrown.com. May 17.

70. Smith, David Livingstone. 2011. *Less Than Human: Why We Demean, Enslave, and Exterminate Others*. New York: St. Martin's Press. 13.

71. Anderson, Theo. 2015. "The Danger of Dehumanizing Others." *Kellogg Insight*. December 8.

72. Goff, Phillip Atiba, Jennifer L. Eberhardt, Melissa J. Williams, and Matthew Christian Jackson. 2008. "Not Yet Human: Implicit Knowledge, Historical Dehumanization, and Contemporary Consequences." *Journal of Personality and Social Psychology*. Vol. 94, No. 2. 292–306.

73. Rudman, Laurie A., and Kris Mescher. 2012. "Of Animals and Objects: Men's Implicit Dehumanization of Women and Likelihood of Sexual Aggression." *Personality and Social Psychology Bulletin*. Vol. 38, No. 6. 734–746.

74. Theodoridis, Alexander, and James Martherus. 2018. "Trump Is Not the Only One Who Calls Opponents 'Animals.' Democrats and Republicans Do It to Each Other." *The Washington Post*. May 21. Skinner, Allison. 2018. "The Slippery Slope of Dehumanizing Language." *The Conversation*. June 4. Zhao, Christina. 2018. "Fox News Host Jeanine Pirro Blasts Dianne Feinstein and Her 'unhinged lunatic demon rats.'" *Newsweek*. September 16.

75. Kalmoe and Mason. 2019. *Lethal Mass Partisanship: Prevalence, Correlates, and Electoral Contingencies*. National Capital Area Political Science Association Meeting.

76. Theodoridis, Alexander G., James Martherus, and Andy Martinez. 2019. "Party Animals? Extreme Polarization and Dehumanization." *Political Behavior*. July.

77. *Ibid*.

78. Klein, Ezra. 2020. *Why We're Polarized*. New York: Avid Reader Press. 71–72.

79. Kalmoe and Mason. 2019. *Lethal Mass Partisanship: Prevalence, Correlates, and Electoral Contingencies*. National Capital Area Political Science Association Meeting.

80. *Ibid*.

81. Salvanto, Anthony, Jennifer De Pinto, Fred Backus, and Kabir Khanna. 2021. "Majority Favor Conviction as Impeachment Trial Begins, but Many Republicans Urge Loyalty to Trump—CBS News poll." *CBS News*. February 9.

82. Kalmoe and Mason. 2019. *Lethal Mass Partisanship: Prevalence, Correlates, and Electoral Contingencies*. National Capital Area Political Science Association Meeting.

83. *Ibid*.

84. Laughland, Oliver, and Jon Swaine. 2017. "Virginia Shooting: Gunman Was Leftwing Activist with Record of Domestic Violence." *The Guardian*. June 15.

85. Date, Jack. 2019. "Mail Bomber Cesar Sayoc Obsessed with Trump, Fox News, Chilling New Court Filings Show." *ABC News*. July 23. Robertson, Lind, Sarah Blaskey, and Martin Vassolo. 2018.

"Bombing Suspect Cesar Sayoc, Lost and Angry, Found His Tribe with Trump." *Miami Herald*. October 27.

86. Mason, Lilliana. 2018. *Uncivil Agreement: How Politics Became Our Identity*. Chicago: The University of Chicago Press. 2.

87. Sorkin, Aaron. 2013. *The Newsroom*. Burbank, CA: Home Box Office. Season 1, Episode 1.

88. Feynman, Richard P., and Edward Hutchings. 1985. *Surely, You're Joking, Mr. Feynman!* New York: W.W. Norton & Company Ltd. 343.

89. Several of these questions are based on Mael and Tetrick's measure of social identity: Mael, Fred, and Louis Tetrick. 1992. "Identifying Organizational Identification." *Educational and Psychological Measurement*. 54: 813–24.

90. Galef, Julia. 2021. *The Scout Mindset: Why Some People See Things Clearly and Others Don't*. New York: Penguin.

91. Mael, Fred, and Louis Tetrick. 1992. "Identifying Organizational Identification." *Educational and Psychological Measurement*. 54: 813–24.

92. Berreby, David. 2005. *Us and Them: The Science of Identity*. Chicago: The University of Chicago Press. 19.

93. Bacon, Perry, and Dhrumil Mehta. 2018. "Religious Democrats, Young Republicans: What the Stereotypes Miss About Both Parties." *FiveThirtyEight*. March 23.

94. Levendusky, Matthew S. 2018. "Americans, Not Partisans: Can Priming American National Identity Reduce Affective Polarization?" *Journal of Politics*. Vol. 80, No. 1. 59–70.

95. Ripley, Amanda. 2019. "The Least Politically Prejudiced Place in America." *The Atlantic*. March 4.

96. Eberhardt, Jennifer L. 2019. *Biased: Uncovering the Hidden Prejudice That Shapes What We See, Think, and Do*. New York: Viking. Pettigrew, Thomas F., and Linda R. Tropp. 2006. "A Meta-Analytic Test of Intergroup Contact Theory." *Journal of Personality and Social Psychology*. Vol. 90, No. 5. 751–783.

97. Pettigrew, Thomas F., Linda R. Tropp, Ulrich Wagner, and Oliver Christ. 2011. "Recent Advances in Intergroup Contact Theory." *International Journal of Intercultural Relations*. Vol. 35, No. 3. 271–80.

98. Pew Research Center. 2016. "Partisanship and Political Animosity in 2016." *Pew Research Center*. June 22.

99. Pew Research Center. 2017. "The Partisan Divide on Political Values Grows Even Wider." *Pew Research Center*. October 5.

100. NPR Staff. 2016. "Ginsburg and Scalia: 'Best Buddies.'" *NPR*. February 15.

101. Klein, Ezra. 2020. *Why We're Polarized*. New York: Avid Reader Press. 71.

Chapter 2

1. Resnick, Brian. 2017. "Trump Is a Real-World Political Science Experiment." *Vox*. October 11.

2. Hibbing, John, Kevin Smith, and John Alford. 2014. *Predisposed: Liberals, Conservatives, and the Biology of Political Differences*. New York: Routledge. Lyons, Jeffrey. 2016. "The Family and Partisan Socialization in Red and Blue America." *Political Psychology*. Vol. 20, No. 20. Beattie, Peter. 2017. "The Chicken-and-Egg Development of Political Opinions: The Roles of Genes, Social Status, Ideology, and Information." *Politics and the Life Sciences*. Vol. 36. No. 1.

3. Kane, John V., Lilliana Mason, and Julie Wronski. 2020. "Who's at The Party? Group Sentiments, Knowledge, and Partisan Identity." *The Journal of Politics*. September 3.

4. Campbell, Angus, Philip E. Converse, Warren E. Miller, and Donald E. Stokes. 1960. *The American Voter*. Chicago: The University of Chicago Press. Kinder, Donald R., and Nathan P. Kalmoe. 2017. *Neither Liberal nor Conservative: Ideological Innocence in the American Public*. Chicago: The University of Chicago Press.

5. Levendusky, Matthew. 2009. *The Partisan Sort: How Liberals Became Democrats and Conservatives Became Republicans*. Chicago: The University of Chicago Press.

6. Lavine, Howard, Christopher Johnston, and Marco Steenbergen. 2012. *The Ambivalent Partisan: How Critical Loyalty Promotes Democracy*. New York: Oxford University Press. 166.

7. Levendusky, Matthew. 2009. *The Partisan Sort: How Liberals Became Democrats and Conservatives Became Republicans*. Chicago: The University of Chicago Press.

8. McCarty, Nolan. 2019. *Polarization: What Everyone Needs to Know*. New York: Oxford University Press.

9. Lavine, Howard, Christopher Johnston, and Marco Steenbergen. 2012. *The Ambivalent Partisan: How Critical Loyalty Promotes Democracy*. New York: Oxford University Press. 87.

10. *Ibid*.

11. Cummings, William. 2019. "'A WALL is a WALL!' Trump Declares. But the Definition Has Shifted a lot Over Time." *USA Today*. January 31.

12. Ekins, Emily. 2019. "Americans Used to Support a Border Wall. What Changed Their Minds?" *CATO Institute*. January 14.

13. Pew Research Center. 2019. "Most Border Wall Opponents, Supporters Say Shutdown Concessions Are Unacceptable." *Pew Research Center*. January 16.

14. Edwards-Levy, Ariel. 2018. "Republicans Support Tougher Gun Background Checks, Unless It's Obama Suggesting Them." *Huffington Post*. May 31.

15. Edwards-Levy, Ariel. 2018. "Republicans Like Obama's Ideas Better When They Think They're Donald Trump's." *Huffington Post*. May 31.

16. Gillespie, Patrick. 2016. "Trump Hammers America's 'worst trade deal.'" *CNN*. September 27.

17. Bandler, Aaron. 2017. "Trump Effect: New Poll Shows More Democrats Support NAFTA Than Republicans. The Margin Will Stun You." *Daily Wire*. February 25.

18. Cohen, Geoffrey L. 2003. "Party Over Policy: The Dominating Impact of Group Influence on Political Beliefs." *Journal of Personal and Social Psychology*. Vol. 85, No. 5. 808–822.

19. *Ibid*., 808.

20. *Ibid*., 811–812.

21. Barber, Michael, and Jeremy C. Pope. 2018. "Does Party Trump Ideology? Disentangling Party and Ideology in America." *American Political Science Review*. Vol. 113, No. 1.

22. Whitman, Walt. 2016. "Song of Myself," Part 51. IA: Iowa University Press. 180.

23. Groenendyk, Eric W. 2013. *Competing Motives in the Partisan Mind: How Loyalty and Responsiveness Shape Party Identification and Democracy*. New York: Oxford University Press. 137.

24. Pogosyan, Marianna. 2017. "On Belonging: What Is Behind Our Psychological Need to Belong?" *Psychology Today*. April 11.

25. Beck, Julie. 2019. "This Article Won't Change Your Mind: The Facts on Why Facts Alone Can't Fight False Belief." *The Atlantic*. December 11.

26. Groenendyk, Eric W. 2013. *Competing Motives in the Partisan Mind: How Loyalty and Responsiveness Shape Party Identification and Democracy*. New York: Oxford University Press. 110–111.

27. Simler, Kevin, and Robin Hanson. 2018. *The Elephant in the Brain: Hidden Motives in Everyday Life*. New York: Oxford University Press.

28. Hardin, Garrett. 1969. "The Tragedy of the Commons." *Science*. Vol. 162, Issue 3859.

29. Kahan, Dan M. 2017. "Misconception, Misinformation, and the Logic of Identity-Protective Cognition." *Yale Law & Economist Research Paper*. No. 575.

30. Pinker, Steven. *Enlightenment Now: The Case for Reason, Science, Humanism, and Progress*. New York: Viking. 358.

31. *Ibid*.

32. Armstrong, Eric. 2017. "Are Democrats the Party of Science? Not Really." *The New Republic*. January 10.

33. Davenport, Coral, and Eric Lipton. 2017. "How G.O.P. Leaders Came to View Climate Change as Fake Science." *The New York Times*. June 3.

34. Tavris, Carol and Elliot Aronson. 2007. *Mistakes Were Made (but not by me): Why We Justify Foolish Beliefs, Bad Decisions, and Hurtful Acts*. Orlando: Harcourt.

35. Groenendyk, Eric W. 2013. *Competing Motives in the Partisan Mind: How Loyalty and Responsiveness Shape Party Identification and Democracy*. New York: Oxford University Press. 49–63.

36. Anson, Ian. 2016. "A Tale of Two GDPs: Why Republicans and Democrats Live in Different Economic Realities." *The Conversation*. August 28.

37. *Ibid*., 179.

38. Finkel, Eli J., Christopher A. Bail, Mina Cikara, Peter H. Ditto, Shanto Iyengar, Samara Klar, Lilliana Mason, Mary C. McGrath, Brendan Nyhan, David G. Rand, Linda J. Skitka, Joshua A. Tucker, Jay J. Van Bavel, Cynthia S. Wang, and

James N. Druckman. 2020. "Political Sectarianism in America." *Science*. Vol. 370, Issue 6516.

39. Mason, Lilliana. 2018. *Uncivil Agreement: How Politics Became Our Identity*. Chicago: The University of Chicago Press. 74–76.

40. Lawson, Rebecca. 2006. "The Science of Cycology: Failure to Understand How Everyday Objects Work." *Memory and Cognition*. Vol. 34. 1667–1675.

41. Kahneman, Daniel. 2011. *Thinking, Fast and Slow*. New York: Farrar, Straus, and Giroux. 199–202.

42. Fernbach, Philip M., Todd Rogers, Craig R. Fox, and Steven A. Sloman. 2013. "Political Extremism Is Supported by an Illusion of Understanding." *Psychological Science*. Vol. 20, Issue 10. 1–8.

43. Pope, Alexander. 1711. *An Essay on Criticism*. London: W. Lewis. 14.

44. Petrocelli, John V. 2021. *The Life-Changing Science of Detecting Bullshit*. New York: St. Martin's Press.

45. Lavine, Howard, Christopher Johnston, and Marco Steenbergen. 2012. *The Ambivalent Partisan: How Critical Loyalty Promotes Democracy*. New York: Oxford University Press. 21.

46. *Ibid.*, 94.

47. *Ibid.*, 95–96.

48. *Ibid.*, 25.

49. Saslow, Eli. 2016. "The White Flight of Derek Black." *The Washington Post*. October 15.

50. *Ibid.*

51. *Ibid.*

52. *Ibid.*

53. *Ibid.*

54. *The Daily Show with Trevor Noah*. 2018. Comedy Central. September 19.

55. Washington, George. 1796. "Transcript of President Washington's Farewell Address." ourdocuments.gov. Accessed February 2021.

Chapter 3

1. Seife, Charles. 2014. *Virtual Unreality: Just Because the Internet Told You, How Do You Know It's True?* New York: Viking. 73.

2. Festinger, Leon, Henry W. Riecken, and Stanley Schachter. 2009. *When Prophecy Fails: A Social and Psychological Study of a Modern Group that Predicted the Destruction of the World*. New York: Harper & Row Publishers. 62.

3. *Ibid.*, 139–173.

4. *Ibid.*, 228–229.

5. Mason, Lilliana. 2018. *Uncivil Agreement: How Politics Became Our Identity*. Chicago: The University of Chicago Press. 55.

6. Pew Research Center. 2017. "The Partisan Divide on Political Values Grows Even Wider." *Pew Research Center*. October 5. Pew Research Center. 2016. "Partisanship and Political Animosity in 2016." *Pew Research Center*. June 22.

7. Guess, Andrew, Benjamin Lyons, Brendan Nyhan, and Jason Reifler. "Avoiding the Echo Chamber About Echo Chambers: Why Selective Exposure to Like-Minded Political News Is Less Prevalent Than You Think." *Knight Foundation*. 1–25.

8. Gleason, Abbott, and Martha C. Nussbaum. 2005. *On Nineteen Eighty-Four: Orwell and Our Future*. Princeton: Princeton University Press. 1.

9. Guess, Andrew, Benjamin Lyons, Brendan Nyhan, and Jason Reifler. "Avoiding the Echo Chamber About Echo Chambers: Why Selective Exposure to Like-Minded Political News Is Less Prevalent Than You Think." *Knight Foundation*. 1–25.

10. Stroud, Natalie J. 2011. *Niche News: The Politics of News Choice*. New York: Oxford University Press. 14–20.

11. Lodge, Milton, and Charles S. Taber. 2013. *The Rationalizing Voter*. New York: Cambridge University Press. 162.

12. Stroud, Natalie J. 2011. *Niche News: The Politics of News Choice*. New York: Oxford University Press.

13. *Ibid.*, 76.

14. Frimer, Jeremy, Linda Skitka, and Matt Motyl. 2017. "Liberals and Conservatives Have One Thing in Common: Zero Interest in Opposing Views." *The Los Angeles Times*. January 4.

15. Iyengar, Shanto, and Kyu S. Hahn. 2009. "Red Media, Blue Media: Evidence of Ideological Selectivity in Media Use." *Journal of Communication*. Vol. 59. 19–39.

16. Druckman, James N., Matthew S. Levendusky, and Audrey McLain. 2018. "No Need to Watch: How the Effects of Partisan Media Can Spread via Interpersonal

Discussions." *American Journal of Political Science*. Vol. 62, No. 1. 99–112.

17. Stroud, Natalie J. 2011. *Niche News: The Politics of News Choice*. New York: Oxford University Press. 54.

18. Levendusky, Matthew. 2013. *How Partisan Media Polarizes America*. Chicago: The University of Chicago Press. 14.

19. Stroud, Natalie J. 2011. *Niche News: The Politics of News Choice*. New York: Oxford University Press. 59.

20. Himelboim, Itai, Stephen McCreery, and Marc Smith. 2013. "Birds of a Feather Tweet Together: Integrating Network and Content Analyses to Examine Cross-Ideology Exposure on Twitter." *Journal of Computer-Mediated Communication*. Vol. 18. 154–174.

21. Bakshy, Eytan, Solomon Messing, and Lada A. Adamic. 2015. "Exposure to Ideologically Diverse News and Opinion on Facebook." *Science*. Vol. 348, No. 6239.

22. Peterson, Andrea. 2014. "Liberals Are More Likely to Unfriend You Over Politics—Online and Off." *The Washington Post*. October 21.

23. El-Bermawy, Mostafa M. 2016. "Your Filter Bubble Is Destroying Democracy." *Wired*. November 18.

24. Thompson, Derek. 2014. "The Algorithm Economy: Inside the Formulas of Facebook and Amazon." *The Atlantic*. March 12.

25. Bleiberg, Joshua, and Darrell M. West. 2015. "Political Polarization on Facebook." Brookings. May 13.

26. Eakin, Emily. 2004. "Study Finds a Nation of Polarized Readers." *The New York Times*. March 13.

27. Tufekci, Zeynep. 2018. "YouTube, the Great Radicalizer." *The New York Times*. March 10.

28. *Ibid*.

29. Lewis, Rebecca. 2018. "Alternative Influence: Broadcasting the Reactionary Right on YouTube." *Data and Society*. September 18.

30. Ledwich, Mark, and Anna Zaitsev. 2019. "Algorithmic Extremism: Examining YouTube's Rabbit Hole of Radicalization." *arXivLabs*. December 24.

31. Levendusky, Matthew. 2013. *How Partisan Media Polarizes America*. Chicago: The University of Chicago Press. 94–109.

32. *Ibid*.

33. *Ibid*., 117–129.

34. *Ibid*., 94–109.

35. Stroud, Natalie J. 2011. *Niche News: The Politics of News Choice*. New York: Oxford University Press. 136.

36. Levendusky, Matthew. 2013. *How Partisan Media Polarizes America*. Chicago: The University of Chicago Press. 51.

37. Sunstein, Cass R. 2017. *#Republic: Divided Democracy in the Age of Social Media*. Princeton: Princeton University Press. 68.

38. *Ibid*., 69.

39. *Ibid*.

40. Levendusky, Matthew. 2013. *How Partisan Media Polarizes America*. Chicago: The University of Chicago Press. 67.

41. Druckman, James N., Matthew S. Levendusky, and Audrey McLain. 2018. "No Need to Watch: How the Effects of Partisan Media Can Spread via Interpersonal Discussions." *American Journal of Political Science*. Vol. 62, No. 1.

42. Stroud, Natalie J. 2011. *Niche News: The Politics of News Choice*. New York: Oxford University Press. 131.

43. *Ibid*., 119–125 and 175–177.

44. Mason, Lilliana. 2018. *Uncivil Agreement: How Politics Became Our Identity*. Chicago: The University of Chicago Press. 141.

45. Ketcham, Ralph, ed. 1986. "Brutus, Essay I." *The Federalist Papers and the Constitutional Convention Debates*. New York: Mentor. 277.

46. Wills, Garry, ed. 1982. "Federalist No. 70." *The Federalist Papers by Alexander Hamilton, James Madison, and John Jay*. New York: Bantam Books. 358.

47. Wills, Garry, ed. 1982. "Federalist No. 51." *The Federalist Papers by Alexander Hamilton, James Madison, and John Jay*. New York: Bantam Books. 265.

48. Mercier, Hugo, and Hélène Landemore. 2012. "Reasoning Is for Arguing: Understanding the Successes and Failures of Deliberation." *Political Psychology*. Vol. 33, Issue 2.

49. Sunstein, Cass R. 2017. *#Republic: Divided Democracy in the Age of Social Media*. Princeton: Princeton University Press. 262.

50. Frimer, Jeremy, Linda Skitka, and Matt Motyl. 2017. "Liberals and Conservatives Have One Thing in Common: Zero Interest in Opposing Views." *The Los Angeles Times*. January 4.

51. Guess, Andrew, Benjamin Lyons, Brendan Nyhan, and Jason Reifler. "Avoiding the Echo Chamber About Echo Chambers: Why Selective Exposure to Like-Minded Political News Is Less Prevalent Than You Think." *Knight Foundation.* Stroud, Natalie J. 2011. *Niche News: The Politics of News Choice.* New York: Oxford University Press. 63.

52. Druckman, James N., Matthew S. Levendusky, and Audrey McLain. 2018. "No Need to Watch: How the Effects of Partisan Media Can Spread via Interpersonal Discussions." *American Journal of Political Science.* Vol. 62, No. 1. Guess, Andrew, Benjamin Lyons, Brendan Nyhan, and Jason Reifler. "Avoiding the Echo Chamber About Echo Chambers: Why Selective Exposure to Like-Minded Political News Is Less Prevalent Than You Think." *Knight Foundation.*

53. Guess, Andrew, Benjamin Lyons, Brendan Nyhan, and Jason Reifler. "Avoiding the Echo Chamber About Echo Chambers: Why Selective Exposure to Like-Minded Political News Is Less Prevalent Than You Think." *Knight Foundation.*

54. Leslie, Ian. 2014. *Curious: The Desire to Know and Why Your Future Depends on It.* New York: Basic Books. xix–xx.

55. Kahan, Dan M., Ashley Landrum, Katie Carpenter, Laura Helft, and Kathleen Hall Jamieson. 2017. "Science Curiosity and Political Information Processing." *Political Psychology.* January 26.

56. Clay, Nadine. 2020. "How to Cultivate Your Curiosity." *Medium.com.* July 10.

57. Eikanas, Marvae. 2017. "12 Ways to Cultivate Curiosity." *leadlifewell.com.* November 7.

58. Bail, Christopher, Lisa Argyle, Taylor Brown, John Bumpus, Haohan Chen, M.B. Fallin Hunzaker, Jaemin Lee, Marcus Mann, Friedolin Merhout, and Alexander Volfovsky. 2018. "Exposure to Opposing Views on Social Media Can Increase Political Polarization." *PNAS.* Vol. 115, No. 37. 9216–9221.

59. Klein, Ezra. *Why We're Polarized.* 2020. New York: Avid Reader Press.

60. Levendusky, Matthew. 2013. *How Partisan Media Polarizes America.* Chicago: The University of Chicago Press.

61. Levendusky, Matthew. 2013. *How Partisan Media Polarizes America.* Chicago: The University of Chicago Press. 78.

62. Hess, Amanda. 2017. "How to Escape Your Political Bubble for a Clearer View." *The New York Times.* March 3.

63. Coleman, Peter T. 2021. *The Way Out: How to Overcome Toxic Polarization.* New York: Columbia University Press.

64. Galef, Julia. 2021. *The Scout Mindset: Why Some People See Things Clearly and Others Don't.* New York: Penguin. 182.

65. Lai, Yvonne. 2006. "Never Discuss Politics, Religion, or the Great Pumpkin." *ABC News.* October 27.

66. Mutz, Diana C. 2006. *Hearing the Other Side: Deliberative versus Participatory Democracy.* Cambridge: Cambridge University Press. 71-79.

67. Coleman, Peter T. 2021. *The Way Out: How to Overcome Toxic Polarization.* New York: Columbia University Press.

68. Rossiter, Erin. 2021. "The Consequences of Interparty Conversation on Outparty Affect and Stereotypes." *Work in Progress.* April 1.

69. Druckman, James N., Matthew S. Levendusky, and Audrey McLain. 2018. "No Need to Watch: How the Effects of Partisan Media Can Spread via Interpersonal Discussions." *American Journal of Political Science.* Vol. 62, No. 1.

70. Fishkin, James, Alice Siu, Larry Diamond, and Norman Bradburn. 2021. "Is Deliberation an Antidote to Extreme Partisan Polarization? Reflections on America in One Room." *American Political Science Review.* June 14.

71. Shi, Feng, Misha Teplitskiy, Eamon Duede, and James A. Evans. 2019. "The Wisdom of Polarized Crowds." *Nature Human Behaviour.* 3, 329-336.

72. Erisen, Elif, and Cengiz Erisen. 2012. "The Effect of Social Networks on the Quality of Political Thinking." *Political Psychology.* Vol. 33, No. 6.

73. Page, Scott E. 2007. *The Difference: How the Power of Diversity Creates Better Groups, Firms, Schools, and Societies.* Princeton: Princeton University Press. 153.

74. Mercier, Hugo, and Dan Sperber. 2017. *The Enigma of Reason.* Cambridge: Harvard University Press. 233–234.

75. *Ibid.,* 10.

76. *Ibid.,* 310.

77. *Ibid.,* 310–314.

78. Oldfield, J.R. *Popular Politics and British Anti-Slavery: The Mobilization of Public Opinion Against the Slave Trade,*

1787–1807. London: Routledge. 83.
79. Kaufmann, Chaim D., and Robert Pape. 1999. "Explaining Costly International Moral Action: Britain's Sixty-Year Campaign Against the Atlantic Slave Trade." *International Organization*. Vol. 53, No. 4. 631–688.
80. Mercier, Hugo, and Dan Sperber. 2017. *The Enigma of Reason*. Cambridge: Harvard University Press. 274.
81. Coleman, Peter T. 2021. *The Way Out: How to Overcome Toxic Polarization*. New York: Columbia University Press. 151.
82. Stone, Douglas, Bruce Patton, and Sheila Heen. 2010. *Difficult Conversations: How to Discuss What Matters Most*. New York: Penguin.
83. Coleman, Peter T. 2021. *The Way Out: How to Overcome Toxic Polarization*. New York: Columbia University Press.
84. Boghossian, Peter, and James Lindsay. 2019. *How to Have Impossible Conversations: A Very Practical Guide*. New York: Lifelong Books. 13.
85. Pinsker, Joe. 2020. "If Someone Shares the 'Plandemic' Video, How Should You Respond?" *The Atlantic*. May 9.
86. Boghossian, Peter, and James Lindsay. 2019. *How to Have Impossible Conversations: A Very Practical Guide*. New York: Lifelong Books. 102.
87. Resnick, Brian. 2020. "How to Talk Someone Out of Bigotry." *Vox*. January 29.
88. Boghossian, Peter, and James Lindsay. 2019. *How to Have Impossible Conversations: A Very Practical Guide*. New York: Lifelong Books. 19-22.
89. Mill, John Stewart. 1965. *Principles of Political Economy*. Toronto: University of Toronto Press.
90. Levendusky, Matthew. 2013. *How Partisan Media Polarizes America*. Chicago: The University of Chicago Press. 16.
91. Nyhan, Brendan. 2012. "Biases Abound." *Open Transcripts*. Berkman Klein Center for Internet & Society. March 6.

Chapter 4

1. Hastorf, Albert H., and Hadley Cantril. 1954. "They Saw a Game; a Case Study." *The Journal of Abnormal and Social Psychology*. Vol. 49, No. 1. 129–134.
2. *Ibid.*
3. Kahan, Dan M., David A. Hoffman, Donald Braman, Danieli Evans, and Jeffrey J. Rachlinski. 2012. "They Saw a Protest: Cognitive Illiberalism and the Speech-Conduct Distinction." *Cornell Law Faculty Publications*. Paper 400.
4. *Ibid.*
5. *Ibid.*
6. Swift, Art. 2016. "Americans' Trust in Mass Media Sinks to New Low." *Gallup*. September 14.
7. Vielma, Antonio Jose. 2016. "The Only Things People Hate More Than the Media Are Putin and Trump." *CNBC*. September 21.
8. GSS Data Explorer. 2021. "Confidence in the Press." *NORC at the University of Chicago*. gssdataexplorer.norc.org.
9. Knight Foundation. 2018. "Indicators of News Media Trust." knightfoundation.org. September 11.
10. Niven, David. 2002. *Tilt? The Search for Media Bias*. Westport: Praeger Publishers. ix. Jones, Jeffrey M. 2018. "Americans: Much Misinformation, Bias, Inaccuracy in News." *Gallup*. June 20.
11. Atkins, Larry. 2016. *Skewed: A Critical Thinker's Guide to Media Bias*. New York: Prometheus. 131.
12. Rauch, Jonathan. 2021. *The Constitution of Knowledge: A Defense of Truth*. Washington, D.C.: Brookings Institution Press.
13. Mitchell, Amy, Jefferey Gottfried, Michael Barthel, and Elisa Shearer. 2016. "The Modern News Consumer: Trust and Accuracy." *Pew Research Center*. July 7.
14. D'Alessio, Dave. 2013. *Media Bias in Presidential Election Coverage, 1948–2008*. New York: Lexington Books.
15. D'Alessio, Dave, and Mike Allen. 2000. "Media Bias in Presidential Elections: A Meta-Analysis." *Journal of Communication*. Vol. 50, Issue 4. 133–156.
16. Budak, Ceren, Sharad Goel, and Justin M. Rao. 2016. "Fair and Balanced? Quantifying Media Bias Through Crowdsourced Content Analysis." *Public Opinion Quarterly*. Vol. 80, Issue S1.
17. Niven, David. 2002. *Tilt? The Search for Media Bias*. Westport: Praeger Publishers.
18. D'Alessio, Dave. 2013. *Media Bias in Presidential Election Coverage, 1948–2008*. New York: Lexington Books.
19. Novella, Steven. 2018. *The Skeptics'*

Notes—Chapter 4

Guide to the Universe: How to Know What's Really Real in a World Increasingly Full of Fake. New York: Grand Central Publishing. 30.

20. Baum, Matthew A., and Phil Gussin. 2008. "In the Eye of the Beholder: How Information Shortcuts Shape Individual Perceptions of Bias in the Media." *Quarterly Journal of Political Science*. Vol. 3, No. 1. 1–31.

21. *Ibid.*, 7.

22. *Ibid.*

23. Ladd, Jonathan M. 2010. "The Neglected Power of Elite Opinion Leadership to Produce Antipathy Toward the News Media: Evidence from a Survey Experiment." *Political Behavior*. Vol. 32. 36.

24. Stroud, Natalie J. 2011. *Niche News: The Politics of News Choice*. New York: Oxford University Press.

25. Vallone, R.P., L. Ross, and M. R. Lepper. 1985. "The Hostile Media Phenomenon: Biased Perception and Perceptions of Media Bias in Coverage of the Beirut Massacre." *Journal of Personality and Social Psychology*. Vol. 49, No. 3. 577–585.

26. *Ibid.*

27. *Ibid.*

28. *Ibid.*

29. Dalton, Russel J., Paul A. Beck, and Robert Huckfeldt. 1998. "Partisan Cues and the Media: Information Flows in the 1992 Presidential Election." *American Political Science Review*, 92, 111–126.

30. Schmitt, Kathleen M., Albert G. Gunther, and Janice L. Liebhart. 2004. "Why Partisans See Mass Media as Biased." *Communications Research*. Vol. 31, No. 6. 623–641.

31. D'Alessio, Dave. 2013. *Media Bias in Presidential Election Coverage, 1948–2008*. New York: Lexington Books.

32. Schmitt, Kathleen M., Albert G. Gunther, and Janice L. Liebhart. 2004. "Why Partisans See Mass Media as Biased." *Communications Research*. Vol. 31, No. 6. 623–641.

33. Kiely, Eugene. 2016. "A Guide to Clinton's Emails." *factcheck.org*. July 5. Bump, Philip. 2016. "23 Things Donald Trump Has Said That Would Have Doomed Another Candidate." *The Washington Post*. June 17.

34. Klein, Ezra. 2017. "Was the Democratic Primary Rigged?" *VOX*. November 14.

35. Vallone, Robert P., Lee Ross, and Mark R. Lepper. 1985. "The Hostile Media Phenomenon: Biased Perception and Perceptions of Media Bias in Coverage of the Beirut Massacre." *Journal of Personality and Social Psychology*. Vol. 49, No. 3. 577–585.

36. D'Alessio, Dave. 2013. *Media Bias in Presidential Election Coverage, 1948–2008*. New York: Lexington Books.

37. Hubbard, Ben. 2020. "The Killing of General Qassim Suleimani: What We Know Since the U.S. Airstrike. *The New York Times*. January 4.

38. Lichter, S. Robert, Stanley Rotham, and Linda S. Lichter. 1986. *The Media Elite: America's New Powerbrokers*. New York: Hastings House.

39. O'Toole, Garrison. 2020. "The Duty of Newspapers Is to Comfort the Afflicted and to Afflict the Comforted. *quoteinvestigator.com*.

40. Lichter, S. Robert, Stanley Rotham, and Linda S. Lichter. 1986. *The Media Elite: America's New Powerbrokers*. New York: Hastings House.

41. *Ibid.*, 86.

42. *Ibid.*, 115.

43. D'Alessio, Dave. 2013. *Media Bias in Presidential Election Coverage, 1948–2008*. New York: Lexington Books. 24.

44. Society of Professional Journalists. 2020. Code of Ethics. *spj.org*.

45. D'Alessio, Dave. 2013. *Media Bias in Presidential Election Coverage, 1948–2008*. New York: Lexington Books. 23. Budak, Ceren, Sharad Goel, and Justin M. Rao. 2016. "Fair and Balanced? Quantifying Media Bias Through Crowdsourced Content Analysis." *Public Opinion Quarterly*. Vol. 80, Issue S1.

46. Patterson, Thomas. 2016. "News Coverage of the 2016 General Election: How the Press Failed the Voters." *shorensteincenter.org*.

47. *Ibid.*

48. Kaid, Lynda Lee, and Christina Holtz-Bacha. Eds. "Media Bias." *Encyclopedia of Political Communication*. Online.

49. Hartmann, Margaret. 2017. "How the Roy Moore Allegations Were Covered on the Right." *New York* Magazine. November 10.

50. Kaid, Lynda Lee, and Christina Holtz-Bacha, Eds. "Media Bias."

Encyclopedia of Political Communication. Online.

51. Kovach, Bill, and Tom Rosenstiel. 2010. *Blur: How to Know What's True in the Age of Information Overload.* New York: Bloomsbury.

52. Ibid.

53. Belson, Ken. 2017. "Multiple Weapons Found in Las Vegas Gunman's Hotel Room." *The New York Times.* October 2.

54. Nightly News Full Broadcast. 2017. October 2. https://www.nbcnews.com/nightly-news-netcast/video/nightly-news-full-broadcast-oct-2-1060317763849.

55. Kristof, Nicholas. 2017. "We Can Act Before the Next Mass Shooting." *The New York Times.* October 5, 2017. A23.

56. Hannity, Sean. 2017. "Rich and Kaya Jones Talk Feeling of Unity Before Las Vegas Attack." *foxnews.com.* October 2.

57. Christensen, Tyler. 2018. "Journalism 101: What Is an Editorial, Anyway?" *The Missoulian.* August 5.

58. Budak, Ceren, Sharad Goel, and Justin M. Rao. 2016. "Fair and Balanced? Quantifying Media Bias Through Crowdsourced Content Analysis." *Public Opinion Quarterly.* Vol. 80, Issue S1.

59. Coles, Isabel, Ghassan Adnan, and Michael R. Gordon. 2020. "U.S. Strike Ordered by Trump Kills Key Iranian Military Leader in Baghdad." *The Wall Street Journal.* January 3.

60. Moran, Lee. 2020. "Lou Dobbs Turns His Adulation of Donald Trump Up Yet Another Ridiculous Notch." *huffpost.com.* January 4.

61. The Young Turks. 2020. "The REAL Reason Trump Attacked Iran." *facebook.com.* January 3.

62. Mitchell, Amy, Jeffrey Gottfried, Michael Barthel, and Nami Sumida. 2018. "Distinguishing Between Factual and Opinion Statements in the News." *Pew Research Center.* June 18.

63. Ibid.

64. Axelrod, Tal. 2019. "Poll: 57 percent of Republicans Approve of Trump's Syria Withdrawal." *The Hill.* October 16.

65. Mitchell, Amy, Jeffrey Gottfried, Michael Barthel, and Nami Sumida. 2018. "Distinguishing Between Factual and Opinion Statements in the News." *Pew Research Center.* June 18.

66. Glum, Julia. 2017. "Some Republicans Still Think Obama Was Born in Kenya as Trumps Resurrects Birther Conspiracy Theory." *Newsweek.* December 11.

67. Mitchell, Amy, Jeffrey Gottfried, Michael Barthel, and Nami Sumida. 2018. "Distinguishing Between Factual and Opinion Statements in the News." *Pew Research Center.* June 18.

68. Ibid.

69. Long, Heather. 2019. "U.S. Unemployment Fell to 3.6 Percent, Lowest Since 1969." *The Washington Post.* May 3.

70. Cournoyer, Caroline. 2019. "Trump Promised to Eliminate the National Debt. It Has Risen by $3 Trillion." *CBS News.* October 29.

71. Levendusky, Matthew. 2013. *How Partisan Media Polarizes America.* Chicago: The University of Chicago Press. 11.

72. Ibid., 25–35.

73. Feldman, Lauren. 2011. "Partisan Differences in Opinionated News Perceptions: A Test of the Hostile Media Effect." *Political Behavior.* 33: 407–432.

74. Stroud, Natalie J. 2011. *Niche News: The Politics of News Choice.* New York: Oxford University Press.

75. Feldman, Lauren. 2011. "Partisan Differences in Opinionated News Perceptions: A Test of the Hostile Media Effect." *Political Behavior.* 33: 407–432. Coe, Kevin, David Tewksbury, Bradley J. Bond, Kristin L. Drogos, Robert W. Porter, Ashley Yahn, and Yuanyuan Zhang. 2008. "Hostile News: Partisan Use and Perceptions of Cable News Programming." *Journal of Communication.* 58: 201–219.

76. Mitchell, Amy, Jefferey Gottfried, Michael Barthel, and Elisa Shearer. 2016. "The Modern News Consumer: Trust and Accuracy." *Pew Research Center.* July 7.

77. Gunther, Albert C., Cindy T. Christen, Janice L. Liebhart, and Stella Chih-Yun Chia. 2001. "Congenial Public, Contrary Press, and Biased Estimates of the Climate of Opinion." *Public Opinion Quarterly.* Vol. 65, No. 3. 295–320.

78. Sullivan, Margaret. 2017. "Polls Show Americans Distrust the Media. But Talk to Them, and It's a Very Different Story." *The Washington Post.* December 28.

79. Ibid.

80. Jones, Bradley. 2019. "Majority of Americans Continue to Say That Immigrants Strengthen the U.S." *Pew Research Center.* January 31. Kafura, Craig and

Bettina Hammer. 2019. "Republicans and Democrats in Different Worlds on Immigration." *The Chicago Council on Global Affairs*. October 8.
  81. Davis, Leslie, and Hannah Hartig. 2019. "Two-Thirds of Americans Favor Raising Federal Minimum Wage to $15 an Hour." *Pew Research Center*. July 30.
  82. Mitchell, Amy, Jeffrey Gottfried, Michael Barthel, and Nami Sumida. 2018. "Distinguishing Between Factual and Opinion Statements in the News." *Pew Research Center*. June 18.
  83. Limbaugh, Rush. 2019. "Trump Did It! The American Economy Is the Envy of the World." *rushlimbaugh.com*. May 3.
  84. Sanders, Lindley. 2020. "The Difference Between Which News Outlets Republicans and Democrats Trust." *yougov.com*. June 18.

Chapter 5

  1. Bacon, Francis. 1902. *Novum Organum*. New York: P. F. Collier & Son. 23.
  2. Franklin, Benjamin. 1982. *The Autobiography and Other Writings by Benjamin Franklin*. New York: Bantam Books. 32–33.
  3. Hetherington, Marc, and Jonathan Weiler. 2018. *Prius or Pickup: How the Answers to Four Simple Questions Explain America's Great Divide*. Boston: Houghton Mifflin Harcourt. 134.
  4. Ditto, Peter H., Brittany S. Liu, Cory J. Clark, Sean P. Wojcik, Eric E. Chen, Rebecca H. Grady, Jared B. Celniker, and Joanne F. Zinger. 2018. "At Least Bias Is Bipartisan: A Meta-Analytic Comparison of Partisan Bias in Liberals and Conservatives." *Perspectives on Psychological Science*. Vol. 14, Issue 2.
  5. Lord, Charles G., Lee Ross, and Mark R. Lepper. 1979. "Biased Assimilation and Attitude Polarization: The Effects of Prior Theories on Subsequently Considered Evidence." *Journal of Personality and Social Psychology*. Vol. 37, No. 11. 2100–2101.
  6. Ibid.
  7. Ibid., 2102.
  8. Taber, Charles S., and Milton Lodge. 2011. "Motivated Skepticism in the Evaluation of Political Beliefs." *American Journal of Political Science*. Vol. 50, No. 3. 762.
  9. Ibid.

  10. Nir, Lilach. 2011. "Motivated Reasoning and Public Opinion Perception." *The Public Opinion Quarterly*. Vol. 75, No. 3. 504–532. Druckman, James N. 2012. "The Politics of Motivation." *Critical Review*. Vol. 24, No. 2. 199–216.

Chapter 6

  1. Illing, Sean. 2017. "America's Misinformation Problem Explained: It's Better—and Worse—Than You Think." *Vox*. November 6.
  2. Tillman, Zoe. 2017. "Pizzagate Gunman Is Sentenced to Four Years in Prison." *BuzzFeed News*. June 22. Miller, Michael E. 2021. "The Pizzagate Gunman Is Out of Prison. Conspiracy Theories Are Out of Control." *The Seattle Times*. February 16.
  3. Goldman, Adam. 2016. "The Comet Ping Pong Gunman Answers Our Reporter's Questions." *The New York Times*. December 7.
  4. Boller, Paul F. 1996. *Presidential Campaigns*. New York: Oxford University Press. 9–13.
  5. Ingram, Mathew. 2017. "Fake News Isn't a New Problem, and We're Better Equipped to Fight It Now." *Fortune*. February 8. Guilford, Gwyn. 2016. "Fake News Isn't a Recent Problem in the U.S.—It Almost Destroyed Abraham Lincoln." *Quartz*. November 28.
  6. NPR Staff. 2016. "No, FDR Did Not Know the Japanese Were Going to Bomb Pearl Harbor." *NPR*. December 6. Kaiser, David. 2016. "Ted Cruz Is Not the First Politician to Cause Controversy with a Doctored Photo." *Time*. February 19.
  7. Silverman, Craig. 2016. "This Analysis Shows How Viral Fake Election News Stories Outperformed Real News on Facebook." *BuzzFeed News*. November 16. Gore, D'Angelo. 2016. "A Fake Mike Pence Quote." *factcheck.org*. December 21.
  8. Fagan, Kaylee. 2018. "A Viral Video That Appeared to Show Obama Calling Trump a 'Dipshit' Shows a Disturbing New Trend Called Deepfakes." *Business Insider*. April 17. Ghaffary, Shirin. "Facebook Is Banning Deepfake Videos." *Vox*. January 7.
  9. Santhanam, Laura. 2020. "American Voters Worry They Can't Spot Misleading Information, Poll Finds." *PBS*. January 21.

10. Harper, Craig A., and Thom Baguley. "You Are Fake News! Ideological (A)symmetries in Perceptions of Media Legitimacy." *PsyArXiv*. January 23.

11. *Ibid.*

12. Silverman, Craig, and Jeremy Singer-Vine. 2016. "Most Americans Who See Fake News Believe It, New Survey Says." *BuzzFeed News*. December 6.

13. Fieldstadt, Elisha. 2016. "Don't Get Fooled by These Fake News Sites." *CBS News*. December 2.

14. Sichermann, Stefan. 2018. "Trump Wants to Deport American Indians to India." *The Postillion*. July 6.

15. Caron, Christina. 2017. "Paul Horner, Fake News Writer Who Took Credit for Trump Victory, Dies at 38." *The New York Times*. September 27.

16. *Ibid.*

17. Greenberg, John. 2015. "Donald Trump Says Crime Statistics Show Blacks Kill 81 Percent of White Homicide Victims." *PolitiFact*. November 23.

18. United States Department of Justice. 2015. "Crime in the United States." Retrieved from: ucr.fbi.gov/crime-in-the-u.s/2015/crime-in-the-u.s.-2015/tables/expanded_homicide_data_table_6_murder_race_and_sex_of_vicitm_by_race_and_sex_of_offender_2015.xls.

19. MacGuill, Dan. 2018. "Have Leaked Documents Been Published Showing Donald Trump's 'True' Weight? *Snopes.com*. May 16.

20. Voltaire. 1972. "A Letter to D'Argental." *The Complete Works of Voltaire*. Vol. XXII of the Correspondence. Oxford: The Voltaire Foundation. 76.

21. Boller, Paul F., and John George. 1989. *They Never Said It: A Book of Fake Quotes, Misquotes, and Misleading Attributions*. New York: Oxford University Press.

22. *Ibid.*

23. Bugliosi, Vincent. 2007. *Reclaiming History: The Assassination of President John F. Kennedy*. New York: W. W. Norton & Company. An original recording of the interview can be found at https://www.jfklibrary.org/asset-viewer/archives/JFKWHA/1963/JFKWHA-212-002/JFKWHA-212-002 (13:00–17:00).

24. Campbell, Joseph W. 2016. *Getting It Wrong: Debunking the Greatest Myths in American Journalism*. Oakland: University of California Press.

25. Search the University of Michigan's Collected Works of Abraham Lincoln at: https://quod.lib.umich.edu/l/lincoln/

26. Campbell, Joseph W. 2016. *Getting It Wrong: Debunking the Greatest Myths in American Journalism*. Oakland: University of California Press.

27. Jacobson, Louis. 2011. "Mitt Romney Ad Charges Obama Said, 'If we keep talking about the economy, we're going to lose.'" *PolitiFact*. November 22.

28. Montopoli, Brian. 2011. "Mitt Romney Attack Ad Misleadingly Quotes Obama." *CBS News*. November 23.

29. Carroll, Lauren. 2016. "Super PAC Ad Says Trump Likes War, Even Nuclear, but That Needs Context." *PolitiFact*. June 19.

30. *Ibid.*

31. Benner, Jeffrey. 2001. "He's the Real Tourist Guy." *Wired*. November 20.

32. Johnson, Ken. 2012. "Their Cheating Art: Reality and Illusion." *The New York Times*. October 11.

33. Farid, Hany. 2007. "Digital Doctoring: Can We Trust Photographs?" Hanover: Dartmouth.

34. Seife, Charles. 2014. *Virtual Unreality: Just Because the Internet Told You, How Do You Know It's True?* New York: Viking Press. 100–101.

35. Mikkelson, David. 2002. "Does This Photograph Show President Bush Reading a Book Upside-Down?" *Snopes.com*. September 24.

36. Mikkelson, David. 2015. "False: Barack Obama with Upside Down Telephone." *Snopes.com*. August 9.

37. Mikkelson, David. 2012. "Mitt Romney 'Money' Shirts." *Snopes.com*. March 6.

38. Evon, Dan. 2017. "Did President Trump Experience Diarrhea on a Golf Course?" *Snopes.com*. April 10.

39. Moye, David. 2018. "Fake Photo of Trump 'Rescuing' Flood Victims Goes Viral." *Huffington Post*. September 24.

40. Reuters Staff. 2020. "False Claim: Photograph Shows Joe Biden Groping a Reporter." *Reuters*. April 22.

41. Swenson, Ali. 2021. "Photo Appearing to Show Biden Asleep in Oval Office Is Fake." *Associated Press*. February 8.

42. Sacchi, Dario L. M., Franca Agnoli, and Elizabeth Loftus. 2007. "Changing History: Doctored Photographs Affect

Memory for Past Public Events." *Applied Cognitive Psychology*. Vol. 21. 1005–1022.

43. Frenda, Steven J., Eric D. Knowles, William Saletan, and Elizabeth Loftus. 2013. "False Memories of Fabricated Political Events." *Journal of Experimental Psychology*. Vol. 49. 280–286.

44. http://transcripts.cnn.com/TRANSCRIPTS/0809/07/rs.01.html

45. Jackson, Brooks. 2008. "Picture of Palin Is a Fake. *FactCheck.org*. September 8.

46. Palma, Bethania. 2017. "Did Muslim Federal Judge 'Mahal al Alallaha-Smith' Rule That Two Items of Sharia Law Are Now Legal?" *Snopes.com*. July 25.

47. Lah, Kyung. 2016. "Being a Muslim Judge in the Age of Trump." www.cnn.com/videos/politics/2016/07/06/muslim-judge-trump-lah-pkg.cnn

48. Bump, Phillip. 2018. "Here Are the Tools That Could be Used to Create the Fake News of the Future." *The Washington Post*. February 12.

49. Johnson, Dave. 2020. "Audio Deepfakes: Can Anyone Tell If They're Fake?" *How-To Geek*. August 3.

50. Gault, Matthew. 2016. "After 20 Minutes of Listening, New Adobe Tool Can Make You Say Anything." *Vice*. November 5.

51. Johnson, Dave. 2020. "Audio Deepfakes: Can Anyone Tell If They're Fake?" *How-To Geek*. August 3.

52. Copeland, Cody. 2021. "Is There a Way to Spot Deepfakes?" *Grunge*. April 2.

53. Ibid.

54. Turton, William, and Matthew Justus. 2018. "Deepfake Videos Like That of Gal Gadot Porn Are Only Getting More Convincing—and More Dangerous." *Vice*. August 27.

55. Chesney, Robert, and Danielle Citron. 2018. "Deepfakes and the New Disinformation War: The Coming Age of Post-Truth Geopolitics." *Foreign Affairs*. December 11.

56. Chesney, Robert, and Danielle Citron. 2019. "Deep Fakes: A Looming Challenge for Privacy, Democracy, and National Security." *California Law Review*. Vol. 107, No. 6.

57. Christian, Jon. 2018. "Experts Fear Face-Swapping Tech Could Start an International Showdown." *The Outline*. February 1.

58. Chesney, Robert, and Danielle Citron. 2019. "Deep Fakes: A Looming Challenge for Privacy, Democracy, and National Security." *California Law Review*. Vol. 107, No. 6.

59. Haberman, Maggie, and Jonathan Martin. 2017. "Trump Once Said the 'Access Hollywood' Tape Was Real. Now He's Not Sure." *The New York Times*. November 28.

60. Reuters Staff. 2021. "Fact Check: Donald Trump Concession Video Not a 'confirmed deepfake'" *Reuters*. January 11.

61. O'Sullivan, Donie. 2019. "When Seeing Is No Longer Believing: Inside the Pentagon's Race Against Deepfake Videos." *CNN*. Accessed on April 2, 2021.

62. Villasenor, John. 2019. "Artificial Intelligence, Deepfakes, and the Uncertain Future of Truth." *Brookings*. February 14.

63. Swift, Jonathan. 1710. "Number 15." *The Examiner*. Page 2, Column 1.

64. Klass, Brian. 2019. "Deepfakes Are Coming. We're Not Ready." *The Washington Post*. May 14.

65. Cole, Samantha. 2020. "For the Love of God, Not Everything Is a Deepfake." *Vice*. April 27.

66. Putterman, Samantha. 2020. "This Video Shows Trump Looking 'lost and disoriented.'" *PolitiFact*. September 7.

67. International Fact-Checking Network. 2018. "10 Tips for Verifying Viral Social Media Videos." *Poynter*. Accessed on April 5, 2020.

68. Copeland, Cody. 2021. "Is There a Way to Spot Deepfakes?" *Grunge*. April 2.

69. Conley, Nicholas. 2019. "The Untold Truth of Deepfakes." *Grunge*. August 29.

70. Pennycook, Gordon, Ziv Epstein, Mohsen Mosleh, Antonio A. Arechar, Dean Eckles, and David G. Rand. 2021. "Shifting Attention to Accuracy Can Reduce Misinformation Online." *Nature*. March 17.

71. Pennycook, Gordon. Personal Communication, March 22, 2021.

72. Pennycook, Gordon, Ziv Epstein, Mohsen Mosleh, Antonio A. Arechar, Dean Eckles, and David G. Rand. 2021. "Shifting Attention to Accuracy Can Reduce Misinformation Online." *Nature*. March 17.

73. Osmundsen, Mathias, Alexander Bor, Peter Bjerregaard Vahlstrup, Anja

Bechmann, and Michael Bang Petersen. 2021. "Partisan Polarization Is the Primary Psychological Motivation Behind Political Fake News Sharing on Twitter." *American Political Science Review*. May 6.

74. Rauch, Jonathan. 2021. *The Constitution of Knowledge: A Defense of Truth*. Washington, D.C.: Brookings Institution Press.

75. Fazio, Lisa K., Nadia M. Brashier, B. Keith Payne, and Elizabeth J. Marsh. 2015. "Knowledge Does Not Protect Against Illusory Truth." *Journal of Experimental Psychology*. Vol. 144, No. 5. 993–1002.

76. Pennycook, Gordon, Tyrone Cannon, and David G. Rand. 2018. "Prior Exposure Increases Perceived Accuracy of Fake News." *Journal of Experimental Psychology*. Vol. 147, No. 12. 1865–1880.

77. Pennycook, Gordon, Ziv Epstein, Mohsen Mosleh, Antonio A. Arechar, Dean Eckles, and David G. Rand. 2021. "Shifting Attention to Accuracy Can Reduce Misinformation Online." *Nature*. March 17.

78. Harrison, Guy P. 2017. *Think Before You Like: Social Media's Effect on the Brain and the Tools You Need to Navigate Your Newsfeed*. New York: Prometheus.

79. Pennycook, Gordon, Ziv Epstein, Mohsen Mosleh, Antonio A. Arechar, Dean Eckles, and David G. Rand. 2021. "Shifting Attention to Accuracy Can Reduce Misinformation Online." *Nature*. March 17.

80. Kovach, Bill, and Tom Rosenstiel. 2010. *Blur: How to Know What's True in the Age of Information Overload*. New York: Bloomsbury. 7.

81. *Ibid.*, 197.

Chapter 7

1. Wright, Carroll D. 1890. "Seventh Annual Report of the Bureau of Labor and Industrial Statistics." *Joint Documents of the State of Michigan for the Year 1889*. Lansing: State Printer and Binder. 311.

2. Evans, M. Stanton. 2007. *Blacklisted by History: The Untold Story of Senator Joe McCarthy*. New York: Crown Forum. 180–181.

3. Seife, Charles. 2010. *Proofiness: The Dark Arts of Mathematical Deception*. New York: Penguin Group. 1–2.

4. Jackson, Brooks, and Kathleen Hall Jamieson. 2007. *Unspun: Finding Facts in a World of Disinformation*. New York: Random House. 32.

5. World Health Organization. 2018. "Arsenic Fact Sheet." *W.H.O.* February 15.

6. Seelye, Katharine Q. 2001. "EPA to Adopt Clinton Arsenic Standard." *The New York Times*. November 1.

7. Jackson, Brooks, and Kathleen Hall Jamieson. 2007. *Unspun: Finding Facts in a World of Disinformation*. New York: Random House. 32–33.

8. *Ibid.*, 31.

9. *Ibid.*, 32.

10. Huff, Darrell. 1993. *How to Lie with Statistics*. New York: W.W. Norton & Company. 27–28.

11. Editorial Board. 2003. "Law of Averages." *The Washington Post*. February 21.

12. *Ibid.*

13. *Ibid.*

14. Gearan, Anne. 2015. "Brother, Can You Spare a Dollar? Clinton Asking for $1 Donations as Deadline Nears." *The Washington Post*. June 29.

15. *Ibid.*

16. Jacobson, Louis. 2016. "Clinton Claim on Small Donors Is 'Mostly False,' PolitiFact Finds." *NBC News*. March 21. Kurtzleben, Danielle. 2015. "Five Things We've Learned About 2016 Presidential Fundraising." *NPR*. July 16.

17. *Saturday Night Live*. 2016. "Bern Your Enthusiasm." *NBC*. February 7.

18. Jacobson, Louis. 2016. "Clinton Claim on Small Donors Is 'Mostly False,' PolitiFact Finds." *NBC News*. March 21.

19. Best, Joel. 2004. *More Damned Lies and Statistics: How Numbers Confuse Public Issues*. Berkeley: University of California Press. 43.

20. Reagan, Ronald. 2016. "President Reagan's Address to the Nation on Federal Tax Reduction Legislation, July 27, 1981." *YouTube*. May 12.

21. Smith, Gary. 2014. *Standard Deviations: Flawed Assumptions, Tortured Data, and Other Ways to Lie with Statistics*. New York: Overlook Duckworth. 74.

22. *Ibid.*

23. Greenberg, Scott. 2016. "Looking Back at the Bush Tax Cuts, Fifteen Years Later." *The Tax Foundation*. June 7.

24. Levitin, Daniel J. 2016. *A Field Guide to Lies: Critical Thinking in the*

Information Age. New York: Dutton. 29.

25. Markets Now. 2012. "What Will 'Taxmageddon' Cost You?" *Fox Business*. June 22.

26. Collins, Keith. 2015. "Axis of Evil: The Most Misleading Charts of 2015, Fixed." *Quartz*. December 23.

27. Ibid.

28. Zengerle, Jason. 2018. "How the Trump Administration Is Remaking the Courts." *The New York Times Magazine*. August 22.

29. Gramlich, John. 2021. "How Trump Compares to Other Recent Presidents in Appointing Federal Judges." *Pew Research Center*. January 13.

30. Zengerle, Jason. 2018. "How the Trump Administration Is Remaking the Courts." *The New York Times Magazine*. August 22.

31. Roos, Dave. 2020. "How Political Polling Works." *How Stuff Works*. September 2.

32. Hurley, Patrick J. 2008. *A Concise Introduction to Logic*. Belmont, CA: Thomson Learning, Inc.

33. Lopez, German. 2016. "Donald Trump Won the Debate … According to Useless Website Polls That Mean Nothing." *Vox*. September 27. Farley, Robert. 2020. "Survey Says: Trump Misleads on Debate Performances." *FactCheck.org*. February 21.

34. Stelter, Brian. 2016. "The Problem with Donald Trump's 'we won every poll' Claim." *CNN Business*. September 27.

35. Powell, Austin. 2021. "4chan and Reddit Bombarded Debate Polls to Declare Trump the Winner." *Daily Dot*. January 26.

36. Lopez, German. 2016. "Donald Trump Won the Debate … According to Useless Website Polls That Mean Nothing." *Vox*. September 27.

37. Langer, Gary. 2008. "Sampling Error: What It Means." *ABC News*. October 8.

38. Ibid.

39. Kahneman, Daniel. 2011. *Thinking Fast and Slow*. New York: Farrar, Straus, and Giroux. 367.

40. Ibid.

41. Sussman, Dalia. 2010. "Opinion Polling: A Question of What to Ask." *The New York Times*. February 27.

42. Pew Research Center. 2021. "Questionnaire Design." *Pew Research Center*. May 18.

43. Ladd, Everett C. 1994. "Setting the Record Straight on a Holocaust Denial Poll." *The Christian Science Monitor*. July 1.

44. Kagay, Michael R. 1994. "Poll on Doubt of Holocaust Is Corrected." *The New York Times*. July 8.

45. Quinnipiac University Poll. 2018. "Most U.S. Voters Back Life Over Death Penalty." *Quinnipiac University*. March 22.

46. Di Carlo, Matthew. 2011. "Why Do Most Americans Support 'Assistance to The Poor' But Oppose 'Welfare'?" *Albert Shanker Institute*. November 17.

47. Yamaguchi, Masataka. 2014. "U.S. Estates Tax for Non-U.S. Decedents." *Perkins and Company*. November 3.

48. Jackson, Brooks, and Kathleen Hall Jamieson. 2007. *Unspun: Finding Facts in a World of Disinformation*. New York: Random House.

49. Schaffner, Brian F., and Mary Layton Atkinson. 2009. "Taxing Death or Estates? When Frames Influence Citizens' Issue Beliefs." *Winning with Words: The Origins and Impacts of Political Framing*. New York: Routledge. 121–135.

50. Blanton, Dana. 2010. "Fox News Poll: 55% Oppose Health Care Reform." *Fox News*. March 18.

51. Ibid.

52. Silver, Nate. 2009. "Question Order May Bias Fox News Health Care Polling." *FiveThirtyEight*. October 6.

53. Ibid.

54. Sterling, Joe. 2012. "CNN Fact Check: Obama Went on an Apology Tour, Romney and Others Say." *CNN*. October 23. Fox News. 2011. "President Obama the Campaigner-in-Chief?" *Hannity*. November 29. Montopoli, Brian. 2012. "Is President Obama the Apologizer in Chief?" *CBS News*. August 2.

55. Silver, Nate. 2009. "Question Order May Bias Fox News Health Care Polling." *FiveThirtyEight*. October 6.

56. Ellenberg, Jordan. 2014. *How Not to be Wrong: The Power of Mathematical Thinking*. New York: The Penguin Press. 369.

57. Gallup. 2020. "Abortion." *Gallup*. Accessed March 2021.

58. Ellenberg, Jordan. 2014. *How Not to be Wrong: The Power of Mathematical Thinking*. New York: The Penguin Press.

368.
59. *Ibid.*
60. Hill, David. 2012. "Polls on Obamacare Mislead." *The Hill.* March 28.
61. Lincoln, Abraham. 1856. "Speech at Republican Banquet, Chicago Illinois." *Collected Works of Abraham Lincoln.* Vol. 2. Lansing: University of Michigan. 384–386.
62. Staff Writer. 2021. "Absolute v. Relative Change Concepts and Definitions." *Manpower Research and Statistics Department.* March 19.
63. Wheelan, Charles. 2013. *Naked Statistics: Stripping the Dread from the Data.* New York: W. W. Norton & Company. 29.
64. Bump, Philip. 2018. "How to Mislead with Statistics, DHS Secretary Nielsen Edition." *The Washington Post.* January 18.
65. *Ibid.*
66. Kahan, Dan M., Ellen Peters, Erica Dawson, and Paul Slovic. 2013. "Motivated Numeracy and Enlightened Self-Government." *Behavioral Public Policy.* Vol. 1. 54–86.
67. Kaplan, Marty. 2013. "Most Depressing Brain Finding Ever." *Huffington Post.* September 16.
68. Stanovich, Keith. 2009. *What Intelligence Tests Miss: The Psychology of Rational Thought.* New Haven: Yale University Press.
69. Kahan, Dan M., Ellen Peters, Erica Dawson, and Paul Slovic. 2013. "Motivated Numeracy and Enlightened Self-Government." *Behavioral Public Policy.* Vol. 1. 54–86.
70. *Ibid.*
71. Oliphant, Baxter J. 2017. "Bipartisan Support for Some Gun Proposals, Stark Partisan Divisions on Many Others." *Pew Research Center.* June 2013.
72. *Ibid.*
73. *Ibid.*
74. Mooney, Chris. 2013. "Science Confirms: Politics Wrecks Your Ability to do Math." *Mother Jones.* September 4.
75. Starbird, M. 2006. "Meaning from Data: Statistics Made Clear." *The Great Courses.* Chantilly, VA: The Teaching Company. 92.
76. *Ibid.*

Chapter 8

1. O'Toole, Garson. 2018. "He Who Will Not Reason Is a Bigot; He Who Cannot Is a Fool; He Who Dares Not Is a Slave." *Quote Investigator.* September 25.
2. Druckman, James N., Erik Peterson, and Rune Slothuus. 2013. "How Elite Partisan Polarization Affects Public Opinion Formation." *American Political Science Review.* Vol. 107, No. 1.
3. *Ibid.*, 67.
4. Schick, Theodore, and Lewis Vaughn. 2014. *How to Think About Weird Things: Critical Thinking for a New Age.* New York: McGraw Hill. 41.
5. *Ibid.*, 37.
6. *Ibid.*
7. *Ibid.*, 36.
8. Hurley, Patrick J. 2008. *A Concise Introduction to Logic.* California: Wadsworth Cengage Learning.
9. *Ibid.*, 64.
10. Browne, M. Neil, and Stuart M. Keeley. 2010. *Asking the Right Questions: A Guide to Critical Thinking.* New Jersey: Prentice Hall. 90.
11. Levendusky, Matthew. 2013. *How Partisan Media Polarize America.* Chicago: University of Chicago Press. 16–17. Vosoughi, Soroush, Deb Roy, and Sinan Aral. 2018. "The Spread of True and False News Online." *Science.* Vol. 359, Issue 6380. 1146–1151.
12. Groves, Robert M. 2010. "The Structure and Activities of the U.S. Federal Statistical System: History and Recurrent Challenges." *The Annals of the American Academy of Political and Social Science.* August 9.
13. Bureau of Labor Statistics: https://data.bls.gov/timeseries/lns14000000
14. Bryan, Bob. 2017. "Trump Once Called the Jobs Report 'one of the biggest hoaxes in modern politics'—Now He Accepts 'those numbers very proudly.'" *Business Insider.* July 20.
15. Staff Reporter. 2016. "Fact Check: Trump Wildly Inflates Unemployment." *WGRZ News.* February 10.
16. Ingraham, Christopher. 2017. "Nineteen Times Trump Called Jobs Numbers Fake Before They Made Him Look Good." *The Washington Post.* March 10.
17. McKinless, Thomas. 2018. "Schumer Calls on Trump to Address 'Soaring' Gas Prices." *Roll Call.* May 23.
18. Staff Reporter. 2019. "Iran Nuclear

Deal: Key Details." *BBC News.* June 11.

19. Landler, Mark. 2018. "Trump Abandons Iran Nuclear Deal He Long Scorned." *The New York Times.* May 8.

20. Farley, Robert. 2018. "Who's to Blame for Higher Gas Prices?" *FactCheck.org.* May 25.

21. Glader, Paul. 2017. "10 Journalism Brands Where You Find Real Facts Rather than Alternative Facts." *Forbes.* February 1.

22. NPR Ethics Handbook: https://www.npr.org/about-npr/688875732/these-are-the-standards-of-our-journalism. The Society of Professional Journalists Code of Ethics: https://www.spj.org/ethicscode.asp.

23. Flaherty, Anne, and Calvin Woodward. 2018. "AP Fact-Check: 2014 Photo Wrongly Used to Hit Trump Policies." *Associated Press.* May 30.

24. Kiefer, Michael. 2014. "First Peek: Immigrant Children Flood Detention Center." *The Arizona Republic.* June 18.

25. Flaherty, Anne, and Calvin Woodward. 2018. "AP Fact-Check: 2014 Photo Wrongly Used to Hit Trump Policies." *Associated Press.* May 30.

26. Willingham, Daniel T. 2012. *When Can You Trust the Experts: How to Tell Good Science from Bad in Education?* San Francisco: Jossey-Bass. 100–102.

27. Rosenzweig, Cynthia, David Karoly, Marta Vicarelli, Peter Neofotis, Qigang Wu, Gino Casassa, Annette Menzel, Terry L. Root, Nicole Estrella, Bernard Seguin, Piotr Tryjanowski, Chunzhen Liu, Samuel Rawlins, and Anton Imeson. 2008. "Attributing Physical and Biological Impacts to Anthropogenic Climate Change." *Nature.* Vol. 453. 353–357.

28. National Academies of Sciences, Engineering, and Medicine. 2017. *Innovations in Federal Statistics: Combining Data Sources While Protecting Privacy.* Washington, D.C.: The National Academies Press.

29. McGann, James G. 2005. "Think Tanks and Policy Advice in the U.S." *Foreign Policy Research Institute.* August.

30. Davis, Richard. 2001. *The Press and American Politics: The New Mediator.* Upper Saddle River, NJ: Prentice Hall. 144–146.

31. Locke, Susannah. 2015. "8 Ways to Be a More Savvy Science Reader: Your Guide on How to Evaluate Scientific Evidence." *Vox.* May 20.

32. Carroll, Aaron E. 2018. "Peer Review: The Worst Way to Judge Research Except for All the Others." *The New York Times.* November 5.

33. Nichols, Tom. 2017. *The Death of Expertise: The Campaign Against Established Knowledge and Why It Matters.* New York: Oxford University Press. 170–208.

34. Hume, David. 1912. *An Enquiry Concerning Human Understanding.* Chicago: The Open Court Publishing Co. 116.

35. Dorfman, Jeffrey. 2016. "A Look Back at the Year 2016 in Economic Data." *Forbes.* December 30.

36. Jaffe, Amy Myers. 2018. "Iranian Oil Sanctions: Myths and Realities of U.S. Energy Independence." *Council on Foreign Relations.* November 5.

37. Taub, Amanda. 2018. "How Liberals Got Lost on the Story of Missing Children on the Border." *The New York Times.* May 31.

38. Cook, John, Dana Nuccitelli, Arah A. Green, Mark Richardson, Bärbel Winkler, Rob Painting, Robert Way, Peter Jacobs, and Andrew Skuce. 2013. "Quantifying the Consensus on Anthropogenic Global Warming in the Scientific Literature." *Environmental Research Letters.* Vol. 8, No. 2.

39. Vaughn, Lewis. 2018. *Concise Guide to Critical Thinking.* New York: Oxford University Press.

40. Muschert, Glenn W. 2007. "Research in School Shootings." *Sociology Compass.* July 18.

41. Scher, Bill. 2019. "The Real Reason Obama Didn't Pass Gun Control." *Politico.* August 16.

42. Peter, Laurence J. 1977. *Quotations: Ideas for Our Time.* New York: William Morrow & Co. 425.

43. Corasaniti, Nick. 2016. "Ted Cruz Ad Goes After Donald Trump's Stance on Planned Parenthood." *The New York Times.* February 15.

44. Ibid.

45. Bullock, Penn. 2016. "Transcript: Donald Trump's Taped Comments About Women." *The New York Times.* October 8.

46. CQ Transcript Wire. 2016. "Transcript of the Second Debate." *The New York Times.* October 10.

47. Obama, Barack. 2011. "Full Text: President Obama and VP Biden's Remarks to the National Governors Association."

The Oakland Press. February 28.

48. Schick, Theodore, and Lewis Vaughn. 2014. *How to Think About Weird Things: Critical Thinking for a New Age*. New York: McGraw Hill. 52.

49. Gerstein, Josh, Danny Vinik, Katy O'Donnell, Timothy Noah, and Doug Palmer. 2016. "Trump's RNC Address: Fact or Fiction?" *Politico*. July 21.

50. https://ucr.fbi.gov/crime-in-the-u.s/2016/crime-in-the-u.s.-2016/topic-pages/tables/table-1

51. https://www.ucrdatatool.gov/Search/Crime/State/RunCrimeStatebyState.cfm

52. https://www.dictionary.com/browse/anecdote

53. https://en.oxforddictionaries.com/definition/evidence

54. Neporent, Liz. 2013. "Obamacare Explained (Like You're an Idiot)." *ABC News*. December 23.

55. Obama, Barack. 2014. "Remarks by the President on the Affordable Care Act." *The White House*. April 1.

56. Powell, Jared. 2015. "I Am a 62-Year-Old Widow and Have Lost My Insurance Coverage." *Gop.gov*. March 23.

57. Zakaria, Tabassum. 2010. "President Obama Questions Sarah Palin's Nuclear Acumen." *Reuters*. April 8.

58. Novella, Steven. 2018. *The Skeptics Guide to the Universe*. New York: Grand Central Publishing.

59. Wong, Curtis M. 2015. "Here's Why Pat Robertson Insists That Gay Marriage Is Still Illegal." *Huffington Post*. October 26.

60. Obama, Barack. 2013. "Statement by the President." *The White House*. April 17.

61. Staff Writer. 2013. "Background Checks Could Lead to Gun Confiscation, Many Voters Tell Quinnipiac University National Poll; But 91 Percent Want Universal Gun Checks." *Quinnipiac University*. April 4.

62. Hanks, Craig. 2021. "False Dilemma." *Texas State Department of Philosophy*. June 26.

63. http://www.livingroomcandidate.org/commercials/2004/wolves#4327

64. Jackson, Brooks, and Kathleen Hall Jamieson. 2007. *Unspun: Finding Facts in a World of Disinformation*. New York: Random House.

65. Rapoza, Kenneth. 2012. "In Attack Ad, Paul Ryan Kills Grandma in Wheelchair. *Forbes*. August 12.

66. Drobnic, Holan A., and Jacobson, L. 2011. "Throw-Granny-from-the-Cliff Ad Asks What the U.S. Would be 'Without Medicare'?" *Politifact*. May 25.

67. Jung, Nadine., Christina Wranke, Kai Hamburger, and Markus Knauff. 2014. "How Emotions Affect Logical Reasoning: Evidence from Experiments with Mood-Manipulated Participants, Spider Phobics, and People with Exam Anxiety." *Frontiers in Psychology*. 570.

68. Coleridge, Samuel Taylor. 2019. *The Collected Works of Samuel Taylor Coleridge*. Eds. Kathleen Coburn and B. Winer. Volume 14: Table Talk, Part II.

69. Auer, J. Jeffrey. 1962. "The Counterfeit Debates." In *The Great Debates: Background—Perspective—Effects*. Ed. Sidney Kraus. Bloomington, IN: Indiana University Press.

Chapter 9

1. Washington, George. 1913. "Farewell Address." New York: Houghton Mifflin Co.

2. Hamilton, Edith. 1998. *Mythology*. New York: Back Bay Books.

3. *Ibid*.

4. *Ibid*.

5. Burian, Peter, and Alan Shapiro. 2011. *The Complete Aeschylus, Volume 1: The Oresteia*. New York: Oxford University Press.

6. *Ibid*., 156

7. *Ibid*., 158.

8. *Ibid*., 167.

9. *Ibid*., 166–167.

10. *Ibid*., 178–183.

11. *Ibid*., 19.

12. Breyer, Daniel. 2019. "Understanding the Dark Side of Human Nature." Lecture. Retribution and Revenge. *The Great Courses*. Chantilly: The Teaching Company.

13. Burian, Peter, and Alan Shapiro. 2011. *The Complete Aeschylus, Volume 1: The Oresteia*. New York: Oxford University Press. 178–183.

14. Goldstein, Katherine. 2012. "Liberal Schadenfreude Is Out of Control: Why Gloating After the Election Is Nastier Than Ever." *Slate*. November 9.

15. *Ibid*.

16. Munson, Kyle. 2017. "How This Iowan Became a Worldwide Meme for

Those Gloating Over Trump's Win." *Des Moines Register.* January 11.

17. Stokols, Eli. 2016. "Trump Rubs Salt in the Wounds of His Rivals." *Politico.* December 1.

18. Seipel, Arnie. 2016. "Fact Check: Trump Falsely Claims A 'Massive Landslide Victory'" *NPR.* December 11.

19. Bump, Philip. 2017. "Want a Mug of Liberal Tears? It's Going to Take You Several Months." *The Washington Post.* November 28.

20. Anderson, Christopher J., André Blais, Shaun Bowler, Todd Donovan, and Ola Listhaug. *Losers' Consent: Elections and Democratic Legitimacy.* New York: Oxford University Press. 9.

21. Cassino, Dan, and Krista Jenkins. 2013. "Conspiracy Theories Prosper." Fairleigh Dickinson University's Public Mind Poll. January 17.

22. Hasen, Richard L. 2020. *Election Meltdown: Dirty Tricks, Distrust, and the Threat to American Democracy.* New Haven: Yale University Press. 56.

23. Golshan, Tara. 2016. "Trump's Already Got an Excuse for a November Loss: The Election Will Be 'Rigged'" *Vox.* August 2.

24. Hasen, Richard L. 2020. *Election Meltdown: Dirty Tricks, Distrust, and the Threat to American Democracy.* New Haven: Yale University Press.103.

25. *Ibid.,* 105.

26. Farley, Robert. 2016. "Trumps Bogus Voter Fraud Claims." *FactCheck.* October 19.

27. Levitsky, Steven, and Daniel Ziblatt. 2018. *How Democracies Die.* New York: Crown. 61–62.

28. Staff Writer. 2021. "2016 Presidential Election." *270 to Win.* June 28.

29. Hasen, Richard L. 2020. *Election Meltdown: Dirty Tricks, Distrust, and the Threat to American Democracy.* New Haven: Yale University Press. 43.

30. Frankovic, Kathy. 2018. "Russia's Impact on the Election Seen Through Partisan Eyes." *today.yougov.com.* March 9.

31. Hasen, Richard L. 2020. "The Loser of November's Election May Not Concede. Their Voters Won't Either." *The Washington Post.* January 24.

32. Murray, Mark. 2017. "Who Is Greg Phillips, the Man Trump Name-Checked to Prove Voter Fraud?" *NBC News.* January 27.

33. Restuccia, Andrew. 2016. "Trump's Baseless Assertions of Voter Fraud Called 'Stunning.'" *Politico.* November 27.

34. O'Rourke, Ciara. 2020. "Donald Trump Says He 'won the popular vote if you deduct the millions of people who voted illegally.'" *PolitiFact.* February 26. Levitsky, Steven, and Daniel Ziblatt. 2018. *How Democracies Die.* New York: Crown. 197.

35. Hasen, Richard L. 2020. *Election Meltdown: Dirty Tricks, Distrust, and the Threat to American Democracy.* New Haven: Yale University Press. 118.

36. *Ibid.,* 135.

37. Savransky, Rebecca. 2016. "Republicans Still Doubt Obama's Citizenship." *The Hill.* August 10.

38. Hochschild, Jennifer L., and Katherine Levine Einstein. 2012. *Do Facts Matter? Information and Misinformation in American Politics.* Norman: University of Oklahoma Press. 108–113.

39. Schwartz, Ian. 2015. "Sean Hannity: Obama's 'Not my president.'" *Real Clear Politics.* January 12.

40. Krieg, Gregory. 2016. "14 of Trump's Most Outrageous Birther Claims—Half From After 2011." *CNN.* September 16.

41. Jones, Jeffrey M. 2016. "In U.S., 84% Accept Trump as Legitimate President." *Gallup.* November 11.

42. Associated Press. 2017. "Majority of Young Americans View Trump as Illegitimate President: Poll." *NBC News.* March 19.

43. Francescani, Chris, and Robert Chiarito. 2017. "Anti-Trump Rallies Crop Up Again on 'Not My President's Day.'" *Reuters.* February 20.

44. Reimer, Erich. 2017. "Stop Saying 'Not my president.'" *Washington Examiner.* April 28.

45. Rutenberg, Jim, Jo Becker, Eric Lipton, Maggie Haberman, Jonathan Martin, Matthew Rosenberg, and Michael S. Schmidt. 2021. "77 Days: Trump's Campaign to Subvert the Election." *The New York Times.* January 31.

46. Young, Cathy. 2020. "The Republican Mutiny and 2016 Whataboutism." *Arc Digital Media.* December 17.

47. Kim, Catherine. 2020. "Poll: 70 Percent of Republicans Don't Think the Election Was Free and Fair." *Politico.* November 9.

48. Green, Shayna. 2021. "Fact Check: Did Democrats Object to More States for 2016 Than Republicans for 2020?" *Newsweek*. January 13.

49. Anderson, Christopher J., André Blais, Shaun Bowler, Todd Donovan, and Ola Listhaug. *Losers' Consent: Elections and Democratic Legitimacy*. New York: Oxford University Press. 190.

50. Levitsky, Steven, and Daniel Ziblatt. 2018. *How Democracies Die*. New York: Crown. 107.

51. Barash, David P., and Judith Eve Lipton. *Payback: Why We Retaliate, Redirect Aggression, and Take Revenge*. New York: Oxford University Press. 40.

52. Kennedy, Robert F. 1969. *Thirteen Days: A Memoir of the Cuban Missile Crisis*. New York: Mentor.

53. Rieder, Jonathan. 2013. *Gospel of Freedom: Martin Luther King, Jr.'s Letter from Birmingham Jail and the Struggle That Changed a Nation*. New York: Bloomsbury Press.

54. Klein, Ezra. 2020. *Why We're Polarized*. New York: Avid Reader Press. 260.

55. Anderson, Christopher J., André Blais, Shaun Bowler, Todd Donovan, and Ola Listhaug. *Losers' Consent: Elections and Democratic Legitimacy*. New York: Oxford University Press. 125–138.

56. Esposito, Russell R. 2000. *The Golden Milestone: Over 2500 Years of Italian Contributions to Civilization*. New York: New York Learning Library. 354

57. Bowen, Catherine Drinker. 1986. *Miracle at Philadelphia: The Story of the Constitutional Convention May to September 1787*. Boston: Back Bay Books. 294–295.

58. *Ibid.*, 295-304.

59. *Ibid.*, 305.

60. Gugliotta, Guy. 2012. "New Estimate Raises Civil War Death Toll." *The New York Times*. April 2.

61. Mak, Tim. 2018. "Another 'Civil War'? Pessimism About Political Violence Deepens in a Divided Nation." *NPR*. October 13.

62. Baker, Kevin. 2017. "Bluexit: A Modest Proposal for Separating Blue States from Red." *The New Republic*. March 9.

63. Miller, Ryan W. 2018. "Poll: Almost a Third of U.S. Voters Think a Second Civil War Is Coming Soon." *USA Today*. June 27.

64. Kalmoe, Nathan P., and Lilliana Mason. 2019. "Lethal Mass Partisanship: Prevalence, Correlates, and Electoral Contingencies." National Capital Area Political Science Association Meeting.

65. Levitsky, Steven, and Daniel Ziblatt. 2018. *How Democracies Die*. New York: Crown. 162.

66. Grunwald, Michael. 2016. "The Victory of No: The GOP's unprecedented anti-Obama obstructionism was a remarkable success. And then it handed the party to Donald Trump." *Politico Magazine*. December 4.

67. Nadler, Jerry. 2016. "How We Resist Trump and His Extreme Agenda." Retrieved from: jerrynadler.com/newsclips/how-we-resist-trump-and-his-extreme-agenda.

68. Doherty, Carroll, Jocelyn Kiley, and Bridget Jameson. 2018. "The Public, the Political System, and American Democracy." *Pew Research Center*. April 26.

69. Doherty, Carroll, Jocelyn Kiley, and Bridget Jameson. 2016. "Partisanship and Political Animosity in 2016: Highly Negative Views of the Opposing Party—and Its Members." *Pew Research Center*. June 22.

70. McCain, John. 2008. "I Wish Godspeed to the Man Who Was My Former Opponent and Who Will Be My President." *Journalism of Courage Archive*. November 6.

Conclusion

1. Nichols, Tom. 2017. *The Death of Expertise: The Campaign Against Established Knowledge and Why It Matters*. New York: Oxford University Press. 215.

2. Homer. 1992. *The Odyssey*. New York: Alfred A. Knopf. 210–211.

3. Klein, Ezra. 2020. *Why We're Polarized*. New York: Avid Reader Press. 262.

4. Groenendyk, Eric W. 2013. *Competing Motives in the Partisan Mind: How Loyalty and Responsiveness Shape Party Identification and Democracy*. New York: Oxford University Press. xiii–xvi.

5. *Ibid.*

6. Groenendyk, Eric W. 2013. *Competing Motives in the Partisan Mind: How Loyalty and Responsiveness Shape Party Identification and Democracy*. New York: Oxford University Press. 112 and 129.

7. Roberts, Russ. 2014. *How Adam Smith Can Change Your Life: An*

Bibliography

Abadi, Mark. 2017. "Democrats and Republicans Speak Different Languages—and It Helps Explain Why We're so Divided." *Business Insider.* August 11.

Achen, Christopher H., and Larry M. Bartels. 2016. *Democracy for Realists: Why Elections Do Not Produce Responsive Government.* Princeton: Princeton University Press.

Ahler, Douglas J., and Gaurav Sood. 2018. "The Parties in Our Heads: Misperceptions About Party Composition and Their Consequences." *The Journal of Politics.* Vol. 80, No. 3.

Aldrich, John H. 1995. *Why Parties? The Origin and Transformation of Political Parties in America.* Chicago: The University of Chicago Press.

Anderson, Christopher J., André Blais, Shaun Bowler, Todd Donovan, and Ola Listhaug. 2005. *Losers' Consent: Elections and Democratic Legitimacy.* New York: Oxford University Press.

Anderson, Theo. 2015. "The Danger of Dehumanizing Others." *Kellogg Insight.* December 8.

Anishanslin, Zara. 2019. "What We Get Wrong About Ben Franklin's 'A Republic, if You Can Keep It.'" *The Washington Post.* October 29.

Anson, Ian. 2016. "A Tale of Two GDPs: Why Republicans and Democrats Live in Different Economic Realities." *The Conversation.* August 28.

Armstrong, Eric. 2017. "Are Democrats the Party of Science? Not Really." *The New Republic.* January 10.

Arn, Jackson. 2018. "Why Democrats Are Donkeys and Republicans Are Elephants." *CNN.* November 6.

Asimov, Isaac. 1981. *Asimov's Guide to the Bible: The Old and New Testaments.* New York: Avenel Books.

Associated Press Staff. 2017. "Majority of Young Americans View Trump as Illegitimate President: Poll." *NBC News.* March 19.

Atkins, Larry. 2016. *Skewed: A Critical Thinker's Guide to Media Bias.* New York: Prometheus.

Auer, J. Jeffrey. 1962. "The Counterfeit Debates." In *The Great Debates: Background—Perspective—Effects.* Ed. Sidney Kraus. Bloomington: Indiana University Press.

Axelrod, Tal. 2019. "Poll: 57 Percent of Republicans Approve of Trump's Syria Withdrawal." *The Hill.* October 16.

Bacon, Francis. 1902. *Novum Organum.* New York: P. F. Collier & Son.

Bacon, Perry, and Dhrumil Mehta. 2018. "Religious Democrats, Young Republicans: What the Stereotypes Miss About Both Parties." *FiveThirtyEight.* March 23.

Bail, Christopher, Lisa Argyle, Taylor Brown, John Bumpus, Haohan Chen, M.B. Fallin Hunzaker, Jaemin Lee, Marcus Mann, Friedolin Merhout, and Alexander Volfovsky. 2018. "Exposure to Opposing Views on Social Media can Increase Political Polarization." *PNAS.* Vol. 115, No. 37. 9216–9221.

Baker, Kevin. 2017. "Bluexit: A Modest Proposal for Separating Blue States from Red." *The New Republic.* March 9.

Bakshy, Eytan, Solomon Messing, and Lada A. Adamic. 2015. "Exposure to Ideologically Diverse News and Opinion on Facebook." *Science.* Vol. 348, No. 6239.

Balakian, Peter. 2003. *The Burning Tigris:*

The Armenian Genocide and America's Response. New York: HarperCollins.

Balliet, Daniel, Joshua M. Tybur, Junhui Wu, Christian Antonellis, and Paul A. M. Van Lange. 2018. "Political Ideology, Trust, and Cooperation: In-Group Favoritism Among Republicans and Democrats During a U.S. National Election." *Journal of Conflict Resolution.* Vol. 62, No. 4.

Bandler, Aaron. 2017. "Trump Effect: New Poll Shows More Democrats Support NAFTA Than Republicans. The Margin Will Stun You." *Daily Wire.* February 25.

Barash, David P., and Judith Eve Lipton. *Payback: Why We Retaliate, Redirect Aggression, and Take Revenge.* New York: Oxford University Press.

Barber, Michael, and Jeremy C. Pope. 2018. "Does Party Trump Ideology? Disentangling Party and Ideology in America." *American Political Science Review.* Vol. 113, No. 1.

Baum, A. Matthew, and Phil Gussin. 2008. "In the Eye of the Beholder: How Information Shortcuts Shape Individual Perceptions of Bias in the Media." *Quarterly Journal of Political Science.* Vol. 3, No. 1. 1–31.

Beattie, Peter. 2017. "The Chicken-and-Egg Development of Political Opinions: The Roles of Genes, Social Status, Ideology, and Information." *Politics and the Life Sciences.* Vol. 36, No. 1.

Beck, Julie. 2019. "This Article Won't Change Your Mind: The Facts on Why Facts Alone Can't Fight False Belief." *The Atlantic.* December 11.

Belson, Ken. 2017. "Multiple Weapons Found in Las Vegas Gunman's Hotel Room." *The New York Times.* October 2.

Benen, Steve. 2019. "45 Years Later, Republicans Borrow a Page from Earl Landgrebe." *MSNBC.* December 12.

Benner, Jeffrey. 2001. "He's the Real Tourist Guy." *Wired.* November 20.

Berreby, David. 2005. *Us and Them: The Science of Identity.* Chicago: The University of Chicago Press.

Best, Joel. 2004. *More Damned Lies and Statistics: How Numbers Confuse Public Issues.* Berkeley: University of California Press.

Blanton, Dana. 2010. "Fox News Poll: 55% Oppose Health Care Reform." *Fox News.* March 18.

Bleiberg, Joshua, and Darrell M. West. 2015. "Political Polarization on Facebook." *Brookings.* May 13.

Boghossian, Peter, and James Lindsay. 2019. *How to Have Impossible Conversations: A Very Practical Guide.* New York: Lifelong Books.

Boller, Paul F. 1996. *Presidential Campaigns.* New York: Oxford University Press.

Boller, Paul F., and John George. 1989. *They Never Said It: A Book of Fake Quotes, Misquotes, and Misleading Attributions.* New York: Oxford University Press.

Bowen, Catherine Drinker. 1986. *Miracle at Philadelphia: The Story of the Constitutional Convention May to September 1787.* Boston: Back Bay Books.

Boxell, Levi, Matthew Gentzkow, and Jesse M. Shapiro. 2020. "Cross-Country Trends in Affective Polarization." *National Bureau of Economic Research.* June. 1–43.

Breyer, Daniel. 2019. "Understanding the Dark Side of Human Nature." Lecture. Retribution and Revenge. *The Great Courses.* Chantilly, VA: The Teaching Company.

Brown, Brené. 2018. "Dehumanizing Always Starts with Language." brenebrown.com. May 17.

Brown, Dee. 1970. *Bury My Heart at Wounded Knee: An Indian History of the American West.* New York: Holt, Rinehart, and Winston.

Browne, M. Neil, and Stuart M. Keeley. 2010. *Asking the Right Questions: A Guide to Critical Thinking.* Upper Saddle River, NJ: Prentice Hall.

Bryan, Bob. 2017. "Trump Once Called the Jobs Report 'one of the biggest hoaxes in modern politics'—Now He Accepts 'those numbers very proudly.'" *Business Insider.* July 20.

Budak, Ceren, Sharad Goel, and Justin M. Rao. 2016. "Fair and Balanced? Quantifying Media Bias Through Crowdsourced Content Analysis." *Public Opinion Quarterly.* Vol. 80, Issue S1.

Bugliosi, Vincent. 2007. *Reclaiming History: The Assassination of President John F. Kennedy.* New York: W.W. Norton & Company.

Bullock, Penn. 2016. "Transcript: Donald Trump's Taped Comments About Women." *The New York Times.* October 8.

Bump, Philip. 2016. "23 Things Donald Trump Has Said That Would Have Doomed Another Candidate." *The Washington Post*. June 17.

———. 2017. "Want a Mug of Liberal Tears? It's Going to Take You Several Months." *The Washington Post*. November 28.

———. 2018. "How to Mislead with Statistics, DHS Secretary Nielsen Edition." *The Washington Post*. January 18.

———. 2018. "Here Are the Tools That Could Be Used to Create the Fake News of the Future." *The Washington Post*. February 12.

Burian, Peter, and Alan Shapiro. 2011. *The Complete Aeschylus, Volume 1: The Oresteia*. New York: Oxford University Press.

Butler, Heather A., Christopher Pentoney, and Mabelle R. Bong. 2017. "Predicting Real-World Outcomes: Critical Thinking Ability Is a Better Predictor of Life Decisions Than Intelligence." *Thinking Skills and Creativity*. Vol. 25. 38–46.

Campbell, Angus, Philip E. Converse, Warren E. Miller, and Donald E. Stokes. 1960. *The American Voter*. Chicago: The University of Chicago Press.

Campbell, Joseph W. 2016. *Getting It Wrong: Debunking the Greatest Myths in American Journalism*. Oakland: University of California Press.

Caron, Christina. 2017. "Paul Horner, Fake News Writer Who Took Credit for Trump Victory, Dies at 38." *The New York Times*. September 27.

Carroll, Aaron E. 2018. "Peer Review: The Worst Way to Judge Research Except for All the Others." *The New York Times*. November 5.

Carroll, Lauren. 2016. "Super PAC Ad Says Trump Likes War, Even Nuclear, but That Needs Context." *PolitiFact*. June 19.

Cassino, Dan, and Krista Jenkins. 2013. "Conspiracy Theories Prosper." *Fairleigh Dickinson University's Public Mind Poll*. January 17.

Chang, Iris. 1997. *The Rape of Nanking: The Forgotten Holocaust of World War II*. New York: Basic Books.

Chesney, Robert, and Danielle Citron. 2018. "Deepfakes and the New Disinformation War: The Coming Age of Post-Truth Geopolitics." *Foreign Affairs*. December 11.

———. 2019. "Deep Fakes: A Looming Challenge for Privacy, Democracy, and National Security." *California Law Review*. Vol. 107, No. 6.

Chiu, Allyson. 2019. "'I'm friends with George Bush': Ellen DeGeneres Defends Watching Football with Former GOP President." *The Washington Post*. October 8.

Christensen, Tyler. 2018. "Journalism 101: What Is an Editorial, Anyway?" *The Missoulian*. August 5.

Christian, Jon. 2018. "Experts Fear Face-Swapping Tech Could Start an International Showdown." *The Outline*. February 1.

Clay, Nadine. 2020. "How to Cultivate Your Curiosity." *Medium.com*. July 10.

Coe, Kevin, David Tewksbury, Bradley J. Bond, Kristin L. Drogos, Robert W. Porter, Ashley Yahn, and Yuanyuan Zhang. 2008. "Hostile News: Partisan Use and Perceptions of Cable News Programming." *Journal of Communication*. Vol. 58. 201–219.

Cohen, Geoffrey L. 2003. "Party Over Policy: The Dominating Impact of Group Influence on Political Beliefs." *Journal of Personal and Social Psychology*. Vol. 85, No. 5. 808–822.

Cole, Samantha. 2020. "For the Love of God, Not Everything Is a Deepfake." *Vice*. April 27.

Coleridge, Samuel Taylor. 2019. *The Collected Works of Samuel Taylor Coleridge*. Eds. Kathleen Coburn and B. Winer. Volume 14: Table Talk, Part II.

Coles, Isabel, Ghassan Adnan, and Michael R. Gordon. 2020. "U.S. Strike Ordered by Trump Kills Key Iranian Military Leader in Baghdad." *The Wall Street Journal*. January 3.

Collins, Keith. 2015. "Axis of Evil: The Most Misleading Charts of 2015, Fixed." *Quartz*. December 23.

Congressional Quarterly Transcript Wire. 2016. "Transcript of the Second Debate." *The New York Times*. October 10.

Conley, Nicholas. 2019. "The Untold Truth of Deepfakes." *Grunge*. August 29.

Cook, John, Dana Nuccitelli, Arah A. Green, Mark Richardson, Bärbel Winkler, Rob Painting, Robert Way, Peter Jacobs, and Andrew Skuce. 2013. "Quantifying the Consensus on Anthropogenic Global Warming in the Scientific Literature." *Environmental Research Letters*. Vol. 8, No. 2.

Copeland, Cody. 2021. "Is There a Way to Spot Deepfakes?" *Grunge.* April 2.

Corasaniti, Nick. 2016. "Ted Cruz Ad Goes After Donald Trump's Stance on Planned Parenthood." *The New York Times.* February 15.

Cournoyer, Caroline. 2019. "Trump Promised to Eliminate the National Debt. It Has Risen by $3 Trillion." *CBS News.* October 29.

Cummings, William. 2019. "'A WALL is a WALL!' Trump Declares. But the Definition Has Shifted a lot Over Time." *USA Today.* January 31.

D'Alessio, Dave. 2013. *Media Bias in Presidential Election Coverage, 1948–2008.* New York: Lexington Books.

D'Alessio, Dave, and Mike Allen. 2000. "Media Bias in Presidential Elections: A Meta-Analysis." *Journal of Communication.* Vol. 50, Issue 4. 133–156.

Dalton, Russel J., Paul A. Beck, and Robert Huckfeldt. 1998. "Partisan Cues and the Media: Information Flows in the 1992 Presidential Election." *American Political Science Review.* Vol. 92, No. 1. 111–126.

Date, Jack. 2019. "Mail Bomber Cesar Sayoc Obsessed with Trump, Fox News, Chilling New Court Filings Show." *ABC News.* July 23.

Davenport, Coral, and Eric Lipton. 2017. "How G.O.P. Leaders Came to View Climate Change as Fake Science." *The New York Times.* June 3.

Davis, James F. 1991. *Who Is Black? One Nation's Definition.* University Park: Penn State University Press.

Davis, Leslie, and Hannah Hartig. 2019. "Two-Thirds of Americans Favor Raising Federal Minimum Wage to $15 an Hour." *Pew Research Center.* July 30.

Davis, Richard. 2001. *The Press and American Politics: The New Mediator.* Upper Saddle River, NJ: Prentice Hall.

Delli Carpini, Michael X., and Scott Keeter. 1989. *What Americans Know about Politics and Why It Matters.* New Haven: Yale University Press.

DiCarlo, Matthew. 2011. "Why Do Most Americans Support 'Assistance to The Poor' But Oppose 'Welfare'?" *Albert Shanker Institute.* November 17.

Ditto, Peter H., Brittany S. Liu, Cory J. Clark, Sean P. Wojcik, Eric E. Chen, Rebecca H. Grady, Jared B. Celniker, and Joanne F. Zinger. 2018. "At Least Bias Is Bipartisan: A Meta-Analytic Comparison of Partisan Bias in Liberals and Conservatives. *Perspectives on Psychological Science.* Vol. 14, No. 2. 273–291.

Doherty, Carroll, Jocelyn Kiley, and Bridget Jameson. 2016. "Partisanship and Political Animosity in 2016." *Pew Research Center.* June 22.

_____. 2018. "The Public, the Political System, and American Democracy." *Pew Research Center.* April 26.

Dorfman, Jeffrey. 2016. "A Look Back at the Year 2016 in Economic Data." *Forbes.* December 30.

Doyle, Gerry. 2006. "About Those First Amendment Rights, Doh!" *Chicago Tribune.* March 1.

Drobnic Holan, A., and Jacobson, L. 2011. "Throw-Granny-from-the-Cliff Ad Asks What the U.S. Would be 'Without Medicare'?" *PolitiFact.* May 25.

Druckman, James N. 2012 "The Politics of Motivation." *Critical Review.* Vol. 24, No. 2. 199–216.

Druckman, James N., Erik Peterson, and Rune Slothuus. 2013. "How Elite Partisan Polarization Affects Public Opinion Formation." *American Political Science Review.* Vol. 107, No. 1.

Druckman, James N., Matthew S. Levendusky, and Audrey McLain. 2018. "No Need to Watch: How the Effects of Partisan Media Can Spread via Interpersonal Discussions." *American Journal of Political Science.* Vol. 62, No. 1. 99–112.

Eakin, Emily. 2004. "Study Finds a Nation of Polarized Readers." *The New York Times.* March 13.

Eberhardt, Jennifer L. 2019. *Biased: Uncovering the Hidden Prejudice That Shapes What We See, Think, and Do.* New York: Viking.

Edsall, Thomas B. 2019. "No Hate Left Behind." *The New York Times.* March 13.

Edwards-Levy, Ariel. 2018. "Republicans Like Obama's Ideas Better When They Think They're Donald Trump's." *Huffington Post.* May 31.

_____. 2018. "Republicans Support Tougher Gun Background Checks, Unless It's Obama Suggesting Them." *Huffington Post.* May 31.

Eikanas, Marvae. 2017. "12 Ways to Cultivate Curiosity." *leadlifewell.com.* November 7.

Ekins, Emily. 2019. "Americans Used to Support a Border Wall. What Changed Their Minds?" *CATO Institute.* January 14.

El-Bermawy, Mostafa M. 2016. "Your Filter Bubble Is Destroying Democracy." *Wired.* November 18.

Ellenberg, Jordan. 2014. *How Not to be Wrong: The Power of Mathematical Thinking.* New York: The Penguin Press.

Emerson, Ralph Waldo. 2012. *The Heart of Emerson's Journals.* New York: Dover Publications.

Enda, Jodi. 2012. "When Republicans Were Blue and Democrats Were Red." *Smithsonian Magazine.* October 31.

Esposito, Russell R. 2000. *The Golden Milestone: Over 2500 Years of Italian Contributions to Civilization.* New York: New York Learning Library.

Evans, M. Stanton. 2007. *Blacklisted by History: The Untold Story of Senator Joe McCarthy.* New York: Crown Forum.

Evon, Dan. 2017. "Did President Trump Experience Diarrhea on a Golf Course?" *Snopes.com.* April 10.

Fagan, Kaylee. 2018. "A Viral Video That Appeared to Show Obama Calling Trump a 'Dipshit' Shows a Disturbing New Trend Called Deepfakes." *Business Insider.* April 17.

Farid, Hany. 2007. "Digital Doctoring: Can We Trust Photographs?" Hanover: Dartmouth.

Farley, Robert. 2016. "Trumps Bogus Voter Fraud Claims." *FactCheck.org.* October 19.

_____. 2018. "Who's to Blame for Higher Gas Prices?" *FactCheck.org.* May 25.

_____. 2020. "Survey Says: Trump Misleads on Debate Performances." *FactCheck.org.* February 21.

Fazio, Lisa K., Nadia M. Brashier, B. Keith Payne, and Elizabeth J. Marsh. 2015. "Knowledge Does Not Protect Against Illusory Truth." *Journal of Experimental Psychology.* Vol. 144, No. 5. 993–1002.

Feldman, Lauren. 2011. "Partisan Differences in Opinionated News Perceptions: A Test of the Hostile Media Effect." *Political Behavior.* Vol. 33. 407–432.

Fernbach, Philip M., Todd Rogers, Craig R. Fox, and Steven A. Sloman. 2013. "Political Extremism Is Supported by an Illusion of Understanding." *Psychological Science.* Vol. 20, Issue 10. 1–8.

Festinger, Leon, Henry W. Riecken, and Stanley Schachter. 2009. *When Prophecy Fails: A Social and Psychological Study of a Modern Group that Predicted the Destruction of the World.* New York: Harper & Row Publishers.

Feynman, Richard P. and Edward Hutchings. 1985. *Surely, You're Joking, Mr. Feynman!* New York: W. W. Norton & Company Ltd.

Fieldstadt, Elisha. 2016. "Don't Get Fooled by These Fake News Sites." *CBS News.* December 2.

Fink, Jenni. 2018. "National Tattoo Day: Donald Trump Has Become a Popular Inspiration, For Both Supporters and Critics." *Newsweek.* July 17.

Finkel, Eli J., Christopher A. Bail, Mina Cikara, Peter H. Ditto, Shanto Iyengar, Samara Klar, Lilliana Mason, Mary C. McGrath, Brendan Nyhan, David G. Rand, Linda J. Skitka, Joshua A. Tucker, Jay J. Van Bavel, Cynthia S. Wang, and James N. Druckman. 2020. "Political Sectarianism in America." *Science.* Vol. 370, Issue 6516.

Flaherty, Anne and Calvin Woodward. 2018. "AP Fact-Check: 2014 Photo Wrongly Used to Hit Trump Policies." *Associated Press.* May 30.

Fox News. 2011. "President Obama the Campaigner-in-Chief?" *Hannity.* November 29.

Frail, T.A. 2017. "The Injustice of Japanese-American Internment Camps Resonates Strongly to This Day." *Smithsonian Magazine.* January.

Francescani, Chris and Robert Chiarito. 2017. "Anti-Trump Rallies Crop Up Again on 'Not My President's Day.'" *Reuters.* February 20.

Franklin, Benjamin. 1982. *The Autobiography and Other Writings by Benjamin Franklin.* New York: Bantam Books.

Frankovic, Kathy. 2018. "Russia's Impact on the Election Seen Through Partisan Eyes." *today.yougov.com.* March 9.

Frenda, Steven J., Eric D. Knowles, William Saletan, and Elizabeth Loftus. 2013. "False Memories of Fabricated Political Events." *Journal of Experimental Psychology.* Vol. 49. 280–286.

Frimer, Jeremy, Linda Skitka, and Matt Motyl. 2017. "Liberals and Conservatives Have One Thing in Common: Zero Interest in Opposing Views." *The Los Angeles Times.* January 4.

Galef, Julia. 2021. *The Scout Mindset: Why Some People See Things Clearly and Others Don't*. New York: Penguin.

Gallup. 2020. "Abortion." *gallup.com*. Accessed March 2021.

Gault, Matthew. 2016. "After 20 Minutes of Listening, New Adobe Tool Can Make You Say Anything. *Vice*. November 5.

Gearan, Anne. 2015. "Brother, Can You Spare a Dollar? Clinton Asking for $1 Donations as Deadline Nears." *The Washington Post*. June 29.

Gerstein, Josh, Danny Vinik, Katy O'Donnell, Timothy Noah, and Doug Palmer. 2016. "Trump's RNC Address: Fact or Fiction?" *Politico*. July 21.

Ghaffary, Shirin. "Facebook Is Banning Deepfake Videos." *Vox*. January 7.

Ghose, Tia. 2012. "Why We Care About Our Ancestry." *Live Science*. October 26.

Gillespie, Patrick. 2016. "Trump Hammers America's 'worst trade deal.'" *cnn.com*. September 27.

Glader, Paul. 2017. "10 Journalism Brands Where You Find Real Facts Rather Than Alternative Facts." *Forbes*. February 1.

Gleason, Abbott and Martha C. Nussbaum. 2005. *On Nineteen Eighty-Four: Orwell and Our Future*. Princeton: Princeton University Press.

Glum, Julia. 2017. "Some Republicans Still Think Obama Was Born in Kenya as Trump Resurrects Birther Conspiracy Theory." *Newsweek*. December 11.

Goff, Phillip Atiba, Jennifer L. Eberhardt, Melissa J. Williams, and Matthew Christian Jackson. 2008. "Not Yet Human: Implicit Knowledge, Historical Dehumanization, and Contemporary Consequences." *Journal of Personality and Social Psychology*. Vol. 94, No. 2. 292–306.

Goldman, Adam. 2016. "The Comet Ping Pong Gunman Answers Our Reporter's Questions." *The New York Times*. December 7.

Goldstein. Katherine. 2012. "Liberal Schadenfreude Is Out of Control: Why Gloating After the Election Is Nastier Than Ever." *Slate*. November 9.

Golshan, Tara. 2016. "Trump's Already Got an Excuse for a November Loss: The Election Will Be 'Rigged'" *Vox*. August 2.

Gore, D'Angelo. 2016. "A Fake Mike Pence Quote." *FactCheck.org*. December 21.

Gramlich, John. 2021. "How Trump Compares to Other Recent Presidents in Appointing Federal Judges." *Pew Research Center*. January 13.

Green, Shayna. 2021. "Fact Check: Did Democrats Object to More States for 2016 Than Republicans For 2020?" *Newsweek*. January 13.

Greenberg, John. 2015. "Donald Trump Says Crime Statistics Show Blacks Kill 81 Percent of White Homicide Victims." *PolitiFact*. November 23.

Greenberg, Scott. 2016. "Looking Back at the Bush Tax Cuts, Fifteen Years Later." *The Tax Foundation*. June 7.

Groenendyk, Eric W. 2013. *Competing Motives in the Partisan Mind: How Loyalty and Responsiveness Shape Party Identification and Democracy*. New York: Oxford University Press.

Groves, Robert M. 2010. "The Structure and Activities of the U.S. Federal Statistical System: History and Recurrent Challenges." *The Annals of the American Academy of Political and Social Science*. August 9.

Grunwald, Michael. 2016. "The Victory of 'No.'" *Politico*. December 4.

Guess, Andrew, Benjamin Lyons, Brendan Nyhan, and Jason Reifler. "Avoiding the Echo Chamber About Echo Chambers: Why Selective Exposure to Like-Minded Political News Is Less Prevalent Than You Think." *Knight Foundation*. 1–25.

Gugliotta, Guy. 2012. "New Estimate Raises Civil War Death Toll." *The New York Times*. April 2.

Guilford, Gwyn. 2016. "Fake News Isn't a Recent Problem in the U.S.—It Almost Destroyed Abraham Lincoln." *Quartz*. November 28.

Gunther, Albert C., Cindy T. Christen, Janice L. Liebhart, and Stella Chih-Yun Chia. 2001. "Congenial Public, Contrary Press, and Biased Estimates of the Climate of Opinion." *Public Opinion Quarterly*. 65(3). 295–320.

Haberman, Maggie, and Jonathan Martin. 2017. "Trump Once Said the 'Access Hollywood' Tape Was Real. Now He's Not Sure." *The New York Times*. November 28.

Hamilton, Edith. 1998. *Mythology*. New York: Back Bay Books.

Hanks, Craig. 2021. "False Dilemma." *Texas State Department of Philosophy*. June 26.

Hardin, Garrett. 1969. "The Tragedy of the Commons." *Science*. Vol. 162, Issue 3859.

Harper, Craig A., and Thom Baguley. "You Are Fake News! Ideological (A)symmetries in Perceptions of Media Legitimacy." *PsyArXiv*. January 23.

Harrison, Guy P. 2017. *Think Before You Like: Social Media's Effect on the Brain and the Tools You Need to Navigate Your Newsfeed*. New York: Prometheus.

Hartmann, Margaret. 2017. "How the Roy Moore Allegations Were Covered on the Right." *New York Magazine*. November 10.

Hasen, Richard L. 2020. *Election Meltdown: Dirty Tricks, Distrust, and the Threat to American Democracy*. New Haven: Yale University Press.

———. 2020. "The Loser of November's Election May Not Concede. Their Voters Won't Either." *The Washington Post*. January 24.

Hastorf, Albert H., and Hadley Cantril. 1954. "They Saw a Game; a Case Study." *The Journal of Abnormal and Social Psychology*. 49 (1). 129–134.

Hess, Amanda. 2017. "How to Escape Your Political Bubble for a Clearer View." *The New York Times*. March 3.

Hetherington, Marc, and Jonathan Weiler. 2018. *Prius or Pickup: How the Answers to Four Simple Questions Explain America's Great Divide*. Boston: Houghton Mifflin Harcourt.

Hibbing, John, Kevin Smith, and John Alford. 2014. *Predisposed: Liberals, Conservatives, and the Biology of Political Differences*. New York: Routledge.

Hill, David. 2012. "Polls on Obamacare Mislead." *The Hill*. March 28.

Himelboim, Itai, Stephen McCreery, and Marc Smith. 2013. "Birds of a Feather Tweet Together: Integrating Network and Content Analyses to Examine Cross-Ideology Exposure on Twitter." *Journal of Computer-Mediated Communication*. Vol. 18. 154–174.

Hippel, William von. 2018. *The Social Leap: The New Evolutionary Science of Who We Are, Where We Come From, and What Makes Us Happy*. New York: Harper Wave.

Hitler, Adolf. 1999. *Mein Kampf*. Boston: Houghton Mifflin Company.

Hochschild, Jennifer L., and Katherine Levine Einstein. 2012. *Do Facts Matter? Information and Misinformation in American Politics*. Norman: University of Oklahoma Press.

Homer. 1992. *The Odyssey*. New York: Alfred A. Knopf.

Hubbard, Ben. 2020. "The Killing of General Qassim Suleimani: What We Know Since the U.S. Airstrike." *The New York Times*. January 4.

Huff, Darrell. 1993. *How to Lie with Statistics*. New York: W.W. Norton & Company.

Hume, David. 1912. *An Enquiry Concerning Human Understanding*. Chicago: The Open Court Publishing Co.

Hurley, Patrick J. 2008. *A Concise Introduction to Logic*. Belmont, CA. Thomson Learning, Inc.

Illing, Sean. 2017. "America's Misinformation Problem Explained: It's Better—and Worse—Than You Think." *Vox*. November 6.

Ingraham, Christopher. 2017. "Nineteen Times Trump Called Jobs Numbers Fake Before They Made Him Look Good." *The Washington Post*. March 10.

Ingram, Mathew. 2017. "Fake News Isn't a New Problem, and We're Better Equipped to Fight it Now." *Fortune*. February 8.

Iyengar, Shanto, and Kyu S. Hahn. 2009. "Red Media, Blue Media: Evidence of Ideological Selectivity in Media Use." *Journal of Communication*. Vol. 59. 19–39.

Iyengar, Shanto, and Sean J. Westwood. 2015. "Fear and Loathing across Party Lines: New Evidence of Group Polarization." *American Journal of Political Science*. Vol. 59, No. 3. 690–707.

Iyengar, Shanto, Gaurav Sood, and Yphtach Lelkes. 2012. "Affect Not Ideology: A Social Identity Perspective on Polarization." *Public Opinion Quarterly*. Vol. 76, Issue 3. 405–431.

Jackson, Brooks. 2008. "Picture of Palin Is a Fake." *FactCheck.org*. September 8.

Jackson, Brooks, and Kathleen Hall Jamieson. 2007. *Unspun: Finding Facts in a World of Disinformation*. New York: Random House.

Jacobson, Louis. 2011. "Mitt Romney Ad Charges Obama Said, 'If we keep talking about the economy, we're going to lose.' *PolitiFact*. November 22.

———. 2016. "Clinton Claim on Small

Donors is 'Mostly False,' PolitiFact Finds." *NBC News*. March 21.

Jaffe, Amy Myers. 2018. "Iranian Oil Sanctions: Myths and Realities of U.S. Energy Independence." *Council on Foreign Relations*. November 5.

Jaksa, Kari L. 2011. "Sports and Collective Identity: The Effects of Athletics on National Unity." *SAIS Review of International Affairs*. Vol. 31, No. 1. 39–41.

Jardina, Ashley, and Michael Traugott. 2018. "The Genesis of the Birther Rumor: Partisanship, Racial Attitudes, and Political Knowledge." *Journal of Race, Ethnicity, and Politics*. Vol. 4, Issue 1. 60–80.

Johnson, Dave. 2020. "Audio Deepfakes: Can Anyone Tell If They're Fake?" *How-To Geek*. August 3.

Johnson, Ken. 2012. "Their Cheating Art: Reality and Illusion." *The New York Times*. October 11.

Jones, Bradley. 2019. "Majority of Americans Continue to Say That Immigrants Strengthen the U.S." *Pew Research Center*. January 31.

Jones, Jeffrey M. 2016. "In U.S., 84% Accept Trump as Legitimate President." *Gallup*. November 11.

———. 2018. "Americans: Much Misinformation, Bias, Inaccuracy in News." *Gallup*. June 20.

Jung, Nadine, Christina Wranke, Kai Hamburger, and Markus Knauff. 2014. "How Emotions Affect Logical Reasoning: Evidence from Experiments with Mood-Manipulated Participants, Spider Phobic, and People with Exam Anxiety." *Frontiers in Psychology*. Vol. 5. 570.

Kafura, Craig, and Bettina Hammer. 2019. "Republicans and Democrats in Different Worlds on Immigration." *The Chicago Council on Global Affairs*. October 8.

Kagay, Michael R. 1994. "Poll on Doubt of Holocaust Is Corrected." *The New York Times*. July 8.

Kahan, Dan M. 2017. "Misconception, Misinformation, and the Logic of Identity-Protective Cognition." *Yale Law & Economist Research Paper*. No. 575.

Kahan, Dan M., Ashley Landrum, Katie Carpenter, Laura Helft, and Kathleen Hall Jamieson. 2017. "Science Curiosity and Political Information Processing." *Political Psychology*. January 26.

Kahan, Dan M., David A. Hoffman, Donald Braman, Danieli Evans, and Jeffrey J. Rachlinski. 2012. "They Saw a Protest: Cognitive Illiberalism and the Speech-Conduct Distinction." *Cornell Law Faculty Publications*. Paper 400.

Kahan, Dan M., Ellen Peters, Erica Dawson, and Paul Slovic. 2013. "Motivated Numeracy and Enlightened Self-Government." *Behavioral Public Policy*. Vol 1. 54–86.

Kahneman, Daniel. 2011. *Thinking, Fast and Slow*. New York: Farrar, Straus, and Giroux.

Kaid, Lynda Lee, and Christina Holtz-Bacha, eds. "Media Bias." *Encyclopedia of Political Communication*. Online.

Kaiser, David. 2016. "Ted Cruz Is Not the First Politician to Cause Controversy with a Doctored Photo." *Time*. February 19.

Kalmoe, Nathan P., and Lilliana Mason. 2019. "Lethal Mass Partisanship: Prevalence, Correlates, and Electoral Contingencies." National Capital Area Political Science Association Meeting.

Kane, John V., Lilliana Mason, and Julie Wronski. 2020. "Who's at The Party? Group Sentiments, Knowledge, and Partisan Identity." *The Journal of Politics*. September 3.

Kaplan, Marty. 2013. "Most Depressing Brain Finding Ever." *Huffington Post*. September 16.

Katz, Josh. 2016. "Duck Dynasty vs. Modern Family: 50 Maps of the U.S. Cultural Divide." *The New York Times*. December 27.

Kaufmann, Chaim D., and Robert Pape. 1999. "Explaining Costly International Moral Action: Britain's Sixty-Year Campaign Against the Atlantic Slave Trade." *International Organization*. Vol. 53, No. 4. 631–688.

Kennedy, Robert F. 1969. *Thirteen Days: A Memoir of the Cuban Missile Crisis*. New York: Mentor.

Ketcham, Ralph, ed. 1986. "Brutus, Essay I." *The Federalist Papers and the Constitutional Convention Debates*. New York: Mentor.

Kiefer, Michael. 2014. "First Peek: Immigrant Children Flood Detention Center." *The Arizona Republic*. June 18.

Kiely, Eugene. 2016. "A Guide to Clinton's Emails." *FactCheck.org*. July 5.

Kiley, Jocelyn, and Shiva Maniam. 2016. "Lesbian, Gay, and Bisexual Voters Remain a Solidly Democratic Bloc." *Pew Research Center*. October 25.

Kim, Catherine. 2020. "Poll: 70 Percent of Republicans Don't Think the Election Was Free and Fair." *Politico*. November 9.

Kinder, Donald R., and Cindy D. Kam. 2009. *Us Against Them: Ethnocentric Foundations of American Opinion*. Chicago: The University of Chicago Press.

Kinder, Donald R., and Nathan P. Kalmoe. 2017. *Neither Liberal nor Conservative: Ideological Innocence in the American Public*. Chicago: The University of Chicago Press.

Klass, Brian. 2019. "Deepfakes Are Coming. We're Not Ready." *The Washington Post*. May 14.

Klein, Ezra. 2017. "Was the Democratic Primary Rigged?" *Vox*. November 14.

———. 2020. *Why We're Polarized*. New York: Avid Reader Press.

Knight Foundation. 2018. "Indicators of News Media Trust." *knightfoundation.org*. September 11.

Kovach, Bill, and Tom Rosenstiel. 2010. *Blur: How to Know What's True in the Age of Information Overload*. New York: Bloomsbury.

Krieg, Gregory. 2016. "14 of Trump's Most Outrageous Birther Claims—Half from After 2011." *CNN*. September 16.

Kristof, Nicholas. 2017. "We Can Act Before the Next Mass Shooting." *The New York Times*. October 5. A23.

Kurtzleben, Danielle. 2015. "Five Things We've Learned About 2016 Presidential Fundraising." *NPR*. July 16.

Ladd, Everett C. 1994. "Setting the Record Straight on a Holocaust Denial Poll." *The Christian Science Monitor*. July 1.

Ladd, Jonathan M. 2010. "The Neglected Power of Elite Opinion Leadership to Produce Antipathy Toward the News Media: Evidence from a Survey Experiment." *Political Behavior*. Vol. 32. 36.

Lai, Yvonne. 2006. "Never Discuss Politics, Religion, or the Great Pumpkin." *ABC News*. October 27.

Landler, Mark. 2018. "Trump Abandons Iran Nuclear Deal He Long Scorned." *The New York Times*. May 8.

Langer, Gary. 2008. "Sampling Error: What It Means." *ABC News*. October 8.

Laughland, Oliver, and Jon Swaine. 2017. "Virginia Shooting: Gunman Was Left-wing Activist with Record of Domestic Violence." *The Guardian*. June 15.

Lavine, Howard, Christopher Johnston, and Marco Steenbergen. 2012. *The Ambivalent Partisan: How Critical Loyalty Promotes Democracy*. New York: Oxford University Press.

Lawson, Rebecca. 2006. "The Science of Cycology: Failure to Understand How Everyday Objects Work." *Memory and Cognition*. Vol. 34, 1667–1675.

LeBlanc, Steven A. 2003. *Constant Battles: The Myth of the Peaceful Noble Savage*. New York: St. Martin's Press. 69–70, 113.

Ledwich, Mark, and Anna Zaitsev. 2019. "Algorithmic Extremism: Examining YouTube's Rabbit Hole of Radicalization." *arXivLabs*. December 24.

Leslie, Ian. 2014. *Curious: The Desire to Know and Why Your Future Depends on It*. New York: Basic Books.

Levendusky, Matthew. 2009. *The Partisan Sort: How Liberals Became Democrats and Conservatives Became Republicans*. Chicago: The University of Chicago Press.

———. 2013. *How Partisan Media Polarizes America*. Chicago: The University of Chicago Press.

———. 2018. "Americans, Not Partisans: Can Priming American National Identity Reduce Affective Polarization?" *Journal of Politics*. Vol. 80, No. 1. 59–70.

Levitin, Daniel J. 2016. *A Field Guide to Lies: Critical Thinking in the Information Age*. New York: Dutton.

Levitsky, Steven, and Daniel Ziblatt. 2018. *How Democracies Die*. New York: Crown.

Lewis, Rebecca. 2018. "Alternative Influence: Broadcasting the Reactionary Right on YouTube." *Data and Society*. September 18.

Lichter, S. Robert, Stanley Rotham, and Linda S. Lichter. 1986. *The Media Elite: America's New Powerbrokers*. New York: Hastings House.

Limbaugh, Rush. 2019. "Trump Did It! The American Economy Is the Envy of the World." *rushlimbaugh.com*. May 3.

Lincoln, Abraham. 1856. "Speech at Republican Banquet, Chicago Illinois." *Collected Works of Abraham Lincoln*. Vol. 2. Lansing: University of Michigan. 384–386.

Locke, Susannah. 2015. "8 Ways to Be a More Savvy Science Reader: Your Guide on How to Evaluate Scientific Evidence." *Vox.* May 20.

Lodge, Milton, and Charles S. Taber. 2013. *The Rationalizing Voter.* New York: Cambridge University Press.

Lombrozo, Tania. 2016. "Is the Mind's Approach More Like a Scientist or a Trial Lawyer?" *NPR.* April 11.

Long, Heather. 2019. "U.S. Unemployment Fell to 3.6 Percent, Lowest Since 1969." *The Washington Post.* May 3.

Lopez, German. 2016. "Donald Trump Won the Debate ... According to Useless Website Polls That Mean Nothing." *Vox.* September 27.

Lord, Charles G., Lee Ross, and Mark R. Lepper. 1979. "Biased Assimilation and Attitude Polarization: The Effects of Prior Theories on Subsequently Considered Evidence." *Journal of Personality and Social Psychology.* Vol. 37, No. 11. 2100–2101.

Lyons, Jeffrey. 2016. "The Family and Partisan Socialization in Red and Blue America." *Political Psychology.* Vol. 20, No. 20.

MacGuill, Dan. 2018. "Have Leaked Documents Been Published Showing Donald Trump's 'True' Weight? *Snopes.com.* May 16.

Mael, Fred, and Louis Tetrick. 1992. "Identifying Organizational Identification." *Educational and Psychological Measurement.* 54: 813–24.

Mak, Tim. 2018. "Another 'Civil War'? Pessimism About Political Violence Deepens in a Divided Nation." *NPR.* October 13.

Marietta, Morgan, and David C. Barker. 2019. *One Nation, Two Realities: Dueling Facts in American Democracy.* New York: Oxford University Press.

Marks, Joseph, Eloise Copland, Eleanor Loh, Cass R. Sunstein, and Tali Sharot. 2018. "Epistemic Spillovers: Learning Others' Political Views Reduces the Ability to Assess and Use Their Expertise in Nonpolitical Domains." *Cognition.* Vol. 188. 74–84.

Martin, James. 2008. "Catholics Will No Longer Recite 'And Also with You.'" *NPR.* April 11.

Mason, Lilliana. 2018. *Uncivil Agreement: How Politics Became Our Identity.* Chicago: The University of Chicago Press.

McCain, John. 2008. "I Wish Godspeed to the Man Who Was My Former Opponent and Who Will Be My President." *Journalism of Courage Archive.* November 6.

McCarty, Nolan. 2019. *Polarization: What Everyone Needs to Know.* New York: Oxford University Press.

McGann, James G. 2005. "Think Tanks and Policy Advice in the U.S." *Foreign Policy Research Institute.* August.

McKinless, Thomas. 2018. "Schumer Calls on Trump to Address 'Soaring' Gas Prices." *Roll Call.* May 23.

Mercier, Hugo, and Dan Sperber. 2017. *The Enigma of Reason.* Cambridge: Harvard University Press.

Mercier, Hugo, and Hélène Landemore. 2012. "Reasoning Is for Arguing: Understanding the Successes and Failures of Deliberation." *Political Psychology.* Vol. 33, Issue 2.

Mikkelson, David. 2002. "Does This Photograph Show President Bush Reading a Book Upside-Down?" *Snopes.com.* September 24.

———. 2012. "Mitt Romney 'Money' Shirts." *Snopes.com.* March 6.

———. 2015. "False: Barack Obama with Upside Down Telephone." *Snopes.com.* August 9.

Mill, John Stewart. 1965. *Principles of Political Economy.* Toronto: University of Toronto Press.

Miller, Michael E. 2021. "The Pizzagate Gunman Is Out of Prison. Conspiracy Theories Are Out of Control." *The Seattle Times.* February 16.

Miller, Ryan W. 2018. "Poll: Almost a Third of U.S. Voters Think a Second Civil War Is Coming Soon." *USA Today.* June 27.

Mitchell, Amy, Jefferey Gottfried, Michael Barthel, and Elisa Shearer. 2016. "The Modern News Consumer: Trust and Accuracy." *Pew Research Center.* July 7.

Mitchell, Amy, Jeffrey Gottfried, Michael Barthel, and Nami Sumida. 2018. "Distinguishing Between Factual and Opinion Statements in the News." *Pew Research Center.* June 18.

Moffett, Mark W. 2019. *The Human Swarm: How Our Societies Arise, Thrive, and Fall.* New York: Basic Books.

Montopoli, Brian. 2011. "Mitt Romney Attack Ad Misleadingly Quotes Obama." *CBS News.* November 23.

———. 2012. "Is President Obama the Apologizer in Chief." *CBS News.* August 2.

Mooney, Chris. 2013. "Science Confirms: Politics Wrecks Your Ability to do Math." *Mother Jones.* September 4.

Moran, Lee. 2020. "Lou Dobbs Turns His Adulation of Donald Trump Up Yet Another Ridiculous Notch." *Huffington Post.* January 4.

Mounk, Yascha. 2019. "Republicans Don't Understand Democrats—And Democrats Don't Understand Republicans." *The Atlantic.* June 23.

Moye, David. 2018. "Fake Photo of Trump 'Rescuing' Flood Victims Goes Viral." *Huffington Post.* September 24.

Munson, Kyle. 2017. "How This Iowan Became a Worldwide Meme for Those Gloating Over Trump's Win." *Des Moines Register.* January 11.

Murray, Mark. 2017. "Who Is Greg Phillips, the Man Trump Name-Checked to Prove Voter Fraud?" *NBC News.* January 27.

Muschert, Glenn W. 2007. "Research in School Shootings." *Sociology Compass.* July 18.

Mutz, Diana C. 2006. *Hearing the Other Side: Deliberative versus Participatory Democracy.* Cambridge: Cambridge University Press.

National Academies of Sciences, Engineering, and Medicine. 2017. *Innovations in Federal Statistics: Combining Data Sources While Protecting Privacy.* Washington, D.C.: The National Academies Press.

Neporent, Liz. 2013. "Obamacare Explained (Like You're an Idiot)." *ABC News.* December 23.

Nichols, Tom. 2017. *The Death of Expertise: The Campaign against Established Knowledge and Why It Matters.* New York: Oxford University Press.

Nir, Lilach. 2011. "Motivated Reasoning and Public Opinion Perception." *The Public Opinion Quarterly.* Vol. 75, No. 3. 504–532.

Niven, David. 2002. *Tilt? The Search for Media Bias.* Westport: Praeger Publishers.

Novella, Steven. 2018. *The Skeptics' Guide to the Universe: How to Know What's Really Real in a World Increasingly Full of Fake.* New York: Grand Central Publishing.

NPR Staff. 2016. "Ginsburg and Scalia: 'Best Buddies.'" *NPR.* February 15.

———. 2016. "No, FDR Did Not Know the Japanese Were Going to Bomb Pearl Harbor." *NPR.* December 6.

Nyhan, Brendan. 2012. "Biases Abound." *Open Transcripts.* Berkman Klein Center for Internet & Society. March 6.

O'Rourke, Ciara. 2020. "Donald Trump Says He 'won the popular vote if you deduct the millions of people who voted illegally.'" *PolitiFact.* February 26.

O'Toole, Garson. 2018. "He Who Will Not Reason Is a Bigot; He Who Cannot Is a Fool; He Who Dares Not Is a Slave." *Quote Investigator.* September 25.

———. 2019. "The Duty of Newspapers Is to Comfort the Afflicted and to Afflict the Comforted." *Quote Investigator.* February 1.

Obama, Barack. 2011. "Full Text: President Obama and VP Biden's Remarks to the National Governors Association." *The Oakland Press.* February 28.

———. 2013. "Statement by the President." *The White House.* April 17.

———. 2014. "Remarks by the President on the Affordable Care Act." *The White House.* April 1.

Oldfield, J.R. *Popular Politics and British Anti-Slavery: The Mobilization of Public Opinion against the Slave Trade, 1787–1807.* London: Routledge.

Oliphant, Baxter J. 2017. "Bipartisan Support for Some Gun Proposals, Stark Partisan Divisions on Many Others." *Pew Research Center.* June 2013.

Orkent, Daniel. 2019. *The Guarded Gate: Bigotry, Eugenics, and the Law That Kept Two Generations of Jews, Italians, and Other European Immigrants Out of America.* New York: Scribner.

Osmundsen, Mathias, Alexander Bor, Peter Bjerregaard Vahlstrup, Anja Bechmann, and Michael Bang Petersen. 2021. "Partisan Polarization Is the Primary Psychological Motivation Behind Political Fake News Sharing on Twitter." *American Political Science Review.* May 6.

Page, Scott E. 2007. *The Difference: How the Power of Diversity Creates Better Groups, Firms, Schools, and Societies.* Princeton: Princeton University Press.

Palma, Bethania. 2017. "Did Muslim Federal Judge 'Mahal al Alallaha-Smith'

Rule that Two Items of Sharia Law Are Now Legal?" *Snopes.com*. July 25.

Pampuro, Amanda. 2019. "Wearing Your Candidate on Your Sleeve: Merchandising the 2020 Race." *Courthouse News Service*. September 13.

Patterson, Thomas. 2016. "News Coverage of the 2016 General Election: How the Press Failed the Voters." shorensteincenter.org.

Pennycook, Gordon, Tyrone Cannon, and David G. Rand. 2018. "Prior Exposure Increases Perceived Accuracy of Fake News." *Journal of Experimental Psychology*. Vol. 147, No. 12. 1865–1880.

Pennycook, Gordon, Ziv Epstein, Mohsen Mosleh, Antonio A. Arechar, Dean Eckles, and David G. Rand. 2021. "Shifting Attention to Accuracy Can Reduce Misinformation Online." *Nature*. March 17.

Peter, Laurence J. 1977. *Quotations: Ideas for Our Time*. New York: William Morrow & Co.

Peterson, Andrea. 2014. "Liberals Are More Likely to Unfriend You Over Politics—Online and Off." *The Washington Post*. October 21.

Petrocelli, John V. 2021. *The Life-Changing Science of Detecting Bullshit*. New York: St. Martin's Press.

Pettigrew, Thomas F. and Linda R. Tropp. 2006. "A Meta-Analytic Test of Intergroup Contact Theory." *Journal of Personality and Social Psychology*. Vol. 90, No. 5. 751–783.

Pettigrew, Thomas F., Linda R. Tropp, Ulrich Wagner, and Oliver Christ. 2011. "Recent Advances in Intergroup Contact Theory." *International Journal of Intercultural Relations*. Vol. 35, No. 3. 271–80.

Pew Research Center. 2016. "Partisanship and Political Animosity in 2016." *Pew Research Center*. June 22.

———. 2016. "Party Affiliation Among Voters, 1992–2016." *Pew Research Center*. September 13.

———. 2017. "The Partisan Divide on Political Values Grows Even Wider." *Pew Research Center*. October 5.

———. 2018. "Trends in Party Affiliation Among Demographic Groups." *Pew Research Center*. March 20.

———. 2019. "Most Border Wall Opponents, Supporters Say Shutdown Concessions Are Unacceptable." *Pew Research Center*. January 16.

———. 2021. "Questionnaire Design." *Pew Research Center*. May 18.

Pinker, Steven. *Enlightenment Now: The Case for Reason, Science, Humanism, and Progress*. New York: Viking.

Pinsker, Joe. 2020. "If Someone Shares the 'Plandemic' Video, How Should You Respond?" *The Atlantic*. May 9.

Pogosyan, Marianna. 2017. "On Belonging: What Is Behind Our Psychological Need to Belong?" *Psychology Today*. April 11.

Pope, Alexander. 1711. *An Essay on Criticism*. London: W. Lewis.

Powell, Austin. 2021. "4chan and Reddit Bombarded Debate Polls to Declare Trump the Winner." *Daily Dot*. January 26.

Powell, Jared. 2015. "I Am a 62-Year-Old Widow and Have Lost My Insurance Coverage." *Gop.gov*. March 23.

Power, Samantha. 2002. *A Problem from Hell: America and the Age of Genocide*. New York: Basic Books.

Putterman, Samantha. 2020. "This Video Shows Trump Looking 'lost and disoriented.'" *PolitiFact*. September 7.

Quinnipiac University Poll. 2013. "Background Checks Could Lead to Gun Confiscation, Many Voters Tell Quinnipiac University National Poll; But 91 Percent Want Universal Gun Checks." *Quinnipiac University*. April 4.

———. 2018. "Most U.S. Voters Back Life Over Death Penalty." *Quinnipiac University*. March 22.

Rapoza, Kenneth. 2012. "In Attack Ad, Paul Ryan Kills Grandma in Wheelchair." *Forbes*. August 12.

Rauch, Jonathan. 2021. *The Constitution of Knowledge: A Defense of Truth*. Washington, D.C.: Brookings Institution Press.

Reagan, Ronald. 2016. "President Reagan's Address to the Nation on Federal Tax Reduction Legislation, July 27, 1981." *YouTube*. May 12.

Reeve, Elspeth. 2012. "People Celebrating Obama's Re-Election Through Tattoos." *The Atlantic*. November 8.

Reimer, Erich. 2017. "Stop Saying 'Not my president.'" *Washington Examiner*. April 28.

Resnick, Brian. 2017. "Trump Is a Real-World Political Science Experiment." *Vox*. October 11.

———. 2020. "How to Talk Someone Out of Bigotry." *Vox.* January 29.
Restuccia, Andrew. 2016. "Trump's Baseless Assertions of Voter Fraud Called 'Stunning.'" *Politico.* November 27.
Reuters Staff. 2020. "False Claim: Photograph Shows Joe Biden Groping a Reporter." *Reuters.* April 22.
———. 2021. "Fact Check: Donald Trump Concession Video Not a 'Confirmed Deepfake'" *Reuters.* January 11.
Rieder, Jonathan. 2013. *Gospel of Freedom: Martin Luther King, Jr.'s Letter from Birmingham Jail and the Struggle That Changed a Nation.* New York: Bloomsbury Press.
Ripley, Amanda. 2019. "The Least Politically Prejudiced Place in America." *The Atlantic.* March 4.
Roberts, Russ. 2014. *How Adam Smith Can Change Your Life: An Unexpected Guide to Human Nature and Happiness.* New York: Penguin.
Robertson, Lind, Sarah Blaskey, and Martin Vassolo. 2018. "Bombing Suspect Cesar Sayoc, Lost and Angry, Found His Tribe with Trump." *Miami Herald.* October 27.
Roos, Dave. 2018. "Human Sacrifice: Why the Aztecs Practiced This Gory Ritual." *History.* October 11.
———. 2020. "How Political Polling Works." *How Stuff Works.* September 2.
Rosenzweig, Cynthia, David Karoly, Marta Vicarelli, Peter Neofotis, Qigang Wu, Gino Casassa, Annette Menzel, Terry L. Root, Nicole Estrella, Bernard Seguin, Piotr Tryjanowski, Chunzhen Liu, Samuel Rawlins, and Anton Imeson. 2008. "Attributing Physical and Biological Impacts to Anthropogenic Climate Change." *Nature.* Vol. 453. 353–357.
Rozansky, Michael. 2017. "Americans Are Poorly Informed About Basic Constitutional Provisions." *Annenberg Public Policy Center.* September 12.
Rudman, Laurie A., and Kris Mescher. 2012. "Of Animals and Objects: Men's Implicit Dehumanization of Women and Likelihood of Sexual Aggression." *Personality and Social Psychology Bulletin.* Vol. 38, No. 6. 734–746.
Rutenberg, Jim, Jo Becker, Eric Lipton, Maggie Haberman, Jonathan Martin, Matthew Rosenberg, and Michael S. Schmidt. 2021. "77 Days: Trump's Campaign to Subvert the Election." *The New York Times.* January 31.
Rutherford, Adam. 2020. *How to Argue with a Racist: History, Science, Race, and Reality.* London: Weidenfeld & Nicolson.
Sacchi, Dario L. M., Franca Agnoli, and Elizabeth Loftus. 2007. "Changing History: Doctored Photographs Affect Memory for Past Public Events." *Applied Cognitive Psychology.* Vol. 21. 1005–1022.
Salvanto, Anthony, Jennifer De Pinto, Fred Backus, and Kabir Khanna. 2021. "Majority Favor Conviction as Impeachment Trial Begins, but Many Republicans Urge Loyalty to Trump—CBS News Poll." *CBS News.* February 9.
Sanders, Lindley. 2020. "The Difference Between Which News Outlets Republicans and Democrats Trust." *yougov.com.* June 18.
Santhanam, Laura. 2020. "American Voters Worry They Can't Spot Misleading Information, Poll Finds." *PBS.* January 21.
Saslow, Eli. 2016. "The White Flight of Derek Black." *The Washington Post.* October 15.
Savransky, Rebecca. 2016. "Republicans Still Doubt Obama's Citizenship." *The Hill.* August 10.
Schaffner, Brian F., and Mary Layton Atkinson. 2009. "Taxing Death or Estates? When Frames Influence Citizens' Issue Beliefs." *Winning with Words: The Origins and Impacts of Political Framing.* New York: Routledge. 121–135.
Scher, Bill. 2019. "The Real Reason Obama Didn't Pass Gun Control." *Politico.* August 16.
Schick, Theodore, and Lewis Vaughn. 2014. *How to Think About Weird Things: Critical Thinking for a New Age.* New York: McGraw-Hill.
Schmitt, Kathleen M., Albert G. Gunther, and Janice L. Liebhart. 2004. "Why Partisans See Mass Media as Biased." *Communications Research.* Vol. 31, No. 6. 623–641.
Schwartz, Ian. 2015. "Sean Hannity: Obama's 'Not my president.'" *Real Clear Politics.* January 12.
Seelye, Katharine Q. 2001. "EPA to Adopt Clinton Arsenic Standard." *The New York Times.* November 1.

Seife, Charles. 2010. *Proofiness: The Dark Arts of Mathematical Deception.* New York: Penguin Group.

———. 2014. *Virtual Unreality: Just Because the Internet Told You, How Do You Know It's True?* New York: Viking.

Seipel, Arnie. 2016. "Fact Check: Trump Falsely Claims A 'Massive Landslide Victory.'" *NPR.* December 11.

Shenkman, Rick. 2008. *Just How Stupid Are We? Facing the Truth About the American Voter.* New York: Basic Books.

Sherman, David K., Leif D. Nelson, and Lee D. Ross. 2003. "Naïve Realism and Affirmative Action: Adversaries Are More Similar Than They Think." *Basic and Applied Social Psychology.* Vol. 25, No. 4.

Shi, Feng, Misha Teplitskiy, Eamon Duede, and James A. Evans. 2019. "The Wisdom of Polarized Crowds." *Nature Human Behaviour.* 3, 329–336.

Sichermann, Stefan. 2018. "Trump Wants to Deport American Indians to India." *The Postillion.* July 6.

Silver, Nate. 2009. "Question Order May Bias Fox News Health Care Polling." *FiveThirtyEight.* October 6.

Silverman, Craig. 2016. "This Analysis Shows How Viral Fake Election News Stories Outperformed Real News on Facebook." *BuzzFeed News.* November 16.

Silverman, Craig, and Jeremy Singer-Vine. 2016. "Most Americans Who See Fake News Believe It, New Survey Says." *BuzzFeed News.* December 6.

Simler, Kevin, and Robin Hanson. 2018. *The Elephant in the Brain: Hidden Motives in Everyday Life.* New York: Oxford University Press.

Skinner, Allison. 2018. "The Slippery Slope of Dehumanizing Language." *The Conversation.* June 4.

Smith, David Livingstone. 2011. *Less Than Human: Why We Demean, Enslave, and Exterminate Others.* New York: St. Martin's Press.

Smith, Gary. 2014. *Standard Deviations: Flawed Assumptions, Tortured Data, and Other Ways to Lie with Statistics.* New York: Overlook Duckworth.

Stanovich, Keith E. 2009. *What Intelligence Tests Miss: The Psychology of Rational Thought.* New Haven, CT: Yale University Press.

Stanovich, Keith E., Richard F. West, and Maggie E. Toplak. 2013. "Myside Bias, Rational Thinking, and Intelligence." *Current Directions in Psychological Science.* Vol. 22, No. 4. 259–264.

Starbird, M. 2006. "Meaning from Data: Statistics Made Clear." *The Great Courses.* Chantilly, VA: The Teaching Company.

Stelter, Brian. 2016. "The Problem with Donald Trump's 'we won every poll' Claim." *CNN Business.* September 27.

Sterling, Joe. 2012. "CNN Fact Check: Obama Went on an Apology Tour, Romney and Others Say." *CNN.* October 23.

Stokols, Eli. 2016. "Trump Rubs Salt in the Wounds of His Rivals." *Politico.* December 1.

Stone, Douglas, Bruce Patton, and Sheila Heen. 2010. *Difficult Conversations: How to Discuss What Matters Most.* New York: Penguin.

Stroud, Natalie J. 2011. *Niche News: The Politics of News Choice.* New York: Oxford University Press.

Sullivan, Margaret. 2017. "Polls Show Americans Distrust the Media. But Talk to Them, and It's a Very Different Story." *The Washington Post.* December 28.

Sunstein, Cass R. 2017. *#Republic: Divided Democracy in the Age of Social Media.* Princeton: Princeton University Press.

Sussman, Dalia. 2010. "Opinion Polling: A Question of What to Ask." *The New York Times.* February 27.

Swenson, Ali. 2021. "Photo Appearing to Show Biden Asleep in Oval Office Is Fake." *Associated Press.* February 8.

Swift, Art. 2016. "Americans' Trust in Mass Media Sinks to New Low." *Gallup.* September 14.

Swift, Jonathan. 1710. "Number 15." *The Examiner.* Page 2, Column 1.

Taber, Charles S., and Milton Lodge. 2011. "Motivated Skepticism in the Evaluation of Political Beliefs." *American Journal of Political Science.* Vol. 50, No.3. 762.

Taub, Amanda. 2018. "How Liberals Got Lost on the Story of Missing Children on the Border." *The New York Times.* May 31.

Tavris, Carol, and Elliot Aronson. 2007. *Mistakes Were Made (but not by me): Why We Justify Foolish Beliefs, Bad Decisions, and Hurtful Acts.* Orlando: Harcourt.

Taylor, Adam. 2017. "How Do People Define Their National Identity? By

Speaking the Language, Study Says." *The Washington Post*. February 1.

Theodoridis, Alexander, and James Martherus. 2018. "Trump Is Not the Only One Who Calls Opponents 'Animals.' Democrats and Republicans Do It to Each Other." *The Washington Post*. May 21.

Theodoridis, Alexander G., James Martherus, and Andy Martinez. 2019. "Party Animals? Extreme Polarization and Dehumanization." *Political Behavior*. July.

Thomas, Hugh. 1997. *The Slave Trade: The Story of the Atlantic Slave Trade, 1440–1870*. New York: Touchstone.

Thompson, Derek. 2014. "The Algorithm Economy: Inside the Formulas of Facebook and Amazon." *The Atlantic*. March 12.

Tillman, Zoe. 2017. "Pizzagate Gunman Is Sentenced to Four Years in Prison." *BuzzFeed News*. June 22.

Tufekci, Zeynep. 2018. "YouTube, the Great Radicalizer." *The New York Times*. March 10.

Turton, William and Matthew Justus. 2018. "Deepfake Videos Like That of Gal Gadot Porn Are Only Getting More Convincing—and More Dangerous." *Vice*. August 27.

Vallone, R. P., L. Ross, and M. R. Lepper. 1985. "The Hostile Media Phenomenon: Biased Perception and Perceptions of Media Bias in Coverage of the Beirut Massacre." *Journal of Personality and Social Psychology*. Vol. 49, No. 3. 577–585.

Vaughn, Lewis. 2018. *Concise Guide to Critical Thinking*. New York: Oxford University Press.

Vielma, Antonio Jose. 2016. "The Only Things People Hate More Than the Media Are Putin and Trump." *CNBC*. September 21.

Villasenor, John. 2019. "Artificial Intelligence, Deepfakes, and the Uncertain Future of Truth." *Brookings*. February 14.

Voltaire. 1972. "A Letter to D'Argental." *The Complete Works of Voltaire*. Vol. XXII of the Correspondence. Oxford: The Voltaire Foundation.

Vosoughi, Soroush, Deb Roy, and Sinan Aral. 2018. "The Spread of True and False News Online." *Science*. Vol. 359, Issue 6380. 1146–1151.

Washington, George. 1796. "Transcript of President Washington's Farewell Address." *ourdocuments.gov*.

Wheelan, Charles. 2013. *Naked Statistics: Stripping the Dread from the Data*. New York: W. W. Norton & Company.

White, Kenneth R. 2007. "Scourge of Racism: Genocide in Rwanda." *Journal of Black Studies*. Vol. 39, No. 3. 471–481.

White, Matthew. *The Great Big Book of Horrible Things: The Definitive Chronicle of History's 100 Worst Atrocities*. New York: W.W. Norton. 2012.

Whitman, Walt. 2016. "Song of Myself," Part 51. Ames: Iowa University Press.

Willets, Megan. 2014. "How to Order a Beer Like a True German." *Business Insider*. March 31.

Willingham, Daniel T. 2012. *When Can You Trust the Experts: How to Tell Good Science from Bad in Education*? San Francisco: Jossey-Bass.

Wills Garry, ed. 1982. "Federalist No. 70." *The Federalist Papers by Alexander Hamilton, James Madison, and John Jay*. New York: Bantam Books.

Wong, Curtis M. 2015. "Here's Why Pat Robertson Insists That Gay Marriage Is Still Illegal." *Huffington Post*. October 26.

Wright, Carroll D. 1890. "Seventh Annual Report of the Bureau of Labor and Industrial Statistics." *Joint Documents of the State of Michigan for the Year 1889*. Lansing: State Printer and Binder. 311.

Yamaguchi, Masataka. 2014. "U.S. Estates Tax for Non-U.S. Decedents." Perkins and Company. November 3.

Young, Cathy. 2020. "The Republican Mutiny and 2016 Whataboutism." *Arc Digital Media*. December 17.

Zakaria, Tabassum. 2010. "President Obama Questions Sarah Palin's Nuclear Acumen." *Reuters*. April 8.

Zengerle, Jason. 2018. "How the Trump Administration Is Remaking the Courts." *The New York Times Magazine*. August 22.

Zhao, Christina. 2018. "Fox News Host Jeanine Pirro Blasts Dianne Feinstein and Her 'unhinged lunatic demon rats.'" *Newsweek*. September 16.

Zuppello, Suzanne. 2019. "When Tattoos Become Political Statements." *Inside Out*. July 5.

Index

ABC News 66, 89, 91, 107
abortion 59, 70, 77–78, 95, 138–139, 161
absolute change 6, 121, 140–142, 187
Abu Ghraib 22
academic journals 153, 157, 160
Access Hollywood 116
Achen, Christopher 1
Adamic, Lada 60
Adams, Amy 115
Adams, John 104
Adobe Photoshop 112
Adobe VoCo 114
adversarial bias (media) 85–88, 184–185
Aegisthus 168–169
Aeschylus 169–172
affective polarization 4, 18, 62, 69
affirmative action 37, 58–59, 63, 102
African Americans 16, 19, 23
Agamemnon 168–169
aged voters 19
Agenda Project 166
aggregation (of opinion poll results) 138–140, 187
Aglaus 168–169
Agnoli, Franca 112
Ahmadinejad, Mahmoud 113
algorithms 61–62
Allen, Mike 79
Amazon 61–62
The Ambivalent Partisan 35
American Journal of Psychology 157
American Political Science Review 157
Amnesty International's YouTube Data viewer 117
amygdala 166–167
Anderson, Christopher 172, 176
Annenberg Public Policy Center 1, 155, 159–160
Annual Review of Astronomy and Astrophysics 157
Anson, Ian 44
argumentation 71–73, 147–167, 187

Armenian genocide 13
Armstrong, Eric 41
Arpaio, Joe 175
arsenic 121–122
ascent of man scale 24
Asian Americans 16
Asking the Right Questions 153
Aspen Institute 155
Associated Press 156, 160
Athena 170–172, 179–180
Atkinson, Mary Layton 137
The Atlantic 30
Atreus 168–169, 171, 180
audio files (fake) 6, 114–118, 186
The Autobiography of Benjamin Franklin 99
average (misleading use of) 6, 121, 123–126, 186
Ayres, Whit 42
Aztec 13

baby bonds 70
background checks 36
Bacon, Francis 99
Bacon, Perry 30
Bader Ginsburg, Ruth 31
Baguley, Thom 105
Bail, Christopher 68
Bakshy, Eytan 60
Bannon, Steve 86
Barber, Michael 38
Bartels, Larry 2
baseball 15, 29–30
Baum, Matthew 81
Beatrice Hall, Evelyn 108
Beck, Paul Allen 82
behavioral contagion 7
Beirut Massacre 82
Belson, Ken 88
Berreby, David 11, 30
Best, Joel 126
Bible 14

228　Index

bicycle 47–48, 53
Biden, Joe 74, 112, 116, 117, 135, 175, 177
Big Brother 58
Bipartisan Policy Center 155
Birmingham, AL 177
birther conspiracy 92–93, 107, 115, 175
Black, Derek 51–53
Black, Don 51–53
Black Lives Matter 115, 118
Black Mirror 21–22
Blais, André 172
Bloomberg News 156
Blur 88, 119
Boehner, John 21
Boetcker, William John 110
Boller, Paul 108
border wall 36
Bowen, Catherine Drinker 178
Bowler, Shaun 172
Bradburn, Norman 70
Breitbart 134
Breyer, Daniel 171
Britain 71–73, 104
British Broadcasting Corp. 156
Broder, John 148
Brookings Institution 61, 148
Browne, Neil 153
Budak, Ceren 79
budget 92
Bump, Philip 142
Bureau of Census 154
Bureau of Economic Analysis 154
Bureau of Justice Statistics 154
Bureau of Labor Statistics 93, 153–154, 159
Bureau of Transportation Statistics 154
Buscemi, Steve 115
Bush, George H.W. 82, 131–132, 163
Bush, George W. 21, 26, 81, 110, 112–113, 121–122, 124–125, 128–129, 131–132, 163, 165–166

Cage, Nicolas 115
Cambodian genocide 13
Canada 5
cancel culture 19
Cannon, Tyrone 118–119
Cantril, Hadley 77
cap-and-trade 48
Capitol building (assault on) 116, 176, 179
Cárdenas, Mauricio 148
Carlson, Tucker 90
Carnegie Endowment for International Peace 155
Carpenter, Katie 67
Carter, Jimmy 82, 131, 163
Catholics 12–13, 17

CBS News 66, 89, 91, 93–94, 109, 110
Center for Responsive Politics 125
Chambers, Kim 114
Chesney, Robert 115–116
Christ, Oliver 31
Churchill, Winston 108
Circe 182
Citizens Against Handguns 58
Citron, Danielle 115–116
civil war 178–179
Clarkson, Thomas 71–73
Clemens, Roger 113
climate change 41–42, 48, 59, 63, 157, 160
Clinton, Bill 82, 86–87, 121–122, 131–132, 163
Clinton, Hillary 27, 61–62, 83, 86, 89, 96, 106, 125–126, 134, 172–174
Clytemnestra 169
CNBC 134
CNN 59–60, 81, 113–114, 162
cognitive dissonance 43
cognitive responsibilities of citizenship 43–46, 49–51, 183
Cohen, Geoffrey 37–38
coin toss 158–159
Coleman, Joshua 74
Coleman, Peter 69, 73
Coleridge, Samuel Taylor 167
Collileon 168–169
The Comeback Kid 12
Committee to End Preferences 58
Competing Motives in the Partisan Mind 40
compromise (bipartisan) 63, 177, 179
A Concise Introduction to Logic 152
conclusion (of an argument) 150–153, 187
confirmation bias 6, 100–102
Confucius 109
conjoint premises 152–153
Constitution (U.S.) 1, 65, 178
Constitutional Convention 1
content analysis 84–85, 97, 184
conversation (cross-party) 30–31, 69–75, 84–85, 97, 181, 185, 188
conversation (like-minded) 63–64, 67–68, 184
Conway, Kellyanne 106
Cooper, Anderson 162
Coors beer 17
Council on Foreign Relations 155, 160
cricket 15
crime 140, 162–163
Crime Statistics Bureau of San Francisco 107
Cronkite, Walter 109
Crusades 13

Index 229

Cruz, Ted 161
Cuban Missile Crisis 176
Cultural Anthropology 157
curiosity 67–68, 184, 187
Curious 67
Current TV 91

Daily Kos 66, 91
D'Alessio, Dave 79
Dalton, Russel 82
dangling comparative 6, 121–122, 186
Dartmouth College 76–77
Dawson, Erica 143–144
death penalty 70, 100–102, 136
DeepFaceLab 115
deepfakes 114–118, 186
Deepware (deepware.ai) 117, 186
Deepwater Horizon 147
defense spending 138
Deferred Action for Childhood Arrivals (DACA) 70
deficit 138
DeGeneres, Ellen 21
dehumanization 21–25, 40, 183
Democracy in America 3
Democratic National Committee (DNC) 83, 121–122
Department of Health and Human Services 156
Department of Homeland Security 141–142
Department of State 83, 120
Department of the Treasury 94
Development, Relief, and Education for Alien Minors Act (DREAM Act) 147–150
Dhanidina, Halim 114
diagram (an argument) 7, 151–153, 187–188
Diamond, Larry 70
disconfirmation bias 6, 100–102
discrimination (partisan) 20–21, 183
disinformation 104
Disraeli, Benjamin 146
divided government 177
Dobbs, Lou 91
Donovan, Todd 172
"don't ask, don't tell" 77–78
Druckman, James 64, 148–151
Drudge Report 66, 134
Drummond, William 147
Duck Dynasty 17
Duede, Eamon 70
Duke, David 51
Dunkin' Donuts 17
Dunne, Finley Peter 85

Ebert, Roger 115
Economic Research Service 154
The Economist 59, 97, 156, 174
Edsall, Thomas 19
Edwards-Levy, Ariel 134
Einstein 109
Eisenhower, Dwight 162
Election Meltdown 173
Electoral College 174, 176
electric vehicles 152–153
Ellenberg, Jordan 138–140
Emerson, Ralph Waldo vi
Energy Information Administration 154
The Enigma of Reason 71–73
Environmental Research Letters 160
Erinyes 170–172, 180
Erisen, Cengiz 70
Erisen, Elif 70
Escape Your Bubble 68
An Essay on Criticism 48
estate tax 137
ethnicity 13, 16
European Americans 16
evangelicals 17, 19
Evans, Danieli 77
Evans, James 70
expectation bias 79, 184

Facebook 27, 60, 61, 65, 68–69, 112–113, 116–117, 153
FactCheck.org 113, 116, 155, 186
factual statements (definition) 92
Fairleigh Dickinson University 173
fake news 104, 106–107, 118–119
false information 103–119
Family Guy 17
Farid, Hany 116
Favreau, Jon 156
fear 25–26, 165–167
Federal Bureau of Investigation (FBI) 10, 163
Federal Statistical System of the United States 153–154, 158–159
federalism 177
The Federalist 91
The Federalist Papers No. 51 65
The Federalist Papers No. 70 65
Feldman, Lauren 94
Feng Shi 70
Fernbach, Philip 48
Festinger, Leon 56–57
Feynman, Richard 28
First Amendment 1
Fishkin, James 70
FiveThirtyEight 30
flat tax 48–49

230 Index

Flip Feed 69
The Flip Side 69
folk theory of democracy 2–3, 7–8, 181
football 21, 29–30
Foreign Affairs 156
Fox Business 128–129
Fox News 24, 28, 59–60, 62, 64–65, 68, 81, 89–91, 94, 96–98, 107, 137, 153, 173, 175, 183
Fox News Sunday 68, 90, 110–111, 161
framing effect 135–136
France 108
Frank, Jeff 148
Franklin, Ben 1, 99–100
Franklin, Ross 156
Freedom House 155
Frenda, Steven 113
The Friends of Voltaire 108
Frimer, Jeremy 59, 66
Fuller, Thomas 150

Gadot, Gal 115
Galef, Julia 69
Galileo Galilei 67
Gallup 78, 138–139, 175
gas prices 148–150, 155
Gaynor, Gloria 115
Gentzkow, Matthew 16
George, John 108
Gergen, David 128
Germany 12, 22
girther conspiracy 107–108
Gleason, Abbott 58
Goel, Sharad 79
Goff, Philip 23
Golden Globes 115
Goldstein, Katherine 172
Gospel of Freedom 177
graduation rate (high school) 130–131
Graham, Lindsay 175
graphic organizer (policy) 48–49, 188
graphs (misleading use of) 6, 121, 126–132, 186, 188
Great Recession 110
Green Party 5
Groenendyk, Eric 40, 187–188
Gross Domestic Product 159
Guess, Andrew 67
gun control 58–59, 89–90, 102, 143–146, 160–161, 164–165
Gussin, Phil 81

Hall Jamieson, Kathleen 67, 121–122, 165
Hamilton (musical) 21
Hamilton, Alexander 65–66
Hannity 89–90, 173

Hannity, Sean 89–90, 161, 175
Hardin, Garrett 41
Harper, Craig 105
Harrison, Guy 119
Hasen, Richard 173–174
Hastie, Reid 63
Hastorf, Albert 76–77
HBO 28
health care 37, 50–51, 87, 92, 137, 139–140, 163
Hearing the Other Side 69
Helft, Laura 67
Henry, Patrick 178
Herszenhorn, David 148
Hetherington, Marc 17
Hillis, Burton 161
Himelboim, Itai 60
Himmler, Heinrich 22
Hindus 13
Hispanic Americans 16
Hitler, Adolf 13
hockey 15
Hodgkinson, James 27
Hoffman, David 77
Holocaust 13
Holocaust denial 61, 136
Holt, Lester 89
Homer 182
Homo sapiens 11
hostile media effect 81–85, 184
How Adam Smith Can Change Your Life 188
How Not to Be Wrong 138–140
How Partisan Media Polarizes America 60
How to Lie with Statistics 123–124
How to Think About Weird Things 150
Huckabee, Mike 175
Huckfeldt, Robert 82
Huff, Darrell 123–124
Huffington Post 36, 66, 91
human sacrifice 162
The Human Swarm 12
Hume, David 159
humility (epistemic) 48–49, 68, 182, 188
Hurley, Patrick 152
Hurricane Florence 112
Hurricane Katrina 113

illusion of truth effect 118–119, 186
illusion of understanding 48–49, 68, 183, 188
immigration 19, 92, 95–96, 106–107, 141–142, 147–150, 156
India 106
Infowars 174

Index

infrastructure 162
Inglourious Basterds 12
Ingraham, Laura 91
Inhofe, Jim 157
Instagram 117
Invasion, U.S.A. 14–15
Iphigenia 169
Iran 84
Iran nuclear deal 155, 160
Iraq 92
Iraq War 111
Islamic State of Iraq and Syria (ISIS) 92–93, 116, 162
issue reorientation 43–44
issue reprioritization 43
It's the Great Pumpkin, Charlie Brown 69
Iyengar, Shanto 20

Jackson, Andrew 104
Jackson, Brooks 121–122, 165–166
James A. Baker III Institute for Public Policy 155
Japanese 22–23, 111
Japanese internment 14
Jefferson, Thomas 73, 167
Jewish 16, 22
JFK (movie) 109–110
Jin, Zeyu 115
Johansson, Scarlett 115
Johnston, Christopher 35, 49–51
Jones, Alex 174
Journal of Finance 157
Journal of Political Economy 157
Journal of the American Medical Association 157
journalist code of ethics 82–83, 86, 88, 156
judicial appointments 130–132

Kahan, Dan 41, 67, 77–78, 142–146
Kahneman, Daniel 135–136
Kaiser Family Foundation 155
Kalmoe, Nathan 26
Kasich, John 110
Kazmaier, Dick 76
Keeley, Stuart 153
Kennedy, John 109, 176
Kennedy, Robert 176
Kerry, John 26, 81, 122, 165–166
Key, Keegan-Michael 115
Khamenei, Ayatollah Ali 84
Khrushchev, Nikita 176
King, Martin Luther Jr. 177
Klass, Brian 117
Klein, Ezra 25, 31, 177, 187–188
Koran 114

Kovach, Bill 88, 119
Kraus, Clifford 148
Kristof, Nicholas 89–90, 91
Kteily, Nour 23

Ladd, Jonathan 81
Landgrebe, Earl 3
Landrum, Ashley 67
language 14, 15–16
Lawrence, Jennifer 115
Las Vegas (shooting) 88–90
lateral reading 106–108, 185
Lavine, Howard 35, 49–51
Lawson, Rebecca 47–48, 53
Led Zeppelin 80
Ledwich, Mark 62
legalization (marijuana) 59
Lepper, Mark 82, 100–102
Leslie, Ian 67
Less Than Human 22
lethal partisanship 25–27, 116, 176, 179, 183
Levendusky, Matthew 35, 60, 64, 68, 74, 94
Levitin, Daniel 129
Levitsky, Steven 174, 176
Lewis, Rebecca 62
LGB (as in LGBTQ+) 18, 19, 77–78
liars dividend 116
Libertarian Party 5
Lichter, Linda 85–86
Lichter, Robert 85–86
Limbaugh, Rush 96
Lincoln, Abraham 104, 109–110, 140, 162, 178
Listhaug, Ola 172
Living History 61
Lodge, Milton 58, 102
Loftus, Elizabeth 113
logic 150, 160
logical fallacies 7, 160–167, 187
Lombardo, Joseph 88
Lord, Charles 100–102
Losers' Consent (book) 172
losers' consent (to election outcomes) 63, 171–176, 178–180, 187
Luntz, Frank 137
Lyons, Benjamin 67

Maddow, Rachel 90
Madison, James 65–66, 178
Maiese, Michelle 22
Mall of America 119
Marist Institute for Public Opinion 104
markers (of tribal identity) 12–15
marriage 21
Martherus, James 24

Martin, Dorothy 56–57, 74
Martinez, Andy 24
Mason, Lilliana 18, 19, 26, 28, 46–47, 65
Mather, Cotton 22
Mayflower 13
McCain, John 87, 110, 113, 179–180
McCarthy, Joe 104, 120
McCarthy, Kevin 179
McCarty, Nolan 4
McConnell, Mitch 179
McCormick Tribune Freedom Museum 1
McCreery, Stephen 60
McLain, Audrey 64
McLure Hotel 120
mechanistic explanation of policy 48–49
media bias (partisan) 78–98
The Media Elite 85
Medicaid 92, 163
Medicare 92, 138, 166
Medina, Jennifer 88
mega-identity (party as) 18, 25–26
Mehta, Dhrumil 30
Mein Kampf 13
Men Against Fire 21–22
Mercier, Hugo 71, 73
Mescher, Kris 23
Messing, Solomon 60
Metternich, Klemens von 176
midterm elections 177
migrant caravan 118
Mill, John Stuart 74
Milner, Jeff 80
minimum wage 95–96
misinformation 104
misinterpreting favorable opinion as fact 95–98, 185
misinterpreting unfavorable fact as opinion 92–94, 185
misperception 76–77
Moffett, Mark 12, 14
Moore, Roy 86–87
More Damned Lies and Statistics 126
Mormon 16
Morning Consult 174
motivated reasoning (partisan) 6–7, 99–102
Motyl, Matt 59, 66
MSNBC 28, 59–60, 62, 64–65, 68, 94, 96–98, 153, 183
Mulaney, John 12
Muslims 13
Mutz, Diana 69

Nadler, Jerry 179
Naked Statistics 141
Nanjing Massacre 13

NASCAR 17, 21
NASDAQ 74
The Nation 59
National Academies of Sciences, Engineering, and Medicine 155
National Agricultural Statistics Service 154
National Association for the Advancement of Colored People (NAACP) 58
National Bureau of Economic Research 155
National Center for Education Statistics 154
National Center for Health Statistics 154
national debt 93, 96
National Governors Association 162
National Review 59, 91
National Rifle Association (NRA) 58, 89
National Science Foundation 154
Native Americans 13, 22, 106–107
Nature (journal) 157
NBC News 66, 78, 89, 91, 175
negative partisanship 3, 5–6, 181
The New England Journal of Medicine 157
The New Republic 42, 178–179
New York (magazine) 24
New York City 21, 113, 116
The New York Times 68, 84, 87, 88–91, 108, 148, 156, 160
The New York Times Magazine 130–132
New Zealand 5
news content 88–92, 185
news organizations 153, 156, 158, 160
Newsmax 175
The Newsroom 28
NFL 21
Niche News 59
Nichols, Tom 181
Nielsen, Kirstjen 142
Nineteen Eighty-Four 58
non-believers (religious) 16, 19
North American Free Trade Agreement (NAFTA) 37
North Korea 111
"not my president" 175, 187
NPR 104
nuclear power 41–42
nuclear weapons 111, 155, 164
numeracy 121, 142–146
Nussbaum, Martha 58
NWA 115
Nyhan, Brendan 67, 74

Obama, Barack 15, 21, 27, 36–37, 74, 86, 92–93, 104–105, 110, 112–113, 115, 118,

Index

130–132, 137, 147–148, 153–156, 160, 162–165, 172, 175, 179–180
Obama, Michelle 21, 104, 118
O'Donnell, Lawrence 91
Odysseus 182
The Odyssey 182
Office of Research, Evaluation, and Statistics 154
offshore drilling 147–151
One America News Network 175
op-ed page 90
opinion-based content 88–92, 185
opinion polls 6, 121, 132–140, 186
opinion statements (definition) 92
Orchomenus 168–169
O'Reilly, Bill 107
Oresteia 169–171
Orestes 169–171
Organization of the Petroleum Exporting Countries (OPEC) 155
Orwell, George 58
outlier (in a data set) 123–126, 159

Palin, Sarah 113, 119, 164
Pandora 67
Paris Accord 42
Parliament (British) 72–73
partisan misperception 77–78
partisan selective exposure 6, 58–75, 183
The Partisan Sort 35
partisanship 3, 5–6, 181
partition of India 13
party polarization 3–4
PBS 91
PBS NewsHour 64–65, 104, 156
Pearl Harbor 104
Peele, Jordan 114–115
peer review 157–158, 160
Pelops 168–169
Pelosi, Nancy 84, 104
Pence, Mike 21, 104
Pennycook, Gordon 118–119
Pérez-Peña 88
Peters, Ellen 143–144
Peterson, Erik 148–150
Pettigrew, Thomas 31
Pew Research Center 14, 16–17, 31, 78, 92, 95, 155, 179
Pew Research Journalism Project 60
Phillips, Gregg 174
photographs (fake) 6, 111–114, 186, 188
Pinker, Steven 41
Pirro, Jeanine 24
pizzagate 103
Planned Parenthood 161
Pogosyan, Marianna 40

Polarization 4
policy depolarization 69–71
policy polarization 3–4, 6, 63–65
policy views 5, 34–46, 49–51, 148–150, 188
political elections (evaluation of) 7, 168–180
political parties (purpose of) 7
political tribalism (definition) 3
Politico 174, 176
PolitiFact 109–111, 113, 116–117, 166, 174, 186
Pope, Alexander 48
Pope, Jeremy 38
Pope Francis 104
premises (of an argument) 6–7, 150–160, 187
presidential debates 134
Princeton University 76–77
Priorities USA Action 111
Prius or Pickup 17
Proofiness 120
Protestants 13, 17
psychosocial costs and benefits of tribalism 40–42, 47
psychosocial responsibilities of citizenship 43–46, 51–53, 183

quality evidence (sources of) 153–157, 187
quantity of evidence 158–160, 187
The Quarterly Journal of Economics 157
question wording (opinion polls) 135–138, 187
Quinnipiac University 136, 165
Quintilian 178
quotations (benefits of) 108
quotations (fake) 6, 108–111, 185–186
Quote Investigator 109–110, 186

race 13, 16
The Rachel Maddow Show 90
Rachlinski, Jeffrey 77
Rand, David 118
RAND Corporation 155
Rao, Justin 79
Rasmussen 179
Rath, Tom 110
Reagan, Ronald 82, 109–110, 127–128, 131–132, 163
Redmond, E.S. 30, 130–131
Reid, Harry 24
Reifler, Jason 67
Reimer, Erich 175
relative change 6, 121, 140–142, 187
relative hostile media effect 94
research institutions 153, 154–155, 158–160

Index

Resnick, Brian 34
Reuters 156
reverse image search 114, 117–118, 186
Riecken, Henry 56
Rieder, Jonathan 177
Ripley, Amanda 30–31
Robbers Cave experiment 10–11, 28
Roberts, Russ 188
Robertson, Pat 164
"rolling coal" 41
Romney, Mitt 110, 112
Roosevelt, Franklin 104
Roper 136
Rorschach ink-blot test 85–86
Rosenstiel, Tom 88, 95, 119
Ross, Lee 82, 100–102
Rossiter, Erin 69
Rothman, Stanley 85–86
Rowling, J.K. 10
Rubio, Marco 84
Rudman, Laurie 23
rugby 15
rural 17–18
Rustling, Jimmy 107
Rwandan genocide 13, 22
Ryan, Paul 166, 179

Sacchi, Dario 112
same-sex marriage 59, 63, 164
sample (opinion poll) 133–135, 187
sampling error 135
Sanders, Bernie 62, 83, 125–126
Sandy Hook Elementary school shooting 160–161, 164–165
Saslow, Eli 51
satanic panic 80
satire 104, 106–107, 114
Saturday Night Live 125
Savage, Michael 22
Sayoc, Cesar 27
Scalia, Antonin 31
Scalise, Steve 27
Schachter, Stanley 56
schadenfreude (partisan) 171–172, 186
Schaffner, Brian 137
Schick, Theodore 150–151, 162
Schkade, David 63
Schumer, Chuck 155
Science (journal) 41, 157
The Scout Mindset 69
segregation (partisan) 13, 21, 57–58, 65–66
Seife, Charles 56, 111, 120
selective categorization 82–85, 184
self-selection bias 134
September 11 attacks 62, 111, 166

Shakespeare, William 83–84
sharia law 114
Sherif, Muzafer 10–11
shibboleth 14
Shorenstein Center on Media, Politics, and Public Policy 86
Silver, Nate 137
Simon, Scott 1
Sirens (Greek mythology) 182
Skitka, Linda 59, 66
slave trade 71–73
slavery 13, 65, 162
Slothus, Rune 148–150
Slovic, Paul 143–144
Smith, David Livingstone 22, 23
Smith, Gary 128
Smith, Marc 60
Snopes 109–110, 113, 116, 186
social security 92
Society for Effecting the Abolition of the Slave Trade 71–73
Song of Myself 39
sorted voters 3–4, 35–36, 40, 43–47
Southern Poverty Law Center 52–53
Soviet Union 176
Spataro, Dave 16
Sperber, Dan 71, 73
Spicer, Sean 154
sports 15
"Stairway to Heaven" 80
Starbird, Michael 146
Starbucks 17
Statistics of Income Division 154
Steenbergen, Marco 35, 49–51
Stephens, Bret 91
stereotyping (partisan) 18–19, 69, 183
Stevenson, Adlai 1
Stevenson, Matthew 52
stock market 44, 159
Stone, Oliver 109–110
Stormfront 14
Stroud, Natalie 59–60, 94
structural bias (media) 85, 86–88, 184–185
Sui, Alice 70
Suleimani, Qassim 84, 91
Sunstein, Cass 63–64, 66
Swift, Jonathan 116
Switzerland 5
Syria 92

Taber, Charles 58, 102
table tennis 15
talk radio (political) 60, 62
Tantalus 168–169
Tarantino, Quentin 12
tattoos 15

Tax Policy Center 125
taxes 39, 48, 70, 122, 124–125, 127–129, 138, 141
Teplitskiy, Misha 70
Theodoridis, Alexander 24
thermometer scale (partisan affect) 18, 31, 62
They Never Said It 108
Thinking, Fast and Slow 135
Thirteen Days 176
Thirty Years' War 13
Thorson, Emily 103, 106
Thyestes 168–169
Tiananmen Square 113
Time magazine 82, 134
TinEye 113–114, 117–118, 186
Tocqueville, Alexis de 3
tone (of news content) 91, 97, 185
TownHall 66, 178
tragedy of the commons 41–42, 188
tribal theory of democracy 2–3, 5, 181
tribalism 11–12, 15
tribe 11
Trojan War 169
Tropp, Linda 31
Trump, Donald 15, 16, 24, 27, 29, 36–39, 42, 61–62, 74, 83–84, 86–87, 89, 91–93, 96, 104–108, 111–112, 115–118, 130–132, 134, 141–142, 153–156, 159–163, 172–179
Trump, Eric 24, 106
Trump: The America We Deserve 61
Trump: The Art of the Deal 61
trust (cross-party) 62
trustworthy source effect 95, 96–98, 185
Tucker Carlson Tonight 90
Tufekci, Zeynep 61–62
Twain, Mark 109, 146
Twitter 60, 67–69, 84, 107, 130, 134, 153, 156, 174, 184, 188
Tydings, Millard 104

Udall, Tom 84
UFO 56–57, 74
Uncivil Agreement 18
unemployment rate 93, 96, 140, 153–154, 159
uniforms (partisan) 14
unsorted voters 35–36
Unspun 121
urban 17–18
Us and Them 11

USA Today 91
Uygur, Cenk 91

Vallone, Robert 82
Vaughn, Lewis 150–151, 162
video files (fake) 6, 114–118, 186
Vietnam War 87, 109, 165
Villaraigosa, Antonio 156
Virtual Unreality 111
Voltaire 108
voter fraud 173–176, 187
voter suppression 174, 187

Wagner, Ulrich 31
The Wall Street Journal 61, 78, 89, 91, 108, 156
Wallace, Chris 90, 111
Walmart 17
Washington, George 22, 53, 168, 176
The Washington Post 51, 68, 91, 93, 108, 116, 142, 156
Watergate 3
Watertown, NY 30–31
Weiler, Jonathan 17
Welch, Edgar Maddison 103
welfare 37–38, 136
Westwood, Sean 20
What Happened 61
Wheelan, Charles 141
When Prophecy Fails 56–57
white nationalists 14, 51–53, 61
Whitman, Walt 39
Whole Foods 17
Why We Are Polarized 25, 177
Wikipedia 70
winners' magnanimity 171–172, 176–178, 187
Wright, Carroll 120

Yang, Andrew 16
Yates, Robert 65–66
Young Democrats 20
Young Republicans 20
The Young Turks 91
YouTube 61–62, 153

Zaitsev, Anna 62
Zao 115
Zeus 168
Ziblatt, Daniel 174, 176